A NEW HEART

INTERNATIONAL THEOLOGICAL COMMENTARY

Fredrick Carlson Holmgren and George A. F. Knight
General Editors

Volumes now available

Forthcoming in 1991

A NEW HEART

A Commentary on the Book of
Ezekiel

BRUCE VAWTER, C.M.
and
LESLIE J. HOPPE, O.F.M.

WM. B. EERDMANS PUBLISHING CO., GRAND RAPIDS
THE HANDSEL PRESS LTD, EDINBURGH

First published 1991 by William B. Eerdmans Publishing Company,
255 Jefferson Ave. S.E., Grand Rapids, Michigan 49503
and
The Handsel Press Limited
139 Leith Walk, Edinburgh EH6 8NS

Printed in the United States of America

Library of Congress Cataloging-in-Publication Data
Vawter, Bruce.
A new heart: a commentary on the book of Ezekiel /
Bruce Vawter and Leslie J. Hoppe.
p.   cm.   — (International theological commentary)
Includes bibliographical references.
ISBN 0-8028-0331-8
1. Bible. O.T. Ezekiel—Commentaries.   I. Hoppe, Leslie J.
II. Title.   III. Series.
BS1545.3.V29   1991
224'.407—dc20   91-6675
                                             CIP

Handsel Press ISBN 1 871828 09 0

CONTENTS

ABBREVIATIONS

ANEP	*Ancient Near East in Pictures*, ed. James B. Pritchard
ANET	*Ancient Near Eastern Texts*, ed. James B. Pritchard
LXX	Septuagint
MT	Masoretic Text
NAB	New American Bible
NEB	New English Bible
RSV	Revised Standard Version
TEV	Today's English Version

EDITORS' PREFACE

The Old Testament alive in the Church: this is the goal of the *International Theological Commentary*. Arising out of changing, unsettled times, this Scripture speaks with an authentic voice to our own troubled world. It witnesses to God's ongoing purpose and to his caring presence in the universe without ignoring those experiences of life that cause one to question his existence and love. This commentary series is written by front-rank scholars who treasure the life of faith.

Addressed to ministers and Christian educators, the *International Theological Commentary* moves beyond the usual critical-historical approach to the Bible and offers a *theological* interpretation of the Hebrew text. Thus, engaging larger textual units of the biblical writings, the authors of these volumes assist the reader in the appreciation of the theology underlying the text as well as its place in the thought of the Hebrew Scriptures. But more, since the Bible is the book of the believing community, its text has acquired ever more meaning through an ongoing interpretation. This growth of interpretation may be found both within the Bible itself and in the continuing scholarship of the Church.

Contributors to the *International Theological Commentary* are Christians—persons who affirm the witness of the New Testament concerning Jesus Christ. For Christians, the Bible is *one* scripture containing the Old and New Testaments. For this reason, a commentary on the Old Testament may not ignore the second part of the canon, namely, the New Testament.

Since its beginning, the Church has recognized a special relationship between the two Testaments. But the precise character of this bond has been difficult to define. Thousands of books and articles have discussed the issue. The diversity of views represented in these publications makes us aware that the Church is not of one mind in expressing the "how" of this relationship. The authors of this commentary share a developing consensus that any serious explanation of the Old Testament's relationship to the New will uphold the integrity of the Old Testament. Even though Christianity is rooted in the soil of the Hebrew Scriptures, the biblical interpreter must take care lest he or she "christianize" these Scriptures.

Authors writing in this commentary will, no doubt, hold varied views concerning *how* the Old Testament relates to the New. No attempt has been made to dictate one viewpoint in this matter. With the whole Church, we are convinced that the relationship between the two Testaments is real and substantial. But we recognize also the diversity of opinions among Christian scholars when they attempt to articulate fully the nature of this relationship.

In addition to the Christian Church, there exists another people for whom the Old Testament is important, namely, the Jewish community. Both Jews and Christians claim the Hebrew Bible as Scripture. Jews believe that the basic teachings of this Scripture point toward, and are developed by, the Talmud, which assumed its present form about 500 C.E. On the other hand, Christians hold that the Old Testament finds its fulfillment in the New Testament. The Hebrew Bible, therefore, belongs to both the Church and the Synagogue.

Recent studies have demonstrated how profoundly early Christianity reflects a Jewish character. This fact is not surprising because the Christian movement arose out of the context of first-century Judaism. Further, Jesus himself was Jewish, as were the first Christians. It is to be expected, therefore, that Jewish and Christian interpretations of the Hebrew Bible will reveal similarities *and* disparities. Such is the case. The authors of the *International Theological Commentary* will refer to the various Jewish traditions that they consider important for an appreciation of the Old Testament text. Such references will enrich our understanding of certain biblical passages and, as an extra gift, offer us insight into the relationship of Judaism to early Christianity.

An important second aspect of the present series is its *inter-*

national character. In the past, Western church leaders were considered to be *the* leaders of the Church—at least by those living in the West! The theology and biblical exegesis done by these scholars dominated the thinking of the Church. Most commentaries were produced in the Western world and reflected the lifestyle, needs, and thoughts of its civilization. But the Christian Church is a worldwide community. People who belong to this universal Church reflect differing thoughts, needs, and lifestyles.

Today the fastest-growing churches in the world are to be found, not in the West, but in Africa, Indonesia, South America, Korea, Taiwan, and elsewhere. By the end of this century, Christians in these areas will outnumber those who live in the West. In our age, especially, a commentary on the Bible must transcend the parochialism of Western civilization and be sensitive to issues that are the special problems of persons who live outside of the "Christian" West, issues such as race relations, personal survival and fulfillment, liberation, revolution, famine, tyranny, disease, war, the poor, religion and state. Inspired of God, the authors of the Old Testament knew what life is like on the edge of existence. They addressed themselves to everyday people who often faced more than everyday problems. Refusing to limit God to the "spiritual," they portrayed God as one who heard and knew the cries of people in pain (see Exod. 3:7-8). The contributors to the *International Theological Commentary* are persons who prize the writings of these biblical authors as a word of life to our world today. They read the Hebrew Scriptures in the twin contexts of ancient Israel and our modern day.

The scholars selected as contributors underscore the international aspect of the series. Representing very different geographical, ideological, and ecclesiastical backgrounds, they come from over seventeen countries. Besides scholars from such traditional countries as England, Scotland, France, Italy, Switzerland, Canada, New Zealand, Australia, South Africa, and the United States, contributors from the following places are included: Israel, Indonesia, India, Thailand, Singapore, Taiwan, and countries of Eastern Europe. Such diversity makes for richness of thought. Christian scholars living in Buddhist, Muslim, or Socialist lands may be able to offer the World Church insights into the biblical message—insights to which the scholarship of the West could be blind.

The proclamation of the biblical message is the focal concern of the *International Theological Commentary*. Generally speaking, the authors of these commentaries value the historical-critical studies of past scholars, but they are convinced that these studies by themselves are not enough. The Bible is more than an object of critical study; it is the revelation of God. In the written Word, God has disclosed himself and his will to humankind. Our authors see themselves as servants of the Word which, when rightly received, brings *shalom* to both the individual and the community.

Bruce Vawter was working on this volume when he died in the summer of 1986. He had completed the first draft of the introduction and the commentary on chapters 1-24. In the spring of 1987 the editors asked Leslie Hoppe to complete the work begun by Fr. Vawter.

—George A. F. Knight
—Fredrick Carlson Holmgren

INTRODUCTION

THE BOOK OF EZEKIEL

As it stands before us, the book of Ezekiel falls into two almost precisely equal parts, though the two parts are unequal in their complexities. Prophecies of judgment, doom, and condemnation make up the first part (chs. 1–23), while the second part (chs. 25–48) consists of prophecies of restoration and salvation. Israel throughout is the subject of this prophecy: the judgments "against the nations" in chs. 25–32, as condemnatory as anything else in this book, are, from Israel's perspective, "salvation."

The following outline will be pursued in this commentary, recognizing the division and subdivisions of the book as they emerge from an analysis of its contents.

I. The dominant theme of chs. 1–7 is Ezekiel's inaugural vision, his call to prophecy, and some immediately connected ideas

    A. 1:1–3:15   Ezekiel's call
    B. 3:16-21   The watchman of Israel (see ch. 33)
    C. 3:22-27   Ezekiel's dumbness and restraint (see 24:25-27; 33:21-22)
    D. 4:1–5:17   Symbolic acts against Jerusalem
    E. 6:1–7:27   Oracles against Israel

II. The temple vision of chs. 8–11 and its consequences for the dominant theme of chs. 8–14

    A. 8:1–11:25   The temple vision
    B. 12:1-10   Acts symbolic of the Exile

C. 12:21-28   Reflections on those acts
D. 13:1–14:11   False prophets, witches,
                   and magicians
E. 14:12-23   Irrevocability of judgment: there is
                   no righteous person

III. In chs. 15–24 allegories prevail

A. 15:1–19:14   The great allegories with
                   commentaries
B. 20:1-49   Prophecies of judgment
C. 21:1-32   The sword of the LORD
D. 22:1-31   The bloody city
E. 23:1-49   Oholah and Oholibah
F. 24:1-27   Finale on Jerusalem

IV. The oracles against the nations comprise chs. 25–32

A. 25:1-17   Israel's close neighbors
B. 26:1–28:26   Tyre and Sidon
C. 29:1–32:32   Egypt

V. The restoration of Judah is proclaimed in chs. 33–39

A. 33:1-33   The transition to consolation
B. 34:1-31   Israel's shepherds and God's sheep
C. 35:1–36:15   Judgment on Edom, Salvation
                   for Israel
D. 36:16-38   Israel's new heart and spirit
E. 37:1-14   The dry bones will live
F. 37:15-28   The two sticks
G. 38:1–39:29   The Gog and Magog oracles

VI. Chs. 40–48 depict the kingdom of God

A. 40:1–42:20   The temple vision
B. 43:1-12   The return of God's glory
C. 43:13–46:24   Legislation for the temple
D. 47:1–48:35   The land beyond the Temple

From this analysis, evidently the book of Ezekiel reflects a well-organized plan. In the past commentators considered "literary"

2

prophets like Ezekiel primarily as writers. They would have concluded that the book of Ezekiel was the product of a single author written at a single time. Nowadays there exists a more sophisticated appreciation of the nature of the literary prophecy of Israel. It is one that is less dependent on "Western" preconceptions. Also it is more aware of the actual processes through which ancient Near Eastern literature has come down to us. Today few serious students of the book maintain that the charismatic person Ezekiel himself wrote down all that the book ascribes to him and in the order that the book follows. On the other hand, equally few would defend the opposite thesis. The book of Ezekiel is not a literary *tour de force*. It is not the work of some bold author who invented a prophetic figure (Ezekiel, "God makes strong"). Ezekiel is no fictitious hero of a legendary history of Judah in exile from the time of the political debacle of 597 B.C.E. until the final disaster of 586, the destruction of Jerusalem by the Babylonian king Nebuchadnezzar II. Some had proposed such a thesis when scholars abandoned the old idea of literary prophecy. Few hold it today.

Better historical documentation of the period has saved us from such extravagances. Most commentators agree that there was indeed a prophet Ezekiel who stands behind the substance of this book. The book itself is a product of the faith community that treasured the memory and message of the prophet. This community transmitted Ezekiel's words as a living word of God. Faithful disciples remembered and gathered Ezekiel's prophecies. They doubtless discarded some as no longer relevant. They amplified some to adjust them to changed conditions. Finally they subjected all the prophet's words to editing and reorganization before the book as we have it received its present symmetry.

Built into the edited book of Ezekiel is a series of dates that has something to say about the process of its composition. The dating of prophecies was very rare among earlier Israelite prophets (Isa. 6:1, "in the year that King Uzziah died," is an exception that proves the rule), but it became common in later prophecy (see Hag. 1:1; 2:10: Zech. 1:1). Ernst Kutsch has recently devoted a monograph to these dates in Ezekiel *(Die chronologischen Daten des Ezechielbuches)*. Kutsch's dates depart from those that have

3

become conventional in scholarly circles. It is unlikely that the discrepancies will matter much to the readers of this commentary. In the table below, Kutsch's revisions are in brackets. No matter how one dates Ezekiel's oracles, the list is impressive:

1:1 (fifth day of the fourth month, year 30). We shall note in the Commentary what seems signified by this "thirtieth" year. Here it is to be identified with the fifth year of the exile of King Jehoiachin. Therefore:

1:2 (fifth day of the fifth month, year 5). The 5th of Tammuz (31 July 593) [13 July 594/3]

3:16. Seven days after this

8:1 (fifth day of the sixth month, year 6). The 5th of Elul (17 September 592) [28 September 593]

20:1 (tenth day of the fifth month, year 7). The 10th of Ab (14 August 591) [24 August 592]

24:1 (tenth day of the tenth month, year 9). The 10th of Tebet (15 January 588) [the same, see 2 Kgs. 25:1]

26:1 (the first day of ? month, year 11). The first of some month in 586 [13 February or 15 March]

29:1 (twelfth day of the tenth month, year 10). The 12th of Tebet (7 January 587) [17 January 588]

29:17 (first day of the first month, year 27). The 1st of Nisan (Abib) (26 April 571) [8 April 572]

30:20 (seventh day of the first month, year 11). The 7th of Nisan (Abib) (29 April 587) [10 April 588]

31:1 (first day of the third month, year 11). The 1st of Sivan (21 June 587) [2 June 588]

32:1 (first day of the twelfth month, year 12). The 1st of Adar (3 March 585) [15 March 586]

32:17 (the fifteenth of ? month, year 12). The 15th of some month (in the LXX it is "the first" in 586/5) [29 March 586]

33:21 (the fifth day of the tenth month, year 12). The 5th of Tebet (8 January 585) [19 January 586]

40:1 (tenth day of the first month, year 25). The 10th of Nisan (Abib) (28 April 573) [10 April 574]

We note that this dating system does not extend throughout the book. It usually clusters around only certain parts of the material. Neither does it follow a perfect sequence. Such observations confirm our impression that in its present form the book of Ezekiel confronts us with a redaction—a work of editing and reediting. Compilers shaped the material and structured it in accord with the outline we have discerned above. The material these compilers and editors had to work with was diverse. There are involved and strange allegories, sermons, stories about unusual and eccentric acts, visions of an antic kind. They encompass the galaxy of attributes that make the book of Ezekiel unique in the annals of Israelite prophecy. These conclusions force upon us the task of both trying to understand how this book came to be and getting at the character of the charismatic personage who lies behind it.

COMPOSITION OF THE BOOK

That redaction—editorial work—accounts for most, if not all, of the prophetic literature found in the OT should come as no surprise to anyone who is even vaguely aware of present-day critical study of the Bible. The prophets did not, as a rule, write anything at all (just as Jesus did not). Nevertheless, we still refer to the "classical" prophets of Israel (Amos and his successors in Israel and Judah) by the term "literary prophets." This distinguishes them from those others like Elijah, Elisha, or Nathan, for example, of whose prophetic words no substantial literary memorials remain. The distinction is incidental. Prophecy was, in principle, a thing of speaking and hearing, not a thing of writing and reading. People remembered prophetic utterances usually in brief and poetic form and only later did prophetic disciples commit these to writing. These disciples and descendants handed them on, sometimes in their original form but also often in paraphrase and with modifications.

Prophecy became literature late in the history of Israel and of Judaism. The turmoil and historical discontinuity of political extinction and exile led to the commitment of specific oral traditions to written form. Various groups who were the custodians of ancient Israel's many-sided cultural heritage—history, "wisdom," ancient covenant law, old tales and legends, prophecy and reaction to prophecy—carefully preserved these traditions by turning them into literary texts. This was a time not far removed from that of Ezekiel's prophetic ministry.

The prophetic utterances were first generally assembled into small collections, booklets, dealing with some distinct theme. These might exist independently of other booklets put together by other groups equally interested in the prophetic tradition. We may take as an example ch. 21 of Ezekiel, which has collected various pronouncements involving the catchphrase "the sword of the LORD," though these pronouncements may originally have lacked any connection with one another. Later hands have brought together into one topological unit the oracles against the nations (chs. 25–32). The prophet may have uttered these oracles on several different occasions. The final product was the result of combining these minor collections and others like them with further modifications and updating.

The process by which the words of any given prophet have reached us in written form was probably much the same throughout the spectrum of prophecy. Special problems in the book of Ezekiel have caused some to question whether the pattern holds true here. The book contains many essays, extended sermons, treatises, discourses with elaborately involved allegorical expositions, lengthy autobiographical details, wordy and repetitious descriptions of visions, and prophetic "signs." These and other literary forms make it difficult to discern an earlier oral delivery in the presence of a living audience, which was the normal forum of prophecy. It is small wonder that some believe the book of Ezekiel, or at least much of it, is precisely that—a book, "cabinet prophecy." As an out-and-out literary composition from the beginning, Ezekiel lacked a real connection with the historical background it describes. (These scholars believe it to be similar to the book of Daniel in relation to the decline of the Babylonian Empire.) In this construction it matters little whether the book goes back to a historical Ezekiel or to another writer or writers who assumed the guise of a prophet-in-exile between 597-586 B.C.E.

A quick response can be made to these apparently weighty objections. There is nothing in the book of Ezekiel, nor in the contention that this book represents the authentic recollection of a prophet of that name, that cannot be explained as a logical and predictable development within the known history of Israelite prophetism.

The *prophetic instruction* is an art form particularly associated with Ezekiel and possibly, though not necessarily, enhanced by the priestly character of this prophet. This form existed in earlier prophecy. Traditionally the prophet in Israel played a dual role. Prophets were charismatic figures who spoke words they believed were not theirs but the LORD'S. They were also teachers whom God instructed and called to instruct others. That was the *torah* ("instruction," "teaching") of the prophets (see Isa. 8:16). In this respect, Ezekiel differs from his predecessors perhaps in degree, but not in kind. In like vein the prophet as "watchman" (Ezek. 3:16-21; 33)—that is, the one appointed to foresee and if possible to forestall judgment upon the people by warning them and bringing them to repentance—is only one variation on an old theme of the prophet as mediator.

As far as *visions,* we must acknowledge that there is a considerable difference between those of the prophets before and after the Exile—or, in Ezekiel's case, during the Exile. Before the Exile the visions of the prophets tend to be parabolic: they are suggestive rather than descriptive. Amos sees a basket of over-ripe summer fruit *(qayits)* that suggests to him that the end *(qets)* of Israel is coming soon (Amos 8:1-2). Jeremiah sees a branch of an almond tree *(shaqed)* and concludes that the LORD is watching *(shoqed)* over Israel to destroy it (Jer. 1:11-12). These parabolic visions usually involve ordinary things that, viewed without prophetic insight, would attract no remark at all. Notice how different are the visions of a postexilic prophet like Zechariah. These are allegorical throughout. The vision, which is now of strange things, no longer suggests the message but is the message itself, every detail of it corresponding with some revealed reality. Such are also the visions of Ezekiel, where *allegory* is all. With Ezekiel we are also on the verge of *apocalyptic,* a distinct movement of its own with distinct literary forms much given to allegory. Despite these differences, it is still possible to maintain that Ezekiel's visions represent a development of the prophetic tradition rather than an aberration from it. As any reader of the Gospels knows, the parabolic form easily yields to the allegorical.

There are many borderline cases in which it is difficult to tell the two apart.

Ezekiel's *prophetic acts* are often flamboyant, extravagant, even at times tasteless. Sometimes we can hardly assume that the prophet carried them out and, if he did, hardly in the manner described. In this regard we must be reminded that the prophets were, almost by definition, not "normal" people. Ezekiel's acts are often strange. So were some of Isaiah's prophetic actions. The aristocratic Isaiah stripped himself of his loincloth and sandals and walked about naked as a sign of the LORD'S coming judgment (Isa. 20:2-6). Again it seems a matter of kind rather than of degree—a degree that may strain the distinction to the limit, but still a degree.

Another consideration that is very relevant regarding the make-up of the book of Ezekiel is its largely *prose* character. The ordinary medium of the prophetic oracle was poetry, whether rough or polished. The prophetic oracle was usually short and to the point, designed to be quickly grasped and easily remembered. Such poetic devices as parallelism and alliteration were particularly suited for these purposes. Ezekiel's pronouncements tend to be long, sometimes tediously long. They are often prosaic, though the prophet surprises us occasionally by dropping in a point line or two as he goes along. (The Dutch scholar Adrianus van den Born unkindly accused the author of the book of Ezekiel [whom he did not think to be a prophet named Ezekiel] of attempting to write poetry with the vocabulary of the *Code of Canon Law!*)

Several things must be said. The first is that while poetry may have been an ordinary vehicle for early prophecy, we have every reason to think that prose accompanied it. Prose material was usually commentary on and the expansion of ideas found in the poetry. Today in many cultures people convey folk wisdom in this very manner. The rule-of-thumb that determines "authentic" prophecy by the test of its poetic content rests on an unprovable and improbable assumption. In obedience to that assumption, some past scholars took drastic measures to "recover" the poetry of Ezekiel. Georg Fohrer, in his 1955 commentary, invented the category of *Kurzvers,* "short verse," an attempt at converting Ezekiel's prose into poetry by redefining poetry in terms of word clusters. At the other extreme, Jean Steinmann in 1953 brought the prose out of Ezekiel by eliminating as "accretions" any words or phrases that would interfere with the poetic meter of the residual text. Most scholars never took up these leads. By such processes practically any given document, including the driest of statistical lists, could, with appropriate ingenuity, change pedestrian prose into lyric poetry. Another point to bear in mind is one that we have already noted: there *is* poetry in Ezekiel. It is usually imbedded in prose, and it is often difficult to isolate. It turns up in translation more often, perhaps, through the editorial perception of the NAB rather than of the RSV, the NEB, or TEV. Sometimes a piece of poetry emerges in the elaboration of the most complex allegory or the development of a wordy and repetitious instruction. This poem may have been the inspiration of the passage and probably puts us in contact with the living prophetic voice that provided the inspiration.

Ezekiel is richer in *autobiography* than any other prophetical work. Again this is a matter of degree, not of kind. There are ample precedents in Hosea, Jeremiah, Isaiah, and elsewhere. These charismatic figures in Israel felt it important to make known to posterity their personal encounters with the divine. They believed that these had import for the future of the nation and the people. Autobiographical detail about pronouncement and revelation is a peculiarity of Ezekiel, but not a departure from the tradition in which he stood.

Our own idea of what the OT prophets were owes much to later Jewish and Christian perception. The reality as the OT presents is less influential. "Prophet" is our conventional translation of Hebrew *nabi*. The LXX (the ancient Greek translation from which we get our names and divisions of the biblical books and many of our understandings of basic biblical ideas) translated this term as *prophetes*. *Prophetes* in Greek was something different from *nabi* in Hebrew, or at least from what *nabi* had once been in Hebrew. Thus Amos explicitly rejects the title *nabi* (Amos 7:14), and in Jer. 14:18; Hos. 4:5; Isa. 9:15 and elsewhere the *nabi* is a deceiver, someone brought (or bought) into the service of the national establishment, not a reliable guide to the LORD's will. This is not the place to pursue further the semantic development of *nabi* in the Hebrew Bible or of the *prophetes* in the LXX. It is sufficient for our purposes to point out that those whom we designate *the* prophets of the OT were never conscious of forming a "school" or a "tradition" under that name. This can explain their usual independence of one another and their hardly ever citing one another. They were above all else people, each responding to his inner drive. It is therefore pointless to compare one with another as though there had been some deviation from a common norm. By definition, we should expect the gathered prophetic literature to be unpredictable, unusual, and idiosyncratic.

Considering all this, we must still look at the text of Ezekiel with a dispassionate eye. We must conclude, as we have already implied, that it is a document that has undergone very extensive redaction. Lengthy prose commentaries follow snippets of poetry. Legal aphorisms have grown into treatises. Thoughts have become tracts. Symbols have been enlarged extravagantly, and straightforward projections (like the ideal temple-city-state of Ezek. 40–48, for example) have had their point driven deeply in the ground through the relentless literalism of editors and scribes. Later enthusiasts have subjected the book of Ezekiel to more amplifications, more than any other of the prophetic works. They have so augmented and annotated the prophet's words that it is often impossible to separate what is "authentic" from what is "accretional" in the book. For the most part, no attempt at separation will be made in this commentary.

Such a decision is appropriate in this series of commentaries whose purpose is to expound the received, canonical text handed down by and for the community of believers. We are all heirs of this community, and we regard this text in all its developments as sacred Scripture. Anyone who is sensitive to a major distinction of biblical religion, namely that it centers on not simply a revelation of *word* (as in the religions of timeless revelation of much of the rest of the world) but rather of *word in time and specific act,* will want to ask some of the same questions that occur to the biblical critic: the who, the when, the circumstances that surrounded the giving of the word. Therefore we must express some curiosity about the existence and the character of the prophetic figure Ezekiel who stands behind this work.

The Prophet Ezekiel

If we had to rely solely on the received text of the book of Ezekiel itself, there would be no doubt about the life and character of the prophet who has given it his name. He was an exile. The community of these exiles would have included the more important citizens of Judah, whom the Babylonians deported during Nebuchadnezzar's initial conquest in 597 B.C.E. Five years later, on 31 July 593, to be precise, he received in Babylon the call to prophesy to Israel (Ezek. 1:2). What follows, the various visions, instructions, exhortations, sermons, allegories, and so forth, that make up the book of Ezekiel come from this exilic prophet from that date onward until an oracle against Nebuchadnezzar dated 26 April 571 (29:17), the latest date to appear in the work. With the additions and expansions that we have mentioned before, we see the record of a prophetic career lived out in Babylon over a period of some twenty-two years.

The career of Ezekiel is not so easily dealt with, as we shall see in a moment. We no longer have to contend with a position that was once in critical vogue, that "Ezekiel" had no historical but only a literary existence, like the "Solomon" of Ecclesiastes or the book of Wisdom. Scholars such as the late C. C. Torrey (1934), followed by such commentators as Adrianus van den Born (1954), held that not only Ezekiel but the whole story of exile and restoration found in Chronicles-Ezra-Nehemiah were largely figments of romantic imagination. These books were the results of theological speculations that had created history where there was none. In this case, archaeological discoveries such as the Babylonian records of palace rations distributed to "Jehoiachin, king of Judah" dispelled this skepticism (see *ANET,* 308). They validated the biblical picture of things, if not in every detail at least sufficiently to encourage us to take the Bible's history seriously. There is no reason for us to doubt that there was a prophet Ezekiel. This prophet was active from the time of the first Judean deportation to Babylon, five years into the exile of Jehoiachin and his court that had begun in 597 (Ezek. 1:2; 2 Kgs. 24:15-17).

The problem that immediately arises is a puzzle created by the book of Ezekiel itself. Ezekiel claims to have received his call to prophesy as one of the exiles in Babylon (Ezek. 1:3; 3:15), where he lived (3:24). There is no suggestion in the book of any intervening travel by the prophet back and forth between Jerusalem and Babylon. We cannot even be sure that such travel would have been a possibility, let alone that it would have been likely. Yet the prophet displays an intimate knowledge of the circumstances of the city of Jerusalem. Indeed, Ezekiel might be expected to know Jerusalem well. He was among the "officials, and the chief men of the land"—its princes, warriors, craftsmen. All but the very poorest of the people went into exile according to 2 Kgs. 24:14-15. Yet apparently he had knowledge of what was going on in Jerusalem at the very moment he was prophesying against it (see Ezek. 11:13!). This has suggested to more than one commentator that the book of Ezekiel has it wrong. Ezekiel must have divided his prophetic ministry between his homeland and the land of exile. The explanation that makes the most sense to them is that the prophet was active in Jerusalem during the crucial years 597-586. It was only after that, as a participant in the *second* phase of the Exile, that he did what the text says he did in Babylon. The trouble with this hypothesis is that it robs of historical meaning the greater part of Ezekiel's prophecy and effectively makes of him a character of fiction. As we shall see in the commentary, Ezekiel's presence in Babylon is not a geographical incidental but an essential of his prophecy.

What seems the better solution is to recognize that the redactional element runs through the work deeply and thoroughly. If we consider later updating and the assimilation of later intelligence we can explain how it can be said that Ezekiel "saw" the death of Pelatiah the son of Benaiah in Jerusalem at the very same time he was prophesying against the temple (11:13). It is not necessary to place Ezekiel there physically as an eyewitness. Nor is it necessary to hypothesize some kind of clairvoyance by which he was aware of events taking place hundreds of kilometers removed from him—though we cannot eliminate the hypothesis. (The phenomenon of prophecy and its psychology are areas so insufficiently explored, particularly by Western scholars. These scholars tend to treat prophecy as a defunct craft with no present referents, so we would be wary of firmly deciding what a prophet could and could not do.)

This commentary assumes that Ezekiel was throughout a prophet in Babylon, as he and the book claim. He was more than less in the mold of the prophets of Israel and Judah who had preceded him. We are to understand him mainly in reference to them.

There is one aspect to Ezekiel's prophecy that does seem to dissociate him from the "classical" prophets of the 8th and 7th cents. and from his part-time contemporary Jeremiah. It associates him more clearly both with the ancient "preclassical" *nabis* of Israelite prophetism and with some prophets of postexilic Judaism who in this respect may be thought to have followed in his wake. That aspect is the nature of the prophetic vision, a matter already dealt with above but which deserves some additional remarks.

We have maintained that the line from the "parabolic" vision of Ezekiel's predecessors to his "allegorical" vision is a straight one. Yet there is more to the question than that. It is not a matter of content only but also of the medium by which the vision came. In Ezekiel we read of the "hand" or "spirit" of the LORD. Sometimes simply "spirit" without an article appears. It was the "spirit" that "lifted him up" physically and transported him to "*the* plain" where he received his revelations (3:22-23; 37:1-2). Language like this sounds very much like the attempt to describe an ecstatic experience.

All this is very possible. Ezekiel, after all, combined in himself other characteristics that would have been inconceivable in a prophet like, for instance, Amos. Ezekiel was also a priest (1:3) — a calling that, as we shall see, accounts for much that is distinctive about the book of Ezekiel within the prophetic literature. If he also combined with his prophetic character in the Amosian sense another that harked back to more ancient patterns of religion, culture, and structure, this would not be too difficult to credit. Prophecy, we have already argued, was a highly existential thing. Perhaps it was even more so in the exilic and postexilic periods, the final age of Israelite prophetism. In sum, Ezekiel is his own person. We should measure him by himself and no other. In that spirit we go to find him in the book of his name.

THE THEOLOGY OF EZEKIEL

The starting point of Ezekiel's theology was his experience of exile. Ezekiel had to make sense of this tragedy in Judah's life. Like his predecessors who warned Israel of the consequences of its failure to serve Yahweh alone, this prophet believed that Israel's predicament was Israel's responsibility. According to Ezekiel, Israel has shown a persistent resistance to the LORD. No other prophet pronounces as negative a verdict on all of Israel's history as does Ezekiel (chs. 16 and 23). He asserts that Israel was never obedient to the LORD. Ezekiel protests against the corruption of Israelite society, but he saves his most vehement criticism for Israel's cultic offenses (6:13; 20:12, 24, 28; 23:37-38). When Israel defiled God's sanctuary, its guilt was beyond calculation. These sins touched God's "private sphere." Here Ezekiel's priestly background makes its presence felt.

When the prophet speaks of Israel's infidelity, he recognizes the inevitability of the severe judgment that has come and is still to come upon Israel. He believed that Babylon was God's instrument of judgment. The fall of Jerusalem and the destruction of the temple were the inevitable consequences of Israel's chronic disobedience. Still the prophet believed that judgment was not God's last word to Israel. Ezekiel's preaching also intended to help Judah recognize the salvation that he could discern in Israel's future. Though the prophet calls for repentance (16:54-63; 33:10-16), this will not attain redemption for Israel. The prophet spoke confidently about the future because he believed that Israel's new life would come from God (20:37-38; 37:1-14). It is Yahweh who brings judgment upon Israel. It is the same Yahweh who gives the prophet a vision of the salvation he is to proclaim. Chs. 40–48 contain the prophet's specific plans for Israel's new life in its land. Ezekiel believed that these plans were to come to fruition in the close future because of the power of God.

To those who could not believe in that future because of the collective guilt of Israel the prophet insisted that each generation has a direct relationship with God (18:2). Each generation has to assume responsibility for its future. The prophet sees himself as a watchman (chs. 3 and 33) to his generation. He is to confront the people of his generation, warn them, exhort them. Those who heed his warning and act on his exhortations will be ready to live in the future that God's power is bringing into existence. Those who fail to heed the prophet must bear the burden of their intransigence.

The prophet even has an answer for those who believe that Israel is doomed to disobedience and judgment. God will create a new heart and a new spirit for Israel (11:19-20). God gave Israel the commandments to enable Israel to be faithful, but the commandments were not enough (20:40). The new spirit that God will give to Israel will make obedience and fidelity a genuine possibility for Israel. It will replace the spirit of infidelity that ingrained disobedience on Israel's heart.

Like Isaiah (Isa. 6) and Jeremiah (Jer. 1), Ezekiel (Ezek. 1–3) testifies about his experience of the God who called him to announce both judgment and salvation. The God of Ezekiel is a mysterious, transcendent deity whose holiness Israel has defiled (Ezek. 20:30). Ezekiel lacks the hymnic descriptions of God characteristic of Isa. 40–55. His descriptions of his encounter with the deity are phantasmagoric and even bizarre. His theological discourse is direct, blunt, and even crude. For the prophet, God is holy. That should be enough for Israel to understand how it ought to approach its God. Like Jeremiah and Second Isaiah, Ezekiel tries to broaden Israel's understanding of Yahweh. The God of Israel is no mere national deity. Yahweh is the God of all nations. God uses the nations so that all people could recognize Yahweh as God. A formula that concludes most of the prophet's oracles reads: ". . . that they (or 'you') will know that I am Yahweh." Israel and the nations will learn who Yahweh is by witnessing Yahweh's actions toward Israel.

In the midst of the Exile, Ezekiel experienced God's call to be a prophet. He proclaimed the destruction that was to come upon Jerusalem and Judah because of their neglect of God's law. He recognized that destruction was not God's last word to Israel. The prophet believed that salvation was to follow judgment. He saw himself as a watchman calling sinners to return to God. Israel was on the way to its death. God's fidelity would call Israel back to life.

15

EZEKIEL AND ISRAEL'S WORSHIP

Ezekiel played an important role in the profound change that affected the religion of the OT during his lifetime. People have sometimes called Ezekiel "the father of Judaism." There is an element of truth in this title. There is also some truth in a companion title that some have given him: "the father of OT apocalyptic." It depends on what we understand by Judaism. If this means certain seminal ideas and attitudes elaborated in and during the Babylonian Captivity that constituted a program for the radical recasting of the preexilic religion of Israel, then Ezekiel played a major role in the emergence of Judaism. Even in this accounting, one may wonder to what extent his role was that of an initiator of these ideas and attitudes rather than one who simply shared them. If, on the other hand, Judaism refers to the religion promulgated in the Palestine of Ezra and Nehemiah with all the attributes that the Chronicler ascribed to it, then Ezekiel is hardly accountable for this. There is too much here that is directly assignable to the circumstances and realities of the renewed Jewish homeland and to reactions to those circumstances and realities. Ezekiel could not have been responsible for it all, even in principle. There are some aspects of this Judaism, which is the rabbinical Judaism that has passed into our history and remains there, which Ezekiel would hardly have recognized. Conversely, when rabbinical Judaism began the process by which the canon of its Scripture became determined, the book of Ezekiel presented it with a problem because of its conflicts with the Pentateuch.

Ezekiel's contribution to the genesis of Judaism did lie in the part he played in the final formulation of pentateuchal Law, the Torah that is the foundation of Judaism. In this formulation he is to be placed somewhere between the so-called Law of Holiness (Lev. 17–26), which crystallized in Babylon during the Exile, and the Priestly legislation (part of the P source of pentateuchal criticism), which is postexilic and Palestinian. On the Law of Holiness, Ezekiel is dependent, and with the Priestly legislation he sometimes differs—the cause of the canonical problem for the later orthodox rabbis. We have been speaking of formulations and reformulations only. All agree that both the Law of Holiness and

16

the Priestly legislation contained many elements of ancient law going back to Israel's very origins.

The central emphasis of the Law for Ezekiel was the reorganization of the priesthood at the head of this community. The prophet envisaged the restored Israel as a sacral community. This was hardly true of the Judaism of Ezra and Nehemiah. At that time the rabbi with his disciples became the center of religious life. Still later the synagogue became the central religious institution for the ordinary people. This happened because of the historical circumstances that dictated the development of Jewish society both in Palestine and the Diaspora.

Traditionally in Israel the priesthood had become the hereditary prerogative of the Levites, those who belonged to the tribe of Levi. In Deuteronomy and the Deuteronomistic history, preexilic in inspiration though only fixed in writing in later times, "priest" and "Levite" are simply interchangeable terms (e.g., Deut. 18:1). Alongside this "official" priesthood there were others, harkening back to simpler and less organized times. At one time the head of the household or the larger community served as priest, as in the patriarchal period and later (e.g., Judg. 17:1-6). Thus both David (2 Sam. 6:12-15, 20; 24:18-25) and Solomon (1 Kgs. 8:62-64) functioned as priests, as did David's sons (2 Sam. 8:18 — see how the revisionism represented in 1 Chr. 18:17 refused to admit this!). Ezekiel deplored this and legislated against it. He required the separation of the temple from the palace and insisted upon the lay character of the prince of the people (Ezek. 43:6-9; 46:1-8).

With some exceptions, then, throughout most of Israel's preexilic history levitical priests served in the cult places both of the north (Judg. 18:30-31) and the south—places like Nob (1 Sam. 21:1-9) and Anathoth (the city of Jeremiah; see Jer. 1:1; 11:18-23). These priests were of the tribe of Levi or those who had at least become part of it. Levites of one kind or another formed the priesthoods of the local sanctuaries of the north and south. These sanctuaries were the *bamot* (usually translated "high places" but more accurately "cult places") that the Deuteronomic legislation tried to eradicate.

As a rule these priesthoods, hereditary as they were, had simply been inherited when the sanctuaries changed from Canaanite into Israelite places of sacrifice. As the rites were much the same, so were the officiants. Only the worship was now of Yahweh rather than of Baal or whatever local or city deity had been the object of worship. In Jerusalem, after David conquered it and made it his capital and it later became the site of Solomon's temple, we hear particularly of the priestly name Zadok (2 Sam. 8:17; 1 Kgs. 1:32-48). Another priestly name, that of Abiathar, was also prominent in David's time. Solomon deposed Abiathar in favor of Zadok. Abiathar, who had been a priest from the line of Eli of the sanctuary at Shiloh, misplayed the game of palace politics. He favored Adonijah rather than Solomon for the succession (1 Kgs. 2:26-27). Zadok, whose name is resonant of pre-Israelite Jerusalem (cf. Melchizedek in Gen. 14:18; Ps. 110:4; Adonizedek in Josh. 10:1, Zedek [RSV "righteousness"], doubtless the former name of the city deity, in Isa. 1:21), was the Jebusite priestly line now assimilated into Israel. This Zadokite priesthood (including Ezekiel?) was without doubt transported to Babylon by Nebuchadnezzar in 597 B.C.E. with the other influential families of Jerusalem. In the Exile it understandably got a monopoly of the priestly caste. Ezekiel declared it to be the only priesthood of the future Israel, with the consequent demotion of the other Levites to other stations.

The so-called reform of King Josiah around 621 appears to anticipate the demotion of the Levites (2 Kgs. 22–23). Then, at least, many country shrines outside Jerusalem ceased operations, thus leaving the levitical priests who had officiated there without the means of livelihood. (This explains why the legal code of Deuteronomy so often groups the Levites with orphans, widows, and landless aliens as indigent persons in need of charity.) With the Exile, the demotion became complete through another development in what had become the proprieties of the sacrificial cult.

In the preexilic temple Canaanite serfs handled the menial work incidental to the primary business of sacrifice ("Solomon's servants" and the *netinim* of Ezra 2:43-58; cf. Josh. 9). To Ezekiel, this institution was an abomination of the past that had to be rooted out (Ezek. 44:6-8). From then on this work was to be done by the Levites. (From the Ezra passage above it seems clear that during the Exile some at least of "Solomon's servants" and the *netinim* became part of Israel and constituted a subordinate levitical group.) It is obvious from Ezek. 44:10-14 that the new station allotted to the Levites was thought of as a punishment for past shortcomings and lack of fidelity. Their reduced status doubtless accounts for the difficulty experienced by Ezra in persuading Levites to accompany him to Jerusalem to repopulate the land and service the temple (Ezra 8:15-20).

Such, then, was one of the essentials of the holy community-to-be as it was envisioned by Ezekiel, a community gathered about "the sons of Zadok." The Priestly author/redactor of the Pentateuch of the postexilic community also recognizes the subordinate station of the Levites. For him the Zadokites' privileged position is not such an issue: the priests of Israel are all "the sons of Aaron." In 1 Chr. 6:49-53 the Chronicler of postexilic Judaism in the "restoration" (Ezra?) lists Zadok as one of these sons of Aaron.

PART I
THE PROPHET
AND THE PEOPLE

Ezekiel 1:1–7:27

EZEKIEL'S CALL
Ezekiel 1:1–3:15

This narrative of Ezekiel's call to prophecy is a redactional unit, the first of many that the reader encounters in this book. The prophetic literature describes more than once the experience of a divine calling. The prophet appealed to such a calling as constituting his credentials to speak the word of the LORD. Jer. 1:4-10 is one example. Perhaps Isa. 6 is a better example since in the Isaianic text there is a highly symbolic portrayal of the divine majesty similar to the one in Ezekiel. In Amos 7:15 there occurs simply the terse statement that the LORD "took" Amos and sent him to prophesy. It is likely that the biographical/autobiographical narrative of the first three chapters of the book of Hosea intended to do the same. The purpose of these chapters is to relate the series of circumstances under which Hosea assumed his vocation as a prophet.

Some modern versions of the Scripture attempt to reconstruct the presumed original shape of the text by rearranging verses, bracketing out words, and the like. The purpose is to separate what was always there from later glosses and annotations. Such a procedure requires much guesswork. The subject of this commentary is the received and canonical text of Ezekiel. It is therefore possible to keep distinctions between the prophet's words and later additions to a minimum unless necessary for a proper understanding of the text. In its present form, this passage falls into four parts. First comes the introduction (Ezek. 1:1-3), then the vision of the LORD'S glory (1:4-28), the commissioning of Ezekiel (2:1–3:11), and the end of the vision (3:12, 15).

This first vision of Ezekiel immediately sets a pattern that repeats itself in others to come. At first glance the picture that emerges seems full of contradictions of a kind that a redactor would not have introduced, had he any competence for his task. First Ezekiel is in the presence of the exiles when the heavens open and the vision begins. As the vision develops, and especially when the word of the LORD comes to him and commands him to go and speak to the rebellious house of Israel, these third parties obviously are present. Also in 3:12-14 the spirit lifts him up and transports him to the exiles. Simultaneously the hand of the LORD that came upon Ezekiel in 1:3 continues to rest heavily upon him. These apparent inconsistencies resolve themselves easily if we assume that we are reading the account of an ecstatic experience. On this assumption Ezekiel is physically present with the exiles throughout this vision. He is in such a state of spiritual removal that he is oblivious to his surroundings. The prophet is conscious only of the heavenly realities that are appearing in his mind's eye. The illusion of movement back and forth—or the necessity of describing the experience in such terms—is altogether of the same quality as the phantasmagory of visual and tactile images that otherwise overflow the vision.

We shall see how this hypothesis squares with the details of Ezekiel's vision in the verses that follow. Of equal importance will be the source of the images themselves that impress themselves on the prophet's mind.

1:1-3 Two dates attach themselves to the account of this inaugural vision. One locates it during "*the fifth year* of the exile of King Jehoiachin," namely in 593 B.C.E. It is consistent with the rest of the dates found elsewhere in the book. A glossator probably added this date. The years of Jehoiachin's exile would have corresponded to the years of his reign, had the Babylonians not taken him from Jerusalem and made him a hostage at the court of Nebuchadnezzar and his successors (2 Kgs. 25:27-30). Inscriptional material from both Palestine and Babylonia suggests that Jehoiachin continued to bear the title of king even in exile. The people of Judah probably considered his uncle Mattaniah to whom Nebuchadnezzar gave the name Zedekiah (well known for his conflicts with the prophet Jeremiah) and set up to reign in his place, as 2 Kgs. 24:17 has it, to be only a regent for the king.

In Ezek. 1:1—probably in Ezekiel's own words—we also read about a "thirtieth year." Interpreters have debated the significance of this date. The most obvious assumption seems to be that the prophet was referring to his age at the time he received his prophetic call. As Ernst Vogt, among others, has argued, it would be altogether natural to expect from Ezekiel, a man born to the privileged priestly class, a reminder that it was in the time of his full adulthood (cf. Luke 3:23) that God called him to prophesy doom to Judah. If Ezekiel were thirty years old in 593, therefore, he would have been born about 622, during the reign of the pious King Josiah. About 600, when he was some twenty-three years of age, the prophet married. With his wife he went to Babylonia as an exile in 597 at the age of twenty-six. The last dated prophecy of his book (Ezek. 29:17) is that of the year 571, when he would have been fifty-six. Meanwhile he would have lost his wife when he was thirty-seven (24:18).

Ezekiel's vision took place while he was among the exiles "by the river Chebar." The LXX and the Vulgate have preserved the name of the river as "Chobar" (Akkadian *nar kabaru*). This reading is better than that of the Hebrew. There were probably various sites that had this name ("the big river"), though this fact does not preclude the use of the term as a distinct proper name (cf. Guadalquivir, Rio Grande); one is near Nippur in southern Mesopotamia, which would correspond with Ezekiel's reference to "the land of the Chaldeans." The term "river" refers to one of the extensive network of irrigation canals that crisscrossed Mesopotamia in ancient times. These canals enabled the region then to present much less of the forbidding desert vista that is now so much its characteristic. The Jews of the Exile gathered at these water sources because of the extensive ritual washings that played an important role in their worship. Similarly, when Paul visited Philippi and sought out the Jews where there was no synagogue, he found them gathered by the riverside (Acts 16:12-13).

Ezekiel and the redactor of these verses describe the beginning of his visionary experience in several ways. "The heavens were opened" is an expression found only this once in the OT. It refers to the necessary condition for a vision rather than to something itself seen. The unseen spiritual world of God and God's heavenly court is now visible. What becomes visible, the "visions of God," is the revelation given to the prophet. All that follows is his description of what he saw, heard, and felt, and what his fellow exiles neither saw, heard, nor felt. (Compare the various accounts of Paul's vision on the way to Damascus in Acts 9:1-8; 22:4-16; 26:12-20.) "The hand of the LORD" designates something felt rather than seen. It is an awareness of the divine power coming over the prophet's consciousness that enables him to experience these heavenly visions.

1:4-14 First the vision is one of the mysterious "living creatures" (*hayyot,* literally "live ones," "animals"). It is a vision that comes with a storm wind "out of the north." In Jer. 1:13 the prophet had a vision of a pot boiling over that was facing the north: the traditional route by which foreign invasion came to Jerusalem. (Surrounding the city were deep ravines except on the north. The region to the north of the city is higher in elevation. This made invasion from the north not only necessary but ideal.) Here the meaning is different. We are reaching back to older mythological ideas, according to which the home of deity was in the far north. There were many places where Semites settled that bore the name Baal-zephon (cf. Exod. 14:2, 9; Num. 33:7), that is, "Baal of the North." Such place names were popular among seafaring people like the Phoenicians. In Ps. 48:2 Jerusalem, in defiance of all real geography, is supposedly "in the far north, the city of the great King" (cf. also Isa. 14:13). Mythological, too, are the elements of fire, wind, the clouds, lightning, and so forth, all conventional symbols attaching to theophanies and divine revelations.

The "living creatures" of Ezekiel's vision have a vague resemblance to the seraphim of Isa. 6, and for good reason, since the images of the cherubim that overshadowed the historical ark of the covenant inspired both visions (1 Sam. 4:4). (Ezek. 10:20 explicitly identifies these living creatures with the cherubim.) In Ezekiel other motifs appear that bear the stamp of Babylon. His living creatures are cherubs: the half-beast, half-human monsters called *karibu* by the Mesopotamians. In plastic art the *karibu* served as guardians of sacred places and the sign of divine presence. It is reminiscent of the cherub guarding the mythological "garden of God" in 28:14, 16 and Gen. 3:24.

The appearance of the creatures need not occupy too much of our attention. The number "four," it will be noted, predominates. This was then, as it is now ("four-square"), regarded as some kind of perfect number. It becomes a characteristic of apocalyptic language later on to designate the four ages of human history. It remains in our familiar references to the four corners of the earth, the four winds, and so on. Walther Zimmerli points out that the Priestly stratum in the Pentateuch has in mind a scheme of four periods in its outline of world history. Similar schemes occur in the framework of cyclic thought and in its most elaborate form in the Hindu doctrine of the four Jugas of a Kalpa. Also typical of apocalyptic is the proliferation of qualifiers such as "the likeness of," "something like," and so forth, when describing the contents of the vision. This is, on the one hand, a disclaimer required by the nature of the subject. Mystics such as St. Teresa of Avila and John of the Cross also confessed to their inability to describe in adequate words the visions they had received. It can also be, especially in apocalyptic, a device for heightening the impression of the other-worldliness that is the desired effect of the supposed revelation. Ezek. 1:9 and 12 express the chief significance of the living creatures for Ezekiel: their absolute mobility at the disposition of the spirit. There is a subtlety here that goes beyond the affirmation that the God of Israel is universal and omnipresent. We shall understand this better at the conclusion of the vision.

The burning coals that are among the living creatures (v. 13) have no function here, though they do in a similar vision described in ch. 10. The significance of the faces (lion, man, ox, and eagle) is not obvious. Ancient Near Eastern art produced mythical creatures in which parts of different animals and birds were combined with those of a human. For example, the Assyrian cherub combines the face of a human, the forequarters of a lion, the hindquarters of a bull, and the wings of an eagle into a fantastic creature. One creature with four faces has no precedent in the ancient Near East. Early Christian interpreters saw these four faces as symbols of the Evangelists: Matthew (the human face), Mark (the lion), Luke (the ox), and John (the eagle).

1:15-25   The next stage of the vision concerns the "wheelwork" of the throne of God. At Dura-Europos, an ancient site in what is now northern Syria, a synagogue dating from ca. 200 C.E. came to light in 1932. Contrary to Jewish law that forbade pictorial representation of sacred things, many wall paintings (now in the Archaeological Museum of Damascus) decorated this synagogue. They pictured biblical events that were probably of special interest to people of this region, such as the story of Esther and the prophecies of Ezekiel. Among other items of interest in these murals are several representations of the ark of the covenant. The ark in these pictures does not look anything like the object described in the Bible. It is likely enough that these pictures preserve a tradition about the ark that is historically of great value. The Priestly writer's description in the Pentateuch is more theologically oriented. At the time the Priestly writer described the ark, it was no longer in existence. What is of concern now is that the ark, which the Bible conceived as the throne of God, may have been mounted on wheels, at least occasionally, just as Ezekiel's vision implies. Royal thrones in the ancient Near East were often portable objects (cf. Dan. 7:9), and there are many representations in Mesopotamian art of gods enthroned in wheeled carriages. Also in 1 Chr. 28:18 there is a reference to the ark and cherubim as constituting together a "golden chariot." (See Rachel Wischnitzer, *The Messianic Themes in the Paintings of the Dura Synagogue* [Chicago: University of Chicago Press, 1948].)

   Of course the wheels as they appear in the vision are like no other wheels on earth. They gleam like "chrysolite," sharing the aura of the heavenly with which they are associated and which so often is symbolized by the glittering of precious stones (cf. Exod. 24:10; Ezek. 28:13, 14; and 1:26, below). They appear as a wheel within a wheel. Given the identification of the four wheels with the four living creatures, this must mean that the prophet thought that they could turn in all four directions as though positioned on a universal axle. This is impossible as a feat of engineering, but at home in the realm of vision. The "eyes" on the rims of the wheels were probably bosses or studs designed to improve traction on rough and uneven roads. That the prophet fancifully calls these "eyes" is doubtless to suggest the all-seeing character of the chariot and its rider.

Above all, wheels and creatures, is a crystalline "firmament" (v. 22). The same word *(raqia*ʿ*)* appears here that, in the first Genesis story of creation, means the sky. People in antiquity thought of the sky as an inverted bowl of burnished and beaten metal. It served to hold in check the waters above the earth and served as a surface for the sun and moon and stars. Here we have a heavenly sky corresponding to the earthly one.

In our edited and elaborated text the vision now also becomes audition as the prophet hears various sounds: the sound of the creatures' "wings" is like that of "many waters," like "the sound of Shaddai" (thunder; cf. Ps. 29:3), a sound of "tumult" like that of a "host," the bustle of an armed camp, and finally the sound of a human "voice." The last mentioned is in anticipation of the call and commissioning of the prophet that properly begins in Ezek. 1:28b. The other sounds come here from other contexts (e.g., 10:5), simply as what the later redactors took to be the usual accompaniments of Ezekiel's visions.

1:26-28a   Finally Ezekiel sees the actual "throne" of the LORD, and seated upon it the LORD in "human form." The exact meaning of some details of this representation is not too clear. Commentators frequently call attention to a pictorial image of the god Asshur from the period 890-884 *(ANEP,* 538). Here, as in Ezekiel, the god is well-defined from the waist up, gleaming with the lustre of fiery colors. Something of this nature may well have been the inspiration of Ezekiel's portrayal. Below the waist, Ezekiel's figure seems ill-defined. There is "brightness round about him," and the fire engulfs the prophet (the fire in the midst of the living creatures?). Perhaps the intention is to stress again the awesome presence of deity while tying the appearance firmly to the symbolism of the ark of God's presence. That presence, whose mobility has already been and is even now being shown, belongs properly to God's abode in Jerusalem, whither it will return. The light surrounding the human figure has all the colors of the rainbow, as in the picture of Asshur just mentioned.

Ezekiel identifies this appearance as that of "the glory of the LORD." This expression or its equivalent occurs often in Ezekiel, always to designate the visible, numinous appearance of the divine majesty. The Priestly writing uses the same expression for the "pillar of fire" that accompanied the Israelites in their desert wanderings. (The literary relationship between P and the book of Ezekiel is still a mystery.) This fire was visible only at night; during the day a "pillar of cloud" concealed it (Num. 14:14; Exod. 16:10). The Priestly writer, unlike Ezekiel, never represents the glory of the LORD in human form. Clouds, like fire, are a frequent concomitant of theophany (Exod. 19:16; Judg. 5:4), and Ps. 68:4, 33; 104:3 picture the God of Israel as riding in a chariot on the clouds. Ancient Israel borrowed this last imagery from Canaanite myth, which so represented the weather-god Baal.

1:28b–2:7   Ezekiel, who has prostrated himself in the presence of divine majesty, is not only told to stand, he is also physically stood on his feet by "spirit" (not *the* Spirit [of God] but the force of ecstatic experience). The divine apparition addresses him as "son of man." This expression, which occurs 87 times in Ezekiel and once in Dan. 8:17, does not have the same significance as the messianic Son of man of intertestamental Judaism and of the Gospels (cf. Norman Perrin, *A Modern Pilgrimage in New Testament Christology* [Philadelphia: Fortress, 1974]). The latter expression doubtless derives from the "one like a son of man" in the apocalyptic vision of Dan. 7:13. In Ezekiel the expression, though it becomes virtually a title, means nothing more or less than "man," as it does in Ps. 8:4. Particularly in divine communication, its purpose is to call attention to all that otherwise separates the revealer from the one who receives revelation. The humanity of the prophet and his oneness with the people to whom God has sent him constitute the point at issue. Ezekiel is a sinner, but one whom God loves and chooses to be a prophet. This occurs also in Isa. 6:5. Here the prophet's face-to-face encounter with Yahweh the King brings home to him that he is a person of unclean lips and one of a people of unclean lips.

First Ezekiel receives his mission as the messenger of the LORD. The criterion of true prophecy did not lie in visible manifestations of the spirit (cf. 1 Kgs. 22:24), though Ezekiel seems to have had plenty of these. Rather, it is the prophet's certainty that God had sent him (Amos 7:15; Isa. 6:8-10; Jer. 1:4-10). Ezekiel's commission sounds very much like the one that Jeremiah received with its reiterated assurances of strength and support against inevitable opposition and persecution. The one difference is that Jeremiah is a "prophet to the nations," while God sends Ezekiel to "the people of Israel," a people in rebellion. (In Ezek. 2:3 the RSV reads "to the nations" with the Hebrew text [rationalized "nation" = Israel by the Syriac], but it is a gloss, missing in the LXX.)

Israel was first the name of all the people covenanted with Yahweh. Following the end of the dual monarchy under David and Solomon, the northern kingdom used "Israel" as its proper name. Following the fall of the northern kingdom the people of the southern kingdom reappropriated that name, though they were all Judahites. Verse 3 also suggests a more significant reason for the use of Israel in this context. The exiles to whom Ezekiel is immediately being sent, with those who remain in Jerusalem and to whom his mission will later extend, are but the final stage of the total history of Israel. It has been a consistent history of rebellion against God's word. In v. 5 Ezekiel learns that whether the people heed his prophecy or not, "they will know that there has been a prophet among them." This is a "recognition formula," common in Ezekiel. It testifies to the certain efficacy of prophecy, vindicated in time by force of the word itself or by historical sign (Claus Westermann, *Basic Forms of Prophetic Speech* [Philadelphia: Westminster and London: Lutterworth, 1967]; Walther Zimmerli, "The Word of Divine Self-manifestation (Proof-Saying): A Prophetic Genre," in *I Am Yahweh* [Atlanta: John Knox, 1982], 99-110).

2:8–3:3   Ezekiel receives a scroll that he is to devour. This is only the first of an extraordinary series of prophetic "acts" or signs that the prophet will do during his career. This one is personal and private. It is a very graphic confirmation of his commission to take in the word of the LORD that he is to proclaim to the rebellious house of Israel. The outstretched "hand" holding the "scroll" is, in this instance, represented as something visual. Whether it is actually the hand of the LORD or simply a figure made necessary by the visionary symbolism is not important. The scroll, of course, represents the word which Ezekiel is to proclaim.

More than one commentator recognized that this part of

31

Ezekiel's vision may have had as its inspiration a remembrance of the events that Jer. 36 describes. These events could have easily occurred in Ezekiel's sight in the year 604 when he was a young priest of eighteen serving in the Jerusalem temple. The spectacle of the king burning the scroll of Jeremiah's prophecies must have made a profound impression on all who were present at the court/temple. Some people still esteemed Jeremiah as a true messenger of God. The scroll offered to Ezekiel, written "on the front and on the back," appears to have been, like Jeremiah's, a papyrus scroll. Papyrus is edible and could be easily cut in pieces column by column. Another reminiscence of Jeremiah's scroll is that this one, too, contains "lamentation and mourning and woe." Finally Ezekiel eats the scroll, taking in the word of God and with it his prophetic commission. Like Jeremiah (Jer. 15:16), he finds the words "as sweet as honey." Ezekiel accepts his prophetic mission without much hesitation. This contrasts with the example of Jeremiah (Jer. 1:6-8), but very much in the spirit of Isaiah (Isa. 6:8). This passage in Ezekiel served as the model for Rev. 10:8-11. The latter text has caught the spirit of the whole passage accurately. It makes the scroll of God's word sweet to the mouth but bitter in the belly. It is an aftertaste that Ezekiel himself might have anticipated, having read its doleful words when the scroll unfolded before him. The conclusion of the vision that follows spells out this part of the experience.

3:4-15 After Ezekiel's initial pleasure at accepting the call to prophesy, Ezek. 3:4-11 explains the details of his mission. The particulars that will constitute his prophetic career are as grief-stricken as those of any other prophet in Israel. God is not sending him to "people of foreign speech and a hard language" (cf. Isa. 33:19), to Gentiles such as these Chaldeans among whom the exiles were living, but to the even more difficult people who paradoxically are the prophet's own. If it were to the Gentiles that God was sending him, says the voice, perhaps they would listen. The novelty of the message itself would be compelling. This thought may have inspired the later biblical author who composed the book of Jonah. In that book the entire population of the hated city of Nineveh repents at the first sound of the voice of a somewhat flawed prophet! As it is, God is sending Ezekiel to a recalcitrant people who will continue recalcitrant to the end. They are a people "of a hard forehead and of a stubborn heart." Therefore, even as Jeremiah, a timid and diffident man, became a "fortified city" and an "iron pillar" to prevail over the kings of Judah and its people (Jer. 1:18-19), so Ezekiel's brow will become "harder than flint" to enable him to fulfill his mission. (Here "hard" [*hazaq*] may involve a wordplay on the name of Ezekiel [*Yehezqel*].)

We come to the end of this initial vision of Ezekiel. Its description is somewhat confused since there are several glosses in the text. At the beginning of the vision there was no mention of Ezekiel's being moved to any place away from the river Chebar. It was while he was sitting there among the exiles that the heavens opened and he saw what he saw. Now at the end the "spirit" lifts him up and takes him away and he goes *back* to the exiles at the river Chebar. Thus far there is no great difficulty, since ecstatic experience involves a kind of transport, whether it comes across as such or not. This occurred while "the glory of the LORD arose from its place" (a reading derived by conjectural emendation of the Hebrew text), which in context makes no sense. (The Masoretes' change of the text to "blessed be the glory of the LORD" doubtless testifies to their recognition of this fact.) In context, there is no question of the glory of the LORD departing from Ezekiel but of Ezekiel departing from it to return to the mundane world. The reference is, therefore, a gloss introduced by some redactor who was thinking of another vision of the glory of the LORD, the one featured in Ezek. 10–11. It is fitting that the vision should end with "the sound of a great earthquake." The additional note that the sound was really that of the wings of the living creatures and the wheels of 1:5-25 is another gloss. The redactor introduced it to go with the idea of the movement upwards of the glory of the LORD.

The effects of Ezekiel's ecstatic experience remain with him for a week as he sits among his fellow exiles. In Jer. 15:17 there is something similar described as the aftermath of prophetic vision: "the hand of the LORD being strong" upon the person. The "bitterness" and "heat of spirit" which Ezekiel mentions suggest a state of emotional distress: the experience "overwhelmed" him.

The text specifies the home of the exiles among whom Ezekiel lived as "Tel-abib." This is Hebrew for "the hill of ears [of corn]." It represents the exiles' renaming of the Akkadian *til abubi*, a site in the region of Nippur like the "river" Chebar itself. It is possible to render *Til abubi* as "the mound of the flood." It refers to a mound that the ancients believed took form following *the* primordial flood of Near Eastern mythology. It also may refer to a mound of immemorial antiquity, which amounts to the same thing. These mounds, the "tells" of Near Eastern archaeology, are not natural hills. They are what remains of once inhabited sites that have been the scene of successive abandonment and rebuilding through the centuries. These overgrown hills are what attracts archaeologists. Other places in Babylonia where the Jewish exiles settled were also tells: in Ezra 2:59 = Neh. 7:61 we read of Tel-melah ("mound of salt") and Tel-harsha ("mound of the forest" [?]).

When we put all this together, we come to a summary impression of the whole that is satisfyingly coherent. This is true even when we have to make allowances for the redactional elements that sometimes help and sometimes hinder the sequence of thought. Ezekiel the priest, an exile in Babylonia like many others, while seated with his companions at Tel-abib by the river Chebar, suddenly experiences an ecstatic vision. The vision reveals to him, first, that the God of Israel, whom he once knew intimately as resident in Jerusalem, is present to him here in Babylon. Also this God has not abandoned Israel either at home or abroad, despite the people's continuing record of disobedience and rebellion. Ezekiel's own future is intimately bound up with this revelation. He receives a commission to carry God's message to this people of rebellion. They will ignore this message, but Ezekiel must deliver it as a sign of a continual prophetic presence, of God's willed nearness. The prophet receives assurance of the strength of mind and will that will enable him to withstand the opposition and apathy that will greet his preaching. He feels a turmoil of mixed emotions and depression. These feelings are the result of the spiritual catharsis that he has undergone and the contemplation of the magnitude of the task that lies before him. This awesome feeling is more powerful and enduring than the momentary pleasure he experienced in consuming and being consumed by the word of God communicated to him in the vision of the scroll.

PROPHETIC INSTRUCTIONS
Ezekiel 3:16-27

This section of the book of Ezekiel is redactional, involving historical features that are out of place at its very beginning. The redactor put this section here to express at the outset what he regarded as two of the most significant aspects of the prophet's functions. One is positive and the other negative.

3:16-21 The redactor dated this episode "at the end of seven days," that is, when Ezekiel has finished with the aftermath of his inaugural ecstatic vision (Ezek. 3:15). The purpose was to supplement this vision and to depend upon it. What follows pertains to a later stage in the prophet's life. The seven days probably belong with another passage that we shall see below. In the Hebrew text there is a blank space separating v. 16a from v. 16b, that is, the seven days from the rest of the text. This gap shows that it was probably the redactor himself who recognized that the chronological indication did not go well with the following instruction.

In the present text vv. 16b-19 are almost verbatim 33:7-9, while vv. 20-21 echo 18:24-25 = 33:17-18. If there is a rationale in this redactional distribution, it may be in the theme of "watchman." The redactor deemed the theme of the prophet-as-"watchman" as appropriate to preface both Ezekiel's prophecies of doom, which begin here, and his prophecies of Israel's restoration that begin with ch. 33. As for the intervening ch. 18, Adrianus van den Born has pointed out that from ch. 3 to ch. 18 there are fourteen chapters in the book, and from ch. 18 to ch. 33 another fourteen.

The idea that the prophetic office entailed the custodial function of "watchman" for the people seems to pertain especially to the time of Ezekiel. The metaphor probably derives from him. The theme appears expressly in Isa. 21:6, 8 (a passage that dates from exilic times); 52:8; Jer. 6:17; Hab. 2:1. In Ezekiel's own career the theme first emerged after the fall and destruction of Jerusalem in 587/6 B.C.E. It was at this time that he received this new mission in accord with the wholly new circumstance in which the exiles found themselves in relation to their God. This present passage is out of place chronologically. Still it offers, as the redactor intended, a programmatic view of what the enduring significance of Ezekiel was for posterity.

The figure of the watchman is, of course, borrowed from the everyday life of civil and military defense. The watchman is the one charged with the vigilance of the city. He stands at some post of vantage where he can scour the landscape and give warning to his fellow citizens of imminent attack or danger. The metaphor simultaneously identifies the prophet with the people, of whom he is a part and for whom he is responsible. It also identifies the prophet with God, whose intentions he comes to know.

The passage begins with the statement "the word of the LORD came to me." This is not the messenger formula or word-of-God pronouncement of the earlier classical prophecy. Like the preceding vision by the river Chebar, this one belongs to Ezekiel alone. The expression implies, therefore, not the transmission of a communicable word but the experience of a *possessing word* or influence. This is a "living" word coming from the living God. It is not mere information that God wishes the prophet to convey to others. It is similar to the "spirit" or the "hand" of the LORD that we have seen before. It is a word that both instructs the prophet and commissions him in the function he is to carry out.

The text supposes four situations. (1) The first involves the "wicked" person who does not know of impending disaster. "If I say to the wicked, 'You shall surely die,'" does not entail a special revelation from God to this person at some specific time. What this implies is simply the sentence of death that God has pronounced against wickedness, the curtailed life that, according to conventional wisdom, was the punishment for evil ways (cf. Ps. 55:23). A long life, on the other hand, according to the same conventional wisdom, was God's recompense for righteous living.

The wisdom tradition envisioned only a this-worldly sanction for good and evil. If the wicked person has not had God's sentence of death brought home to him by the prophet whose duty it is to do so, then he shall still "die in his iniquity." Evil must be punished. In this case, however, "his blood I will require at your hand": God also will punish the prophet for having failed in his duty.

(2) If the wicked person has, on the contrary, the benefit of the prophet's warning, his iniquitous death will be his responsibility and the prophet will not be accountable.

(3) If a righteous person departs from good and turns to evil, then he will die, and all the good that he did before "shall not matter," for he has chosen the lot of the wicked. If, however, the prophet has not warned such an individual, then again God will hold the prophet responsible. In this instance God places before the righteous person a *mikshol*, "a stumbling block," that is, an occasion of sin. The idea that God tests the fidelity of the righteous is a well-worn biblical theme, most graphically presented in the prose story of the book of Job. In the Lord's Prayer there is a petition that God preserve the believer in the midst of such a test. Elsewhere Ezekiel speaks of stumbling blocks that God has laid in Israel's path in the form of silver and gold (7:19) and idolatry (14:3; 44:12).

(4) The final case. If the righteous person, after receiving a warning, does not succumb to sin, then such a person will live for having heeded the warning. The prophet too will have saved his life for having done his duty.

This list of possibilities is incomplete; other combinations of good/evil and warning/no warning are obviously conceivable. These four were sufficient for the redactor's purpose to illustrate the responsibilities with which God had charged Ezekiel.

3:22-27   These verses are not only an editorial insertion from another context, they are also a redactional creation in the present context. Their purpose is again to set forth at the outset another of Ezekiel's prophetic functions: his role as a sign to Israel. From Ezek. 24:25-27 and 33:21-22, and with the help of 4:4-8, a passage that is also out of place, we can reconstruct the historical circumstances which this scene reflects.

Sometime toward the end of the first period of Ezekiel's prophetic career, he became unable to speak. It was during the period when he had appeared consistently as a prophet of doom for Israel, and shortly before the definitive destruction of Jerusalem by Nebuchadnezzar. He also contracted some incapacitating illness that left him helpless and confined to his bed. These were prophetic signs for Israel: their God had, for the time being, left off speaking to them. God has uttered the final word of impending doom. The people were to see in Ezekiel's helplessness a figure of their certain lot as a totally subjugated people. These were impressive signs that must have left their indelible mark upon all who had witnessed them, once they had come to pass. This happened with the destruction of the city and temple, an event that forever traumatized Israel's soul. Jerusalem after all was the focus of the nation's hopes. We can understand then the redactor's purpose in bringing this in early in his work. He was eager to recall everything that was most significant about Ezekiel. By doing so, however, he left the casual reader open to the impression that Ezekiel was speechless for seven years—from the time of his call in 593 till the devastation of 586—an impression that the following chapters belie. It would make the vision of Ezekiel's call to prophecy meaningless. The redactor also left ch. 24 with some minor incoherences.

In the passage before us, then, 3:24b-26 belongs historically with ch. 24, at home either immediately before or immediately after 24:25. The following verse, 3:27, is the redactor's attempt to explain away what would otherwise be a glaring contradiction: the dumbness of a very vocal prophet. The whole is, as we have said, a redactional creation, made up of bits and pieces found elsewhere in the book. Still the text deserves commentary simply as it stands.

"The hand of the LORD" here merely introduces a new revelation given to the prophet. It is the "he" who speaks to Ezekiel, just as in a moment "spirit" does the same. The "there" where this occurs is presumably Ezekiel's home at Tel-abib by the river Chebar. God orders Ezekiel to "go forth" from his house "into the plain." "The plain"—the word means some wide open space—we encounter again in 37:1, in the famous vision of the dry bones.

The article occurs (again in 8:4) either to suggest some familiar plain that would have been so characterized by the residents of Tel-abib or, as is more likely, to refer to that extraordinary "place" where visions occur. There Ezekiel beholds "the glory of the LORD" as before, and as before "spirit entered" him, set him on his feet, and spoke to him.

God tells Ezekiel to "shut yourself within your house"—the house that he had just left, in the perspective of these verses— and there to remain speechless and without movement. As indicated above, these directions properly belong to ch. 24, to the time of the final siege of Jerusalem. It was then that Ezekiel became, in his inactivity, a sign to the people of the finality of the word of the LORD and of the prolongation of the captivity of Israel. This ran counter to all the vain hopes that would have brought it to a quick end (cf. the prophecy in Jer. 28).

The redactor decided to make this phase in Ezekiel's life exemplary of his entire prophetic career. The result is that he had to compose Ezek. 3:27 so that he could reconcile it with the succeeding chapters. In these chapters the prophet will be very vocal and very active. We can only speculate about the nature of Ezekiel's loss of speech and the "cords" placed upon him that prevented his going out among the people. What this sounds like, however, is a temporary paralysis that deprived him of speech and made him unable to walk. As the apostle Paul would later testify, God makes use of the infirmities and the strengths of people to fulfill the divine will. The LORD had given Ezekiel an adamantine brow. The prophet had to face the stubbornness of Israel (2:8-9). Still the pitiable spectacle of the same prophet's seclusion could be an even more effective sign to them of their helplessness.

SYMBOLIC ACTS
AGAINST JERUSALEM
Ezekiel 4:1–5:17

It is possible that the redactor intended to make the "at the end of seven days" reference of 3:16 to go with the passages that follow, which otherwise lack an introduction except for the routine "And you, son of man. . . ." At least these passages represent the beginning of the prophecy against Israel with which God charged Ezekiel in his inaugural vision. First we have prophecies in action, symbolic acts involving the fate of Jerusalem, and subsequently there will appear prophecies in word.

4:1-3 First, God instructs Ezekiel to take a mud "brick," one of those clay tablets that were common in Babylon both for written documents and for building materials (Gen. 11:3 uses the same word *lebenah*). The prophet is to depict on it "a city" (a gloss adds, unnecessarily, "even Jerusalem") that is under siege. The text pictures Ezekiel as working with still moist clay on which he could draw what he would, showing in some rough form the city walls and all the siegeworks and other armaments that the enemy would bring to bear on them. Among the best-known illustrations that appear in Bible atlases and textbooks of OT history are photographs of the wall friezes (now in the British Museum) from the palace of the Assyrian king Sennacherib at Nineveh. They portray his siege of the city of Lachish in 701 B.C.E. (cf. *ANEP*, 372-73). Their artistry would doubtless have been beyond the capacities of Ezekiel's clay. The friezes picture archers, a battering ram, and all the ferocity of battle, with the impaled bodies of defenders who had been so unlucky as to fall into the merciless hands of their attackers. There is a special significance to this scene in the present connection. Lachish, one

40

of the southern defenses of Jerusalem, was soon again to fall prey to conquest, this time at the hands of Nebuchadnezzar in 588. Added to this image, whose meaning is evident, is the symbol of the "iron plate." This word, which really means a griddle for baking, elsewhere occurs in texts relating to Israel's sacrificial worship (Lev. 2:5; 6:21; 7:9; 1 Chr. 23:29). It probably was part of Ezekiel's priestly vocabulary, or it may be simply that it was a word current at the time that the authors of the Priestly legislation and the Chronicler used. The word may have been a purely "secular" one that only incidentally, in the formation of the Priestly legislation during the Exile, was adapted to sacred use. The context of this passage (cf. in Ezek. 4:3 the "sign for the house of Israel") does, after all, presuppose the presence of Ezekiel's fellow exiles presumably in Ezekiel's house. Nothing could be more commonplace in such a setting than the iron griddle that rested on the coals of the fire for baking bread.

What is the significance of this dual sign? Interpretations have been various. What follows is plausible. The plate presumably represents an iron wall between Ezekiel and the city that is all ready to be under siege. The imagery simply underscores the certainty of Jerusalem's downfall. There will be no protective prophetic intervention possible to turn aside Yahweh's judgment. On the contrary, the prophet himself and his word will form part of the verdict of destruction that God has decreed for Jerusalem. It seems likely that this would be the most logical interpretation of the sign to have occurred to those who were witnessing these actions.

4:4-8 In the symbolic act of these verses Ezekiel takes on a different *persona*. This is a sure indication that we are again in the presence of redactional activity, which has joined these passages because of similarities of theme but has also ignored other discrepancies of chronology and content. While the general theme of these chapters, the siege of Jerusalem, picks up again in vv. 7-8, the rest of these verses seem to deal with the whole of the Israel of old—and by implication with the whole Israel-once-again-to-be of postexilic prophetic anticipation, although, as we shall see, there are difficulties with this interpretation. The passage is a

41

pastiche made up of recollections of Ezekiel's prophecy rather than an actual record of a prophetic act observed.

As commentators have frequently remarked, this episode represents Ezekiel as playing in part the role of the scapegoat of Lev. 16:21-22. Symbolically God lays the guilt (*'awon,* the same word for "punishment") of Israel (the now defunct northern kingdom?) upon Ezekiel while he rests on his left side for 390 days. After that (or concurrently with that?) he bears the guilt of the house of Judah while lying on his right side for 40 days. The days stand for years; this much is plain from the text. What do the separate numbers mean? Forty is easier to account for than 390. By the terms of Num. 14:34 God condemned the Israelites to wander in the wilderness for 40 years, thus to "bear their guilt" as punishment for their disobedience. The allusion to Numbers seems to fit here well. But the 390? We probably should abandon any attempt to relate this to a historical span of years. It is just as difficult to make sense of the variant "190" of the Greek text, which notoriously changes numbers at will in keeping with its own sense of propriety. The figure is undoubtedly symbolic. Perhaps A. van den Born has offered the best solution thus far. According to the "system" of *gematria,* the practice of deriving significant numbers by adding the numerical values of the letters of an important word (like the 318 men "born in [the] house" of Abram [Gen. 14:14] = Eliezer [15:2], "heir of [the] house"), the *yemey matsur,* "days of siege" of Ezek. 4:8, when the letter/numbers are added, yields 390. This solution, though, makes meaningless the distinction between "the house of Israel" and "the house of Judah." Perhaps it is best to acknowledge that the redactors who put this piece together were sometimes working at cross purposes. These verses are in all likelihood reminiscent of events connected with what 3:22-27 describes, which as we have already pointed out are as clear in ch. 24 also.

The final two verses definitely return to the theme of the siege of Jerusalem. We have a new symbolic act that is easy enough to understand: the prophet's bared arm and outstretched fist menacing Jerusalem. Again the "cords" of 3:25 recur. (Another redactional sign is evident in 4:8, which must predate the insertion of v. 6 in this context. In the original historical sequence of prophetic

42

actions related to the siege of Jerusalem, the "binding" of Ezekiel doubtless preceded the symbolism connected with his lying on his left and right side.)

4:9-17 There follow several symbolic actions relating to food. Two separate themes occur here. The first, which is partly in parallel with 12:17-20, has to do with the quality and scarcity of food that the inhabitants of Jerusalem must expect during a siege. (Here, at least, it is plain that the 390 days represent the time of siege.) The bread that God commands Ezekiel to bake is composed of six kinds of grains and legumes, all of which were common both to Babylon and Palestine. The meaning is that food will be hard to come by, and that one must make do with whatever comes to hand. Moshe Greenberg (*Ezekiel, 1–20,* 106) cites the Babylonian Talmud (*Erubin* 81a) to the effect that an experiment had shown that a dog will not eat bread made in this fashion. Even food of this kind, whatever its quality or lack of it, will be severely rationed, as will be water. There are various estimates of the quantities represented by the text's "twenty shekels" of bread and "the sixth part of a hin" of water. Still the general sense is plain enough. Rations will be scarce.

What Ezekiel prophesied here from afar his contemporary Jeremiah experienced. Jeremiah received a ration of a loaf of bread daily during the siege "until all of the bread of the city was gone" (Jer. 37:21). For a time Jeremiah was a prisoner in one of Jerusalem's internal cisterns. Fortunately for him the cistern had gone dry (Jer. 38:6). The "staff of bread" of which the text speaks in Ezek. 4:16 may be a local touch. The expression involves more than our metaphor of bread as the "staff of life." The loaves of the day were, as they still are in many parts of the world, round. They also had holes in the center so that they could be stacked on a staff in the baker's house. If that is what the expression implies, we have a much more graphic picture of the LORD's cutting off the people's food supply by smashing the breadstaffs of the city.

The other theme of this passage appears in vv. 12-15. Here we have to do, not with food of the siege, but with food of the Exile. "Thus shall the people of Israel eat their bread unclean," because they will live in lands where people do not observe the dietary laws (cf. Dan. 1:5-16). For this and for similar reasons—that they were in the realms of alien gods, for example—the OT frequently declares the lands of the Gentiles "unclean" (cf. Amos 7:17; Hos. 9:3). To feature this terrible consequence of the Exile, God orders Ezekiel to do a thing that he regards with revulsion. The prophet had to bake a loaf of bread in the presence of his fellow exiles. The fire had to be fueled by human dung so that they would experience the same revulsion. There is no recorded prohibition in the *kashrut* ("kosher") laws of the Torah regarding the use of human excrement for fuel. The use of dried animal dung for this purpose was and still is in practice throughout the world, and not only in "primitive" societies.

It is evident from Ezekiel's reaction that the command laid upon him violated all his sensibilities. He equated what God was telling him to do with the eating of carrion, something that the law definitely proscribed (Lev. 22:8, a regulation for the priesthood, then extended to the "priestly people" of Israel). The directions for cleanliness of the camp of Israel in Deut. 23:1-14, and what later writers tell regarding the hygienic practices of the Jews, should convince us that what God was asking Ezekiel to do the prophet and his companions regarded with the utmost abhorrence. The point having been made, we probably have the explanation for Yahweh's easy acquiescence to Ezekiel's demurrer. It is an acquiescence—to the first resistance that Ezekiel has shown to any of the charges that God has laid upon him. One might conclude that even God has reservations about issuing commands that violate the rules of propriety which God has instituted.

God then permits Ezekiel to bake his bread in the conventional way. Is that the end of it? Acts 10:14-15 evidently depends on this episode in Ezekiel's life. In Acts Peter remonstrates with God's command only to find that the old rules are no longer in force. What had been unclean was unclean no longer. Ezekiel rebels against a similar "uncleanness," and God allows him to prevail. The divine acquiescence may be deceptive, for God has designs which God will not necessarily reveal all at one time or to one person only.

Despite Ezekiel's determination to pursue his mission to Israel, he was but a man. He was subject to all the limitations of the human being whom God's spirit found and touched. What God revealed to him was immense (we confront this in these pages). It was an immensity that is proportionate to the capacity of the recipient and not the capability of the bestower. Ezekiel had his purpose and his message, also his ability to understand them, but others would have their purposes and messages and understandings. The time was coming that God, through another prophet, would make it known that "the former things have come to pass, and new things I now declare" (Isa. 42:9). In the very land of exile, this prophet would declare a non-Israelite monarch — Cyrus the Persian — to be the paradoxical heir to the messianic expectations God had once encouraged Israel to attach to its Davidic dynasty. Simultaneously people of the utmost goodwill would draw utterly opposite conclusions about the future of Israel, depending on the same premises inherited from the past and appealing to the same spirit of the LORD. Also they would recognize that "my thoughts are not your thoughts, neither are your ways my ways, says the LORD" (Isa. 55:8).

5:1-4a This section describes another of Ezekiel's bizarre actions. It is not the cutting of the hair itself that is bizarre. This was a conventional and therefore easily recognizable sign of mourning obvious to any audience. The bizarre element is the disposition made of the hair, the details of which are sometimes hard to imagine as actually having been acted out. There seems no doubt that there is some affinity of this imagery to Isa. 7:20. In that passage the text pictures Assyria as a "razor" that will shave away all the hair of Jerusalem and Judah — head hair, body hair, and beard alike. In this Ezekiel passage it is a matter of only the head hair and the beard. God tells the prophet to take a sharp sword (the "sword" [*hereb*] could have been any kind of knife such as a dagger or a kitchen utensil). Ezekiel is to act as a barber would in shaving his head and face. Then comes the disposition to be made of the hair.

The symbolism of dividing the hair into three parts is easy to understand, even if the accompanying actions may be hard to follow. First the prophet weighs the hair so that the parts are equal. Weighing and numbering are signs of impending doom and judgment. This is reminiscent of the famous scene at Belshezzar's feast and of Daniel's interpretation of the words that the moving hand wrote in Dan. 5:24-28. One part of the hair is to burn "in the midst of the [representation of] the city." This represents the number of those who will have perished of hunger and plague during the siege itself (cf. Ezek. 5:12 below). A second third Ezekiel is to strike with his knife "round about the city." This can refer to the inhabitants of the villages and defense towns, such as Lachish, surrounding Jerusalem. More likely it involves those who wanted to escape from Jerusalem when its fall was imminent. The Babylonians overtook and destroyed these people, as described in the poignant scene of the blinding of Zedekiah and the execution of his sons in 2 Kgs. 25:4-7. The prophet is to scatter the final third in the wind. These are the new exiles to join those already in exile. Of this final third a further disposition is made (unless this verse-and-a-half is the afterthought of a redactor, as it may very well be since there is no follow-up on it in the explanation of the symbolic actions in Ezek. 5:4b-12). Ezekiel is to bind up a few of the hairs, representing the exiles-to-be, in his skirt. The meaning of this gesture is obscure. It probably signifies that part of the exiles which will survive. They will elude the sword of Yahweh unsheathed against them (cf. the protection symbolized by Boaz's robe in Ruth 3:9), and will form the nucleus of the restored Israel with which Ezekiel will concern himself later. It is significant to the message, no doubt, that this part should be very small. It shall be smaller yet, for some of it the prophet is to throw in the fire to signify that the fate of Jerusalem will be visited on part of the exilic community as well.

5:4b-17 The remainder of this chapter consists of Yahweh's words. First is the LORD'S reproach of Israel for its crimes that have brought upon it the doom that will surely come. Explanations are given for the preceding symbolic actions. There is a final peroration spelling out the severity of Israel's punishment.

The idea expressed in Ezek. 5:5, that Jerusalem is "in the center of the nations," hardly occurs in the OT except with Ezekiel. The same idea reappears in 38:12 where the eschatological Israel resides "at the navel of the earth" (RSV "center"; the same expression in Judg. 9:37 of a holy place associated with Shechem). It has been the persuasion of many peoples throughout history that they stand at the center of things, whether in the order of creation or of the attentions of the gods and fates. They have tended to express this notion geographically. We think of the Chinese "Middle Kingdom," and of the stone in the Roman Forum inscribed *umbilicus orbis,* the selfsame "navel of the world." There are many other examples.

It was not only the ancient cartographers who mirrored on their maps the common prejudices of their time and place. Mercator's projection, upon which most of our contemporary wall maps of the world depend, of course reflects the prejudice of a European of the time. The northern hemisphere is greatly magnified at the expense of the southern, so that South America, Africa, and other landmasses of the south appear much smaller than they really are. We can only surmise what mistaken nations of relative importance have been absorbed through the ages by those who have looked at their *mappa mundi* to see the world as it is and who have instead seen not quite that. Naturally, as people go from country to country today, they will find that the wall maps constantly change their focus about what lies at the center and what on the periphery. A map produced in the United States will normally put the American continents in the center. Europe (including the European part of Russia) will be on the right and the "the Orient" (including the Asiatic part of the Soviet Union) on the left. These maps makes explicit some of our unconscious assumptions.

The intention of the reference in Ezek. 5:5 is hardly of the same spirit as the Chinese "Middle Kingdom" or the Roman *umbilicus orbis.* The idea of "the center of the earth" occurs rarely in the OT. It is not that the Israelites were more realistic than their neighbors and could not imagine their tiny country (at its largest, perhaps 250 km. [150 mi.] N-S by 50-75 km. [30-50 mi.] E-W) being at the heart of things—because they could imagine just that. In Ps. 2, simply to take the first example that comes to mind, a psalmist of the Jerusalem temple—that temple of which Ezekiel will soon be speaking—represents the enthronement of a new Judahite king. That event doubtless occasioned some local unrest in vassal and client tribal areas. It also provoked a revolt by all the kings of the earth. The revolt, the psalmist says, attacks Yahweh and his anointed one, that is, the king of Judah. The LORD, who has set up this king on the holy hill of Zion, laughs at the pretensions of the world's rulers. He promises that his anointed will crush them all and that the anointed's realm will extend to the ends of the earth. Now this is heady language and, if you wish, very unrealistic and pretentious. It is not merely "court style," the rhetoric which envelopes the human person within the language of the ideal, the myth, or the mystique of which he is the embodiment: "Your Grace," "Your Worship," "Your Majesty," "High and Mighty Prince, "The All-Highest." This psalm, among others, clarifies for us the sense in which Ezekiel could make Jerusalem the center of the world.

Not because of its numbers of or any natural attributes did Israel presume to think of itself as at the center of things, but only in virtue of God's election for which there was no accounting save God's love (cf. Deut. 7:7-8). The "nations" and "countries" that have Israel at their center make up the gentile world. Israel was to be unlike them and by that be a witness to what God had done. Israel was to preserve its unique identity by observing Yahweh's "ordinances" and "statutes." These terms, which originally had distinct meanings, probably appear here as synonyms, denoting the whole of the covenant obligations which bound Israel. All the Torah was law of God. It did not matter whether it was what we would call natural law—what is "right," what has commended itself to people as the moral thing to do—or was duty and obligation peculiar to Israel through revelation. In this sense alone is the house of Israel the "center" of the nations— and it had all been in vain.

Israel did not witness to the nations. Israel disregarded Yahweh's ordinances and statutes. It had even surpassed the Gentiles in sinning against them, adopting the ways of the nations instead of the LORD'S. The prophet foresees the doom that is coming upon them. Ezek. 5:1-4a pictures it graphically as fire and sword. In v. 8 we probably should construe Yahweh's initial words somewhat as follows: "Look at me! I am coming at you!" These are words that signal attack, the "on guard!" of the swordsman about to engage his enemy (Paul Humbert, "Die Herausforderungsformel 'hinnenî êlékâ,'" *Zeitschrift für die alttestamentliche Wissenschaft* 51 [1933]: 101-8). They go very well with the motif of Yahweh's sword expressed in v. 2. They also fit with the accompanying assertion that the magnitude of the LORD'S punishment will exceed any that has gone before or is likely to follow (cf. also Isa. 7:17).

The remaining verses in this chapter serve in various ways to underscore and reemphasize the threats which Yahweh has issued against the house of Israel. God swears an oath: "As I live" (Ezek. 5:11)—obviously, there is no one higher by whom the LORD God can swear. There is a reiterated "I, Yahweh, have spoken" (vv. 15, 17). Details of the evils that will fall on the people appear in the conventional language that describes the penalties of covenant violation (e.g., Lev. 26:29-33; Deut. 28:20-24). The sanction of Lev. 26:29 that threatened eating the flesh of sons and daughters recurs with the addition of something even more horrible in Semitic eyes: "sons shall eat their fathers" (Ezek. 5:10). Above all, this highly anthropopathic passage features the "fury" and the "jealousy" of God (v. 13). "Jealousy makes a man furious," wrote the sage, "and he will not spare when he takes revenge" (Prov. 6:34). So the text depicts Yahweh, in one of the most somber of all the prophetic rejections of Israel.

ORACLES AGAINST ISRAEL

Ezekiel 6:1–7:27

Though there is some difference in content, the following two chapters of the text form a unit. The various parts all deal with the inexorability of the doom which Yahweh has pronounced over Israel. In form they are oracles or messages from the LORD. In such passages Ezekiel appears in the guise most characteristic of the prophets of Israel, as the herald of God. Like the preceding redactional section in chs. 4–5, these chapters are part of Ezekiel's "collected works" and are only loosely connected with the chronology that begins in 1:1-12. Just as chs. 4–5 represent, in summary form, certain of the actions and experiences that were most reminiscent of Ezekiel, redactors assembled this collection, or collections, of oracles to typify the message that formed the burden of the first period of his prophetic ministry.

6:1-7 That Ezekiel here assumes the role of herald appears in his assertion: "The word of the LORD came to me." The listener or reader is to construe what follows, then, as Yahweh's words, the oral message which God commands the prophet to convey. Similarly, but without introduction, in 6:11: "Thus says the LORD God." Such formulas, or their equivalents, are the common language of preexilic prophecy. An expression distinctive of Ezekiel occurs immediately when God instructs him: "set your face toward (or 'against') the mountains of Israel." The expression occurs time and again to accompany the prophet's oral messages. It is but a metaphor and does not imply actual physical presence (in 29:2, for example, God tells Ezekiel to set his face toward the pharaoh). Still it seems almost as though sign and gesture so characterize this prophet that they can never be entirely lacking whatever the circumstances.

50

Like "house" of Israel, the "mountains," of course, mean the inhabitants of the mountains. Also it becomes quickly evident that it is not the mountains alone that are in question but also "hills," "ravines," and "valleys." It is the whole land of Israel, that is to say the whole people of Israel, toward and against which the prophet directs this oracle. Why, then, are the mountains singled out? Because, some might say, they were the site of the "high places" with which this prophecy deals. Though Hebrew *bamah* has been so often translated "high place," the translation is not necessarily accurate. (Jer. 7:31 shows us that a *bamah* also could be found in a valley!) Whatever the word might have meant etymologically, its derived and actual meaning is simply that of a cult place, a place of sacrificial worship. Alternatively, it might be imagined that the concern here is literally "the mountains of Israel." Though the oracle's intended audience is the whole of Israel, it is still Jerusalem that is the primary focus. The city lies in the hill country of Judah. Still the rest of the verses seem to oppose such a narrowed focus. The best explanation is that Ezekiel the traditionalist is here reaching back to the language of Israel's origins. He uses terminology that the earliest Israel used to designate the land of its promise and conquest. It was in the hill country of Palestine — "the mountains of Israel" — that the Yahwistic federation of Israel first settled, took shape, and became a people. It is most fitting that the prophet summon the land and people to judgment under the same name. They must hear the sentence of doom that Ezekiel pronounces over them.

It is typical of Ezekiel, priest and prophet, that the thrust of the charge brought against Israel to justify the LORD'S destruction of this people catalogues not its many social sins, in the manner of an Amos or an Isaiah. Rather, Ezekiel concentrates on aberrations in worship. Some interpreters believe that an emphasis of this kind represents a kind of trivializing of the prophetic function. They see Ezekiel wasting it on less than substantive issues at the expense of the greater crimes of Israel that were crying to heaven for vengeance. Among these are a social order that had dedicated itself to the systematic exploitation of the poor and defenseless, corrupted the courts and halls of justice, and unthinkingly pursued an economic and political policy that had already rotted the soul

51

of the nation long before the judgment of God came to declare it officially dead.

In the 8th cent. the prophet Amos had bitterly satirized the conspicuous spending of the privileged of Israel in the face of their tearing away the social fabric of Israel through willful and callous neglect. He also reproached them for not grieving over the ruin that they caused (Amos 6:6). The word "ruin" does not refer to a process of ruin but to a ruin that already·exists, thus implying a most perceptive observation on Amos's part. Observations of this kind, we might think, and what had prompted them, were the real business of prophecy—to get at the real root causes of what ailed Israel.

No one can gainsay the validity of such a judgment. It is at once the glory of Israelite prophecy and its title to a unique status among the analogous institutions of its time that it had this character. It is a character that distinguishes it from the various "prophetic" castes and guilds possessed by the other nations. It would be a mistake to think that in attacking cultic aberrations the prophets were any less radical in their analysis of the evil that had befallen Israel. At that time it was religion more than any other force that made a people one. Religion and cultus determined the people's identity and fidelity to their distinct ethos.

The Deuteronomic authors of the books of Kings have single-mindedly rendered a negative verdict on the monarchies of both north and south. The chief failure of the kings was their failure to eradicate the "high places" throughout Israel. The Deuteronomists have very little else to say about them. They ignore the kings' positive, secular achievements. The Deuteronomists still were not really being superficial in their appraisals.

In recent times inscriptions found at Kuntillet 'Ajrûd (in the eastern Sinai) and Khirbet el-Qôm (near Lachish), both dating from the 8th cent., the time of Amos and Hosea, have given us an inkling of what disturbed the Deuteronomists and Ezekiel. These inscriptions are the product of Israelite worship. Their interpretation is still unclear in details, but it is plain enough that they are the product of a diluted Yahwism. In this aberrant form of ancient Israel's religion, Yahweh shares honors with other deities and possibly has a female consort. Also the Yahweh of one shrine may have been distinct from the Yahweh of another shrine (William G. Dever, "Asherah, Consort of Yahweh? New Evidence from Kuntillet 'Ajrûd," *Bulletin of the American Schools of Oriental Research* 255 [1984]: 21-37; Ziony Zevit, "The Khirbet el-Qôm Inscription Mentioning a Goddess," *Bulletin of the American Schools of Oriental Research* 255 [1984]: 39-47). Such were the "high places."

There is an old rule of *lex credendi lex orandi* or *lex orandi lex credendi*. According to this aphorism, as people believe, so do they pray. From people's worship one may judge their belief. What was distinctive—or what should have been distinctive—about the belief of Israel, what gave this belief the dynamism that accounts for Israelite prophetism and its emphasis on social morality, was its rooting in the historical experience of a God of intervention and change. This was altogether different from serving the timeless, changeless deities of the nature religions who simply personified the continuous cycles of the seasons. When Yahwism became syncretized with these religions in the local shrines that dotted the countryside it inevitably lost its identity. Lost too was its vision of a God who had revealed a way of love and mercy that often transcended nature. This God would hold Israel to a specific code of conduct. With all this in mind, therefore, we can understand the vehemence of Ezekiel's assault on the "altars" (of sacrifice), the "incense altars," and the "idols" of Israel.

The word (*gillulim*) that the prophet repeatedly uses for "idols," which occurs here for the first time, is almost exclusively Ezekiel's. Since it seemed to come from a root meaning "round" or "roll," it was formerly interpreted as "pellets of dung." That may be an afterthought due to the Masoretic editors of the Hebrew Bible. They may have been round objects like totem poles. There can hardly be doubt that it was a pejorative term. Similarly obscure is the reference to "your works" in Ezek. 6:6. The phrase is lacking in the Greek and may be a later addition. In keeping with the cultic emphasis of the prophecy are the particulars of the devastation that will fall upon these places of unhallowed rites. They will be desecrated with the "dead bodies" and the "bones" of the "slain." Contact with corpses, and especially with the remains of those who had died a violent death, caused ritual pollution and defilement.

6:8-10   Some consider these verses to be an addition from a
later time, when the exile had run its course and justice had been
done, and when restoration was in view. Still there is no hint of
restoration to be found here. The verses serve to pile doom upon
doom and to emphasize the inexorability of the judgment that
God has pronounced upon Israel. As we shall see, Ezekiel, like
Jeremiah, looked to a restoration of Israel, and again, like
Jeremiah, he expected that restoration to come out of Babylon.
Unlike Jeremiah, he did not anticipate the restoration taking place
in the lifetime of the present generation of exiles, though they
had "served their time" for their sins and the sins of their ancestors.
As we saw in 5:3-4a—even if these verses are Ezekiel's, which
can be questioned—there was with Ezekiel nothing approximat-
ing the idea of an Isaianic "faithful remnant." In Ezekiel's perspective, the survivors of Yahweh's doom of Israel have little
function except to testify to its thoroughness and finality. In his
view, the whole generation of the exile had to pass away to make
room for the new Israel. After all, the whole generation of the
exodus, Moses included, had to pass away before Israel could enter
its promised land (Num. 14:20-25). The new Israel would be
precisely that, a new creation. Genetically speaking there would
be continuity, but theologically speaking there would be none.

Therefore we should not look in these verses for any hint of a
hope for the future. The survivors will have had their "wanton
heart broken," but there is no mention of a new heart, a new
mind. Their "blinded eyes" will not now necessarily see anything
that is to their future advantage. "They will be loathsome in their
own sight for the evils that they have committed, for all their
abominations." They will be remorseful over the actions and
omissions that have brought them to their present sorry state. All
this is obviously of a wholly different character from that of Jer.
31:2: "The people who survived the sword found grace in the
wilderness." All that the survivors of this generation can do is
attest to the truth of the words of the LORD, who promised to
bring great evil upon them.

6:11-14   Again we have an oracle concerned with idolatry, and
again prophetic gestures accompany it. "Clap your hands, and

stamp your foot" are instructions that intend both to draw attention and to convey a premonition of threat and defiance. The same instruments of God's wrath that feature in the preceding oracle appear again: "famine," "pestilence," "the sword." Again, too, the destruction is total: "he that is far off" and "he that is near" is simply a poetic way of saying "everybody." The text reverts to the consideration of the "high places" with the added mention of the "green tree" and the "leafy oak."

Almost from the very start, the OT takes note of the habitual association of shrines and other holy places with sacred trees (cf. the oak or terebinth of Moreh and Mamre in Gen. 12:6 and 14:13). In Ezek. 6:14 the received Hebrew text reads not "Riblah" but "Diblah." This is undoubtedly due to a scribal confusion of the Hebrew letters "d" and "r," a thing that has occurred several times over in the transmission of the biblical text. Whereas in an earlier age the length and breadth of the land of Canaan might be summed up under the rubric "from Dan to Beer-sheba" (e.g., 1 Sam. 3:20), from the northern- to the southernmost Israelite town, Ezekiel apparently prefers to look at it from south to north. Riblah lay "in the land of Hamath" (2 Kgs. 23:33), and it is this region that Ezekiel (Ezek. 47:15-16; 48:1) made the "ideal" northern boundary of Israel. "The wilderness" that stands for him as the southern boundary is the desert land separating Canaan from Egypt, which in Ezek. 20:36 he calls "the wilderness of the land of Egypt." Riblah was to be the fateful site where Nebuchadnezzar would seal the doom of Jerusalem and Judah after the debacle of 587/6, which Ezekiel is here prophesying (2 Kgs. 25:20-21). It was already a site fraught with significance for Ezekiel's fellow exiles. It was the site where the Pharaoh Neco in 609 took away into exile King Jehoahaz and replaced him on the throne with Jehoiakim. The latter's policies brought on the first exile of 597 of which they were all victims.

7:1-4 Chapter 7 has a series of oracles of doom and judgment that repeat in other words much that the prophet has already said. The word "abominations" frequently occurs to characterize Israel's crimes. This is a cultic term, sometimes used concretely, which designates anything unspeakably offensive to true religion. These introductory verses are general in their expression, but there are a few items that deserve comment.

First one must take literally "the end" of which Ezekiel speaks. Amos (8:1-3) uses the same word, in his case accompanied by a wordplay related to a vision, and to the same effect. The meaning is not that the LORD is simply calling a halt to Israel's wrongdoing. More will happen besides bringing down a punishment that will serve as a warning against similar misconduct in the future. No, Ezekiel means by "end" precisely that, just as Amos did. This is no cautionary warning but a promise of sure extinction. If there is to be a future for Israel it must come as a new revelation. Here there is none. "Then you will know that I am the LORD" implies no hope to be born of this realization, only bitter confirmation of the adage that the wages of sin is death. In Ezek. 7:2 "the four corners (literally, 'extremities,' 'wings') of the land" means the whole earth (cf. Isa. 11:12), but here it is simply an emphatic way of designating the whole of Israel.

7:5-9   These verses make up an oracle that is in close parallel with the one preceding. Though there is some variation in details of language, the catchwords "the end," "abominations," and "you will know that I am the LORD" associate the two oracles closely. In Ezek. 7:7 "the day" that will be only of "tumult," and not of "joyful shouting" as anticipated, introduces a new theme. Development of this theme will occur in the verses that follow.

7:10-13   In Amos 5:18-20 occurs the famous passage:

> Woe to you who desire the day of the LORD!
>   Why would you have the day of the LORD?
> It is darkness, and not light . . .
>   Is not the day of the LORD darkness, and not light,
>   and gloom with no brightness in it?

This prophetic utterance undoubtedly was one of those milestones along the way by which Israelite prophetism journeyed to the fullness of its grandeur. "The day of the LORD" was a byword of popular eschatology. It was a comfortable self-assurance based on confidence in the protection of the national deity. The day was coming—indeed, many days might be coming—when their God would come out in their favor. There will be a rendering of accounts, and it will bring down destruction on their enemies. It was Amos's function to prick the balloon of this misplaced faith. This false confidence rested on the false assumption that theirs was a deity whose role it was to do their bidding rather than the other way round. By thinking thus they merely showed that they had never known Yahweh. Yes, said Amos, there would be a day of the LORD, but the enemies who would meet disaster on that day would be Israel itself. It is in this vein that Yahweh speaks through Ezekiel in these verses. Ezekiel has only "the day" (in Ezek. 7:19, "the day of the wrath of the LORD"). The Greek text accurately translates its sense by "the day of the LORD."

The imagery of plant growth is clear enough. Still it is possible to take the images of blooming and budding, by which Israel's doom is so imaginatively pictured, in two ways. Either Israel's "injustice *(mutteh)* has blossomed" as the RSV would have it, on the analogy of Ezek. 9:9, or, keeping the Masoretic vocalization, "the rod *(matteh)* has blossomed." The "rod" would be Babylonia, even as Isa. 10:5 speaks of Assyria as the rod of Yahweh's wrath. The same ambiguity appears in "pride has budded." In Jer. 50:31 "pride" is a sobriquet for Babylonia. Similarly in Ezek. 7:11, "Violence has grown up into a rod of evil." The "violence" is Israel's; there is no doubt of that. Still, is the image one of its final flowering into adult wickedness or of its growth that has merited the chastisement of the evil rod of Babylon? There is no discrepancy involved in Yahweh's punishing evil by using an instrument that is evil in its own right. Ezekiel's oracles against the nations will make this clear. As stated, the general sense is evident: Israel is ripe for punishment. Unfortunately, the latter part of v. 11 is textually corrupt, and any attempt to get at its meaning must be highly conjectural.

References to buying and selling in the concluding verses may have had something concrete in mind or may be simply by way of example, like the man on the housetop or in the field or the woman with child of Mark 13:15-17. The point is, of course, that buying and selling will have lost their significance in the face of the total disaster that will come on buyer and seller alike. The

RSV has conjectured "wrath" *(haron)* as the reading in Ezek. 7:13, but "vision" *(hazon)* of the Hebrew text is equally likely. It is the vision or oracle of doom that Ezekiel is even now uttering that will not be withdrawn.

7:14-23a The scene changes, and we now have a call to arms — but to a battle that never takes place because the odds are too one-sided. Out of the familiar sources of destruction known to Ezekiel—famine, pestilence, and the sword—there will come universal devastation and demoralization in the city and in the countryside. There is a vivid account of the panic that will follow. The RSV's "all knees [are] weak as water" means "all knees will run water": a euphemism for the loss of bladder control in moments of terror. The "sackcloth" and "baldness" from shaving the head were conventional signs of mourning, though not, in this instance, of a productive repentance. In vv. 19 and 20 Ezekiel's priestly background shows through in his reference to the "unclean thing" that the Israelites' gold will become and that the LORD will make of "their beautiful ornament." This term *(niddah)* has come from the cult, where it referred to anything that was ritually unclean and defiling.

In these verses there appears a mingling of related ideas resulting in some ambiguity. This possibly was due to redactional activity, but just as possibly it may have been the product of the prophet's own exuberant style. The Israelites' silver and gold, he says, have become the "stumbling block of their iniquity." How so? Is it not an occasion of moral corruption that is the result of too much wealth and power? That is the way we might think. It is the way that a prophet like Amos or Isaiah would have meant it. The Israelites' silver and gold are evil because they made use of them to fashion "their abominable images and their detestable things" that have polluted the land and its inhabitants. Is "their (the Hebrew has 'his' or 'its,' probably simply personifying Israel) beautiful ornament," then, their gold and silver that they have "used for vainglory"? From v. 20 it would so appear. As the text goes on, something else seems involved, something that "foreigners," "the wicked of the earth," "robbers" will "despoil," "enter," "profane," and "make a desolation." To compound the confusion,

that something is, in the objective pronouns of vv. 21-22, alternatively masculine (the temple? Israel?) and feminine (the land?
the city?). Also in v. 22 it is Yahweh's "secret place" that is to be
profaned. If it is obvious that the Babylonian conquest and sack
of Jerusalem are in view, it seems equally obvious that in Ezekiel's
stream of consciousness there flow many associated ideas that bob
to the surface at irregular intervals, sometimes showing different
faces. Gold and silver made detestable images that profaned the
temple. These images also polluted the land that is now declared
unclean and will be given over to evil persons for spoliation,
desecration, and desolation.

7:23b-27   In these last verses there is a final and definitive
codicil appended to the sentence that has already been rendered
above. The sentence is also rephrased in almost "secular" terms
to signify the political, social, and the religious *finis* that is now
being written with a flourish at the end of the chronicle of the
nation Israel. Not its holy places only but also all its dwellings
shall pass into the possession of "the worst of the nations." It
would be the most powerful and ruthless of all the world empires
Israel has yet had to face. It was too late for Israel to discover
that it had been playing a game that it could never have won. Its
stakes were far too high for Israel's meager resources. The players
of this high stakes game toyed with Israel as cold-eyed gamblers
will toy with inept players. Israel thought that it could walk the
tightrope of ancient Near Eastern power politics by skillfully
pitting one great power against another. Babylon was vengeful in
the flush of its victories over Assyria and Egypt. The "peace" that
they had so desperately pursued, which their "wise men," their
statesmen, had schemed for (Isa. 5:21) and their kept prophets
had compliantly assured them of (Jer. 23:16-17), will elude them
altogether and forever.
    Ezek. 7:26 is reminiscent of Jer. 18:18. There, when people
were conspiring to destroy Jeremiah's influence, the byword was
that "instruction (law, *torah*) shall not perish from the priest, nor
counsel (*'etsah*) from the wise, nor the word (*dabar*) from the
prophet." In other words, Israel's traditional sources of enlightenment and guidance would never pass away. Here, on the con-

trary, the oracle confirms that they all have passed away: "vision *(hazon)* from the prophet," "instruction from the priest," and "counsel from the elders." There is a total breakdown of society, with "prince" (the added "king," a word that Ezekiel does not use, is an intrusion in the text) and "people" completely distraught.

PART II
JUDGMENT
ON THE PRESENT

Ezekiel 8:1–14:23

THE TEMPLE VISION
Ezekiel 8:1–11:25

The following chapters contain the longest and the most dramatic of Ezekiel's ecstatic visions. With the prophet we arrive at the city of Jerusalem and its temple square. With him we witness successively the abominations practiced there that have profaned it beyond all redemption. The sentence of destruction and death is passed and symbolically carried out. The glory of God, formerly resident in the temple, departs from it. We now know how it was that Ezekiel encountered the glory of the LORD "in the plain" in Babylon at the time of his inaugural vision. In the phantasmagory of the vision we experience more than a trace of the later apocalyptic style that is so often dependent on Ezekiel. The four chapters together make up a satisfying unity. There is no reason not to take the section at face value on the prophet's testimony. Still there are also traces of the inevitable redactional retouching to which the whole of this book has been subject.

8:1-6 These verses set the scene, describe the rapture of Ezekiel, and introduce us to the content of the vision that is soon to unfold. They also supply us with a date corresponding to 17 September 592 B.C.E., therefore something more than a year after Ezekiel had received his prophetic call.

Is it possible to conclude that the elders of Judah lacked houses of their own because the text says that they were sitting about while Ezekiel was sitting in his house? (The elders were the representatives of the important families whom the Babylonians deported in 597.) This is perhaps so. These people were anticipating a speedy end of their exile and a quick return to the

Palestinian homeland, a delusion which was part of Ezekiel's task to dissipate. Also Jeremiah in his letter to the exiles (Jer. 29:1-28) had told them—or was to tell them, since we do not know when the letter was written—to build houses, raise children, and make Babylon their home, since the Exile was going to last for a long time.

As before, the prophet describes the phenomenon of ecstatic seizure in terms of the "hand" of the LORD falling upon him and of the "spirit" lifting him into the air and transporting him in "visions of God." Though we should not expect any strict logical sequence in a vision of this kind, the intervention of the "form that had the appearance of a man" in this series seems to be intrusive and to lead nowhere, so that there is the suspicion that someone has used Ezek. 1:27 to assimilate this vision of Ezekiel to the earlier one. On the other hand, Walther Zimmerli has suggested that in the detail of the prophet's being seized "by a lock of my head" (*Ezekiel 1,* 236), "we may conjecture a basis in the experience of actual bodily pain (and giddiness) felt by the person concerned." At all events, the effect of Ezekiel's ecstatic experience is to bring him to the northern gates of Jerusalem which opened upon the temple area.

The description of Solomon's temple in 1 Kgs. 6:2–7:51 (ultimately the work of persons who had never seen it) is much too theologically motivated to serve as a reliable guide to what it looked like, despite the valiant efforts that countless illustrators have made to reconstruct its particulars from this source. In Ezekiel we have references to the temple from one to whom it had been a familiar sight; but as the prophet's interest in it was slight, the references are casual. Ezekiel's style is, as always, convoluted, and the wooden word-by-word translation of the RSV does not afford the reader much help. As far as can be reasonably determined from the text, Ezekiel first finds himself in the outer courtyard of the temple, standing between two gates. The one gate, which thus far goes unmentioned, would have lain to the north, the direction in which God tells the prophet to face. It was a gateway in the wall that surrounded the royal area of temple and palace that formed one complex (Ezek. 43:7-8). This gate would have led in turn to the northern gate of the city, the Benjamin Gate (Jer. 37:13). Behind Ezekiel as he faced the north was "the entrance of the gateway of the inner court." In the outer court, the intervening area between the two gates, Ezekiel saw two things: "the seat of the image of jealousy, which provokes to jealousy," and "the glory of the God of Israel." It is important to note that the glory of the LORD had already departed the inner precincts of the temple and is now, as it were, poised to quit Jerusalem altogether.

There have been several ways to understand "the seat of the image of jealousy." What the text means here is an unlawful image of some kind which provoked the wrath of the jealous God of Israel. Was its "seat" a niche in the wall which Ezekiel was facing, as thought by William F. Albright in *Archaeology and the Religion of Israel* ([Baltimore: Johns Hopkins University Press, 1956], 165-66)? Possibly, but this may be an attempt to define "seat" too precisely. The Hebrew text here is suspect, and the LXX, which appears to have given up on it, is also of little help. Probably we should read something like this: "I lifted up my eyes toward the north, and behold, north of the gate was an altar" (dispensing with the meaningless "altar gate"), "while this image of jealousy was at the entrance" (i.e., the entrance to the outer court in which Ezekiel was standing, the unmentioned external gate which he was facing).

There was a history of setting up unlawful images and altars in the temple precincts under various circumstances (cf. 2 Kgs. 16:10-16; 21:4-7, etc.). Most likely we have to do here with a votive altar and image of Asherah, "the queen of heaven," a cult which was widespread in Jerusalem at that time (cf. Jer. 7:17-18). Ezekiel's guiding voice calls it a great abomination, great enough to have driven Yahweh from his temple. Yet there are "greater abominations," which the following verses describe.

8:7-18 The remainder of this chapter describes these "greater abominations" in three scenes revealed to the prophet. As we understand the sequence of events and the locales envisaged by the text, God tells Ezekiel first to turn around and enter the gateway to the inner court of the temple. Up to now the prophet had the inner court to his back. To effect his entrance Ezekiel must enlarge a fissure in the wall to reveal the doorway that, for some reason, has been blocked up. There, immediately on his entering, he views the first of the "greater abominations." Proceeding through the gateway the prophet eventually reaches its other entrance, the one facing immediately onto the inner court, where the second abominable scene takes place. Finally, the inner court itself is where he sees the last of these detestable profanations of Yahweh's house. To understand this sequence properly, it is necessary to note that the "gates" of which the text speaks were not simply doors leading immediately from one place to another. They were substantial buildings in their own right, with inner walls and partitions, side room, windows, and entrances fore and aft. The archaeology of Solomonic Israel has acquainted us with the massive character of these gateways, and Ezek. 40:5-16 affords a good description of the kind of "gate" that was in Ezekiel's mind and vision.

The three ritual scenes that follow seem to refer to separate varieties of non-Israelite cult. Theodore H. Gaster has tried to reduce them all to a celebration of the Canaanite feast of ingathering ("Ezekiel and the Mysteries," *Journal of Biblical Literature* 60 [1941]: 289-310). It is probably worthy of note that these rites are "lay" observances. Most likely the altar and image that stood in the outer court also had a "lay" function to the same purpose. They defiled the LORD'S temple no less for that fact. Still the point to notice is that Ezekiel's temple vision portrays the evils committed not by Israel's priesthood. The "house of Israel" itself is guilty, its men and women, its princes and elders.

The first of the scenes of abominations seen by Ezekiel in 8:10-12 cannot be identified with any known non-Israelite cult. This underscores the lay and amateurish character of the travesties of worship that Ezekiel is witnessing. What seems to be the focus of the prophet's disgust is the engravings of "creeping things and loathsome beasts" on the walls of the room in which he finds himself. ("All the idols of the house of Israel" could be the afterthought of some redactor.) Here was multiple affront to a priestly soul. There were the images in the house of the LORD, images of animals that were ritually unclean. There was unclean ritual. We are probably not thinking amiss if we see Egyptian influence at work here. The theriomorphic deities of the Egyptian pantheon were notorious and often an object of amazement and curiosity to the other peoples of their contemporary world. The late King Jehoiakim of Judah, before the Babylonians asserted their hegemony in Palestine, had been a creature of the Egyptians. The tragedy that was now in the making under Zedekiah had as its background the struggle for power and policy between factions in the Judahite community. One group preached conciliation with Babylon. The other advocated resistance through alliances with Egypt. It was likely that a pro-Egyptian faction among the elders of Jerusalem would express its allegiance in an imitation or adaptation of Egyptian cult. Years before, Ahaz had proved his loyalty to Assyria by similar means (2 Kgs. 16:10-18: "because of the king of Assyria"). The presence of "Jaazaniah the son of Shaphan" among the devotees may confirm this impression. We know of Shaphan as high in the administrative circles of the kingdom during the reign of Josiah (2 Kgs. 22). His sons were influential civil servants in Jerusalem at this actual moment (Jer. 29:3; 36:12; 39:14). The disposition of this important personage favoring resistance to Babylon through client status with Egypt was doubtless well known. News came from Jerusalem and reached the exiles by the river Chebar.

That "seventy men of the elders of the house of Israel" enacted this ceremony may be Ezekiel's way of suggesting its more-than-casual nature. The ceremony was exemplary of the people as a whole. On other occasions (e.g., Exod. 24:9-11; Num. 11:24-25) "seventy elders" have represented the entire people of Israel. When the text says that "every man" carried out these rites "in his room of pictures," it does not mean that people were celebrating these rites at random elsewhere throughout the city. It is, after all, the profanation of the temple that concerned the prophet. While the MT has "rooms" in the plural, all the ancient versions read the word in the singular and understand it to refer to this very room in the north gateway.

In Ezek. 8:14-15 God directs Ezekiel to "the entrance of the north gate of the house of the LORD." If the analysis of the progression of this vision that we have offered above is correct, the prophet is still within the northern gateway dividing the inner court of the temple from the outer court. He is now in another room of the gateway that lies upon the threshold of the inner court. Here "sat women weeping for Tammuz." The women had to enter by way of the inner court. The entrance to the gateway facing the outer court was blocked. That fact might have been sufficient to disturb Ezekiel. It is likely that the prophet would have viewed the presence of women in the inner court as a profanation. Still we do not know what were the laws of protocol governing the courts of the preexilic temple that the prophet is describing. We can be sure that there was no exact counterpart in it to the elaborate distinction of multiple courts that later governed the great temple of Herod. In addition, they were "weeping for Tammuz." Tammuz/Dumuzi/Adonis, originally a Sumerian deity, had come into the popular religion of Syria and Canaan from Mesopotamia. He was a prime example of the myth of the dying-and-rising god of vegetation, whose annual death, in the heat and drought of summer, signified the decay of nature. Mourning for him and sympathetic magic led to his resurrection when the winter rains brought new life back to the soil. Weeping for Tammuz was thus a manipulative rite of sympathetic magic. It was a nature cult completely incompatible with the worship of the God of Israel's experience in history.

At last Ezekiel comes into the inner court of the temple itself, where he sees the third of the "greater abominations." Here "twenty-five men"—their character is not further defined—stand with their backs to the temple (whose orientation was East-West) and worship the rising sun in the east. They stand, says the text, "at the door of the temple of the LORD, between the porch and the altar." This precise place, between the entrance to the temple proper and the great altar of sacrifice, apparently was an especially sacred site (2 Kgs. 16:14; Joel 2:17; Matt. 23:35). It has now become a scene of gross sacrilege. The first of the abominations which Ezekiel witnessed in the north gate seemed to be of an Egyptian provenance. The second came from Mesopotamia. The explanation of the third no doubt emerges from Canaan. Though Semitic mythology paid more attention to the moon-god than to the deity identified with the sun, ancient place names like Beth-shemesh ("house [i.e., the shrine or sanctuary] of the sun") suggest that the cult of the "greater light" (Gen. 1:16) was significant. The discoveries at Tell Mardikh (Ebla) have revealed that the sun-god (here under the name Sipish) had worshippers in

Syria/Palestine fully a millennium or more before there was any Israelite presence in this land (Giovanni Pettinato, "The Royal Archives of Tell Mardikh-Ebla," *Biblical Archaeologist* 39 [1976]: 44-52).

The curious expression of Ezek. 8:17, "they put the branch to their nose," becomes easy to understand once one recognizes (with the help of the Hebrew text) that "their" is a "scribal correction" of an original "my." In other words, some scribe among the many who were responsible for the handing down of the biblical texts could not abide its ascribing to the LORD a nose—even though the anthropomorphism here is in Yahweh's own speech—and therefore changed the pronominal modifier. No matter that he sent generations of interpreters scurrying to make sense of his senseless change; he preserved piety. All that the LORD is saying is that in place of the pleasing odor of honest sacrificial worship (Lev. 1:9, etc.), what God is receiving from the Israelites comes as a stench in God's nostrils. In Isa. 17:10 the same word "branch" *(zemorah)* appears in a metaphor of alien practices incompatible with the Israelite profession (Robert Gordis, "'The Branch to the Nose': A Note on Ezekiel VIII$_{17}$," *Journal of Theological Studies* 37 [1934]: 284-88).

9:1-11   Besides the immediate locale, between the temple and the altar of sacrifice ("the bronze altar" of Ezek. 9:2), most everything else in the vision now abruptly changes. From the portrayal of presumably actual happenings in a real world we enter upon a stage of imagination where the protagonists are symbolic and not historical. The "executioners of the city" who appear from the north gate at Yahweh's summons are doubtless "destroying angels" (2 Kgs. 19:35). They come appropriately from the north, since they symbolize the invading Babylonian army, and the route of invasion was invariably from the north. They number seven. There is a distinction because only six of them have a "destroying weapon in his hand" (a club seems to be the meaning). The seventh is "a man clothed in linen, with a writing case at his side": a professional scribe. Angelic presences, for good or for ill, tended to be thought of in sevens at the time of Ezra and Nehemiah and later. The theologians of early Judaism began to organize and adapt to Israelite tradition the spirit world with which it had become acquainted through intimate contact with the gentile religions (cf. Tob. 12:15). Still in this present episode in Ezekiel we perceive a direct Babylonian influence, vague yet unmistakable. In an Aramaic treaty inscription from Assyrian times (the middle of the 8th cent. B.C.E.) found in 1930 at Sefire (ca. 24 km. [15 mi.] SE of Aleppo in Syria), we find invoked as witnesses to the treaty oath the Babylonian gods Nabu (god of wisdom and writing), Erra (god of pestilence and destruction), and the "sevenfold deity," all together (see *Near Eastern Religious Texts,* ed. Walter Beyerlin. Old Testament Library [Philadelphia: Westminster and London: SCM, 1978], 258). There seems to be some similar association and fusion of ideas that lie at the background of Ezekiel's imagery.

The following verses cause some problems. "The glory of the God of Israel" we now find upon the threshold of the temple. As last seen, it was presumably already in the outer courtyard, therefore further advanced in its departure from Jerusalem than it is now. Still we should not press either the chronology or the logic of ecstatic vision, in which picture follows picture in dreamlike succession. For the first time, in this and the following chapters, the "living creatures" that were the support of the LORD'S throne in Ezekiel's inaugural vision of ch. 1 receive the name that properly applies to them: *cherub* in the singular and collective, and in the plural *cherubim.*

The real problem consists in the mission given to the man clothed in linen, who is to mark—evidently that they may survive the general slaughter—all those in the city "who sigh and groan over all the abominations that take place in it." "Put a mark" is, literally, "*taw* with a *taw.*" *Taw,* the last letter of the alphabet, was in the old Hebrew script written as an "X" and had the same function as our X-mark today. While the text does not say explicitly that the man in linen found any candidates suitable for this mark of deliverance, his report of a mission accomplished in 9:11 suggests that he did. (We should remember the blood of the Passover lamb that served as a sign to the destroying angel in Exod. 12:21-27.) In other words, Yahweh's command to the six

70

executioners that they should smite everyone in the city is not an absolute. At the same time, this is not a suggestion that he is making a distinction between the guilty and the innocent: Ezekiel, as we have seen, lacks any notion of a "faithful remnant" from which God is to form the Israel of the future. Still the text does not say that those who sighed and groaned over the abominations of Jerusalem had done anything positively to counteract these evils or that they had merited by that any special consideration for the future. On the other hand, Yahweh's command to the executioners, that they should "show no pity, slay old men outright, young men and maidens, little children and women," does not sound like there is any attempt to segregate the "innocent" from the "guilty." We must conclude that the man clad in linen plays no role other than to acknowledge that there would be those who will have survived the general devastation that descended upon the city and the land.

In Ezek. 9:8 Ezekiel takes on the prophetic role of intercessor, seeking to mitigate the finality of the LORD's doom of Israel. The prophet Amos had earlier assumed this same role and had succeeded in at least delaying the day of judgment (Amos 7:1-6). Yahweh's response to Ezekiel is merely a reaffirmation of the divine will to destroy. Of pity and mercy there will be none.

10:1-8　There is a second commission, different from the first, for the man clothed in linen. It is now that we see the significance of his linen clothing: it is that of a priest (cf. Exod. 28:42-43). It is in his priestly character and not that of the scribe—the writing paraphernalia are no longer mentioned—that the man can touch the sacred fire, fire of the LORD that would spell doom and death for presumptuous, unconsecrated hands (cf. Num. 16:35). Clearly this priestly character is another destroying angel, told to fill his hands with the burning coals "and scatter them over the city." The text does not mention him after Ezek. 10:7, when he receives the coals and goes forth to carry out his new mission. We are to conclude that he finished his new task with the same dispatch he had shown before.

The logistics of these happenings is hard to follow in the existing text. It seems that in the original account of the vision there was no concern with "the glory of Yahweh" and its movements. When the man in linen was told to "go in" amidst the *galgal* ("wheel-work"?) underneath the cherubim" to "take fire" (vv. 2-3 and 6), and when he duly "took it and went out" (v. 7), it was the temple itself and the ark of the covenant in the holy of holies of the temple that were the focus of interest. (We need to remember that we do not know the exact structure of the temple and of the ark of the covenant. Did the ark rest upon wheels? Or do the wheels refer to a portable altar of incense that stood before the ark beneath the overshadowing cherubim, from which, presumably, the burning coals come?)

10:9-17, 20-22   As it stands the text takes pains as before to assimilate all Ezekiel's visions of God's majesty to the model of the one he "had seen by the river Chebar." There are some differences, or modifications, that distinguish the description of ch. 10 from that of ch. 1—calling the "living creatures" cherubim, for example, ascribing hands to them (10:7-8) while explaining how the linen-clad man obtained possession of the fire they guarded—but the overall intention of identification is plain enough. It is also most likely that the process of assimilation has not been in one direction only. Some details in the inaugural vision of ch. 1 appear there by anticipation of the imagery of ch. 10. The redactor probably decided to fit the vision of "the glory of the LORD" to the circumstances of the ark of the covenant.

10:18-19; 11:22-25   Whatever one can say about the description of "the glory of the LORD" and the probable cross-pollination of chs. 1 and 10 in making up this description, the theme of its movement is undoubtedly integral to the temple vision and essential to its message. At the beginning of Ezekiel's vision, the prophet encountered it at the northern gate of the outer court of the temple. It was one of the first things that the prophet saw (8:4). Later it was resting on the threshold of the temple, at the time of the appearance of the destroying angels (9:3). As we have already pointed out, chronology is hardly a matter at issue in the sequences of ecstatic vision. The references of 9:3 and 10:4 that are verbally the same are also probably "chronologically" the same as well. The redactor appears to have introduced a point of confusion here. In this complex "the cherubim" of the text sometimes refer to the agents of the transport of the presence of the glory of the LORD (the "living creatures"). Other times the cherubim refer to the actual sculpted or pictured figures that overshadowed the historical ark of the covenant.

The following seems to have been the original sense of the text. When Ezekiel at last entered the inner court of the temple, he witnessed a progression and a movement of the glory of the LORD. This vision logically was antecedent to the sight he first had of the LORD'S glory in the outer court. The transporting cherubim were "standing on the south side of the house," the shielded, "friendly" side, away from the hostile north (v. 3). After the man clothed in linen had entered the temple (the original sense of the sequence) to take up the sacred fire that he would scatter for the destruction of the profane, "a cloud" of theophany "filled the inner court. It filled the house, and the presence of Yahweh thus departed from the cherubim" overshadowing the ark "to the threshold of the house" (v. 4). There it met the cherubim ("living creatures") of its "transport," and in 11:22-25 we witness its departure from the city. With Ezekiel, we lose sight of it where it pauses "upon the mountain which is on the east side of the city," the Mount of Olives across the Kidron Valley from the temple site. There can be no doubt that as Ezekiel's ecstatic trance ended, when "the vision that I had seen went up from me," among "all the things" he "told the exiles" seated round him was that the divine presence once deemed to be inseparable from the Jerusalem temple (cf. Jer. 7:4) had now abandoned it and that it was this same presence that had appeared to him and constituted him a prophet.

11:1-13 These verses must be interpreted as an alternate account of what the prophet recalled in 8:16-18. We can easily imagine the prophet rehearsing to his fellow exiles the particulars of his ecstatic experiences. Sometimes he may have emphasized one detail over another. The result was that the prophet may have told the same "event" in several versions. We can also easily imagine a redactor of the book preserving all the versions that he had, in fidelity to his mission to perpetuate the memory and message of his prophetic master, and fitting them with editorial splices so that he loses nothing of the heritage he received. This is precisely the kind of technique that governed the literary fixation of most of the oral traditions of the OT that eventually became written down and that accounts for the many "doublets" in OT history.

The circumstances surrounding the "twenty-five men" are the same as in 8:16-18. There they were between the porch of the temple and the altar, their backs to the temple and facing east. Here they are at the "door of the gateway of the east gate" within the inner court. The text says nothing here of the worship of the sun; rather, these twenty-five are emblematic of the complacency and self-sufficiency that have inspired the "wicked counsel" leading to Jerusalem's downfall. The saying ascribed to them in 11:3 is cryptic, so commentators have understood it in various ways. In view of v. 11 particularly, it is hard to avoid the impression that v. 3 intends to exemplify that blindness to the signs of the times and heedlessness of the intentions of divine providence revealed in recent history that account for their wicked counsel. "The time is not near to build houses" probably means that they were thinking of themselves as the only prospective residents of the city where they were safe and secure. There was no cause to contemplate any further change within their generation. That overconfidence recurs in their saying that "the city is the (protective) caldron, and we are the flesh" within its guarding embrace. The text mentions two of the twenty-five by name. They are Jaazaniah the son of Azzur and Pelatiah the son of Benaiah, "princes of the people," presumably counselors of the realm. The first of these is certainly the Jaazaniah of 8:11. Still here the text calls him the son of Azzur rather than of Shaphan. It is likely that the redactor of this passage of Ezekiel, who has chosen to treat the doublet accounts of chs. 8 and 11 sequentially, and thus to introduce Jaazaniah as a new character of the scene, has also altered the name. Azzur was a name well suited to the occasion, associated as it was with the false prophecy of complacency which Jeremiah had opposed in Jerusalem (cf. Jer. 28:1). As for Pelatiah, the name itself ("Yahweh preserves [a remnant]") is significant. It is important in Ezek. 11:13 in the repetition of Ezekiel's intercession of 9:8: "Wilt thou make a full end of the remnant of Israel?" Whether Pelatiah had a real existence apart from Ezekiel's vision, we cannot know. There is no reason to suppose that his death is any less symbolic, or more historically "real," than any other details of the vision.

The LORD'S reiterated sentence of doom in 11:5-12 takes up the saying attributed to the princes of the people and plays on it with several variations. In vv. 6-7 "your slain" introduces a new charge made against the leadership of Jerusalem and Judah. There are no further details. Whether the reference is to political and religious murder or simply to the responsibility of the leaders for the deaths that come about because of their bungling policies, we cannot say.

11:14-21   These verses are an independent oracle, an instruction to Ezekiel. They are connected with the temple vision only casually because of the similarity of the sentiments ascribed to the Jerusalemites in v. 15 to those of v. 3 above. In both cases those who remain in Jerusalem smugly contrast themselves with those who are in exile. The people who remained in Jerusalem look upon themselves as the surviving Israel and upon the exiles as lost forever to any title in the land. As before, Yahweh must shatter this illusion and proclaim that the old Israel is dead. A new Israel will arise only through new creation. One is to look for the new Israel not in reprobate Jerusalem but in the lands of the Exile.

There seems to be no doubt that in these verses we are reading authentic words of Ezekiel. Many of them appear again in later passages from the second and positive phase of the prophet's later career. We will best consider them for commentary at that point. It also would appear that, as such, this passage is a redactional composition, in part anticipating the prophet's later message, which a similar prophecy in Jeremiah has influenced (Jer. 32:36-40). Adrianus van den Born has lined up the parallels convincingly (*Ezechiël.* De Boeken van het Oude Testament 2/1 [Roermond en Maaseik: J. J. Romen, 1954], 74]:

Jeremiah		Ezekiel			
32:37a	=	11:17aα	=	36:24aβ	=	37:21abα
32:37b	=	11:17b	=	36:24b	=	37:21b
32:40	=	11:18b	=	36:25	=	37:23abα
32:39a	=	11:19	=	36:26	=	
32:40	=	11:20a	=	36:27b	=	37:24b
32:38	=	11:20b	=	36:28b	=	37:23bβ, 27aβb

The one element that turns up uniquely in this present passage of Ezekiel is in 11:16. There the LORD'S presence among the exiles is for them "a sanctuary in small measure" (RSV; see note to v. 16). For Ezekiel, as his later prophecies make clear, Yahweh's presence, in any full sense of the word, is inseparable from the land and from the Jerusalem temple. Contrary to the glib self-assurance of the remaining inhabitants of Jerusalem, however, and as we have already seen, the glory of the LORD has departed the city and the temple. Their claim to possession of the land as a gift of God is illusory. Even this illusion is soon to be snatched away. If the God of Israel is present anywhere, that God can only be in the Exile, whence God will bring back a new Israel. Until God establishes the new Israel and the people build a new temple, this is the only presence that Israel-to-be can count on. Still it is presence in a mitigated sense.

ACTS SYMBOLIC
OF THE EXILE
Ezekiel 12:1-28

The twelfth chapter of the book of Ezekiel describes two symbolic actions that God instructs the prophet to do. The LORD gives explanatory instructions. The actions prefigure the coming deportation of the remaining population of Jerusalem—that is, the residual population of princes and leaders of the people whom Ezekiel's fellow exiles had been counting on rejoining in the land of Judah. The first exiles confidently assumed that their stay in Babylon would be of only brief duration. From the reaction of these exiles described in 12:9 we may judge that these prophecies came early in the prophet's career. This was before his message of doom had been so dinned in their ears by constant repetition that there could be no possible misunderstanding about what he was acting out before them.

12:1-7 The first of Ezekiel's symbolic actions unfolds in three stages. First he simulates a person going into exile. He hastily gathers the few belongings. These he will be able to carry with him as he will be led or driven, perhaps fettered, with his companions in woeful procession "to another place." The actual departure will take place "in the evening," the only feasible time for travel after the passing of the heat of the day. Then, we are to assume that unwilling hands will take up the pitiful bundles that were lying alongside the thresholds of houses that were once homes. The journey into exile would then begin.

Between these two signs of preparing the baggage and issuing forth to take it up in the evening, there is an additional sign for Ezekiel to effect. His exile will not be through the doorway; rather, he must "dig through the wall . . . and go out through it." This

77

action would have been much more easily effected in the Mesopotamian than in the Palestinian scene: mud brick as opposed to stone. It applies, nevertheless, to the Palestinian scene, or more specifically to the Jerusalem scene to signify that the exiles' departure will take place from a wasted city whose walls its conquerors have breached and battered down. The further command to "cover your face, that you may not see the land" we might think superfluous, since the prophet went forth in the dark in his obedience to God's instructions. It is given for emphasis. Shame, grief, humiliation, the instinctive furtiveness with which the defeated flee the scene of their disaster—doubtless all these combine in the gesture of covering the face and refusing to look on the land.

12:8-16 In the divine oracle that accompanies these actions and in their interpretation, we find Ezekiel speaking *to* the rebellious house of Israel *about* the rebellious house of Israel. The prophet tells those already in exile that those whose exile is imminent will soon join them. As they formed a single recalcitrant people while yet on the soil of Palestine, a single recalcitrant people they will become again, in Babylon.

We may suspect that Ezekiel himself may have tailored some of the language here to the actual circumstances of Jerusalem's final days as later generations came to know them. Specifically, it would appear that this text presupposes the events narrated in 2 Kgs. 25:3-7 ([= Jer. 39:4-7 =] Jer. 52:5-11) about the fate of King Zedekiah. As we read in 2 Kings, it was Zedekiah's eleventh year, on the ninth day of the fourth month (i.e., July 587), during the siege of the city, that

> a breach was made in the city; the king with all the men of war fled by night by the way of the gate between the two walls, by the king's garden, though the Chaldeans were around the city. And they went in the direction of the Arabah. But the army of the Chaldeans pursued the king, and overtook him in the plains of Jericho; and all his army was scattered from him. Then they captured the king, and brought him up to the king of Babylon at Riblah, who passed sentence upon him. They slew the sons of Zedekiah before his eyes, and put out the eyes of Zedekiah, and bound him in fetters, and took him to Babylon.

It is not simply that the prophet has taken a sign intended to represent the "them" of Jerusalem in Ezek. 12:11 and 15-16 and applied it in vv. 12-14 solely to "the prince" of the people, as we see from some of Ezekiel's later oracles. It is very easy for Ezekiel to personify a whole people in its ruler. On the contrary, it is his changing the meaning of the "not see the land with his eyes," originally a sign of grief, to a literal "not see it" (the land of the Chaldeans) in vv. 12-13. This change of meaning tells us that we must now reflect on the literal physical blindness that Zedekiah's cruel captors inflicted upon him. Also there are the details of the rout and desertion of Zedekiah's pathetic little army and his later death in Babylon. In v. 13 Yáhweh interprets, using a hunting metaphor, the Babylonian vengeance wreaked upon Zedekiah as God's own act. The destruction of the king was like the dropping of a net over a snarling wild beast that the hunter then drags away to an inevitable slaughter. (In its way, this is a larger-than-life portrayal of the dithering Zedekiah whom Baruch reveals in his "life" of Jeremiah.) Only in vv. 14b-15 do we move from the circumstances of Zedekiah's personal debacle to the original context of the general dispersion of the house of Israel. In v. 16 recurs the theme of those who elude the now familiar triad of "sword," "famine," and "pestilence," not as an act of mercy or of grace, but only that they may serve as witnesses to the world of both the efficacy of the LORD's judgment of doom and of the justice with which God inflicted divine judgment upon Judah.

Ezekiel's reference to the king simply as "the prince in Jerusalem" doubtless has dual import. First, the Babylonian records to which we made reference in the Introduction, which have verified the biblical account of the Exile to the extent of mentioning the allowances provided for Jehoiachin in Babylon, suggest that the Babylonians regarded him as the true king of Judah, no matter how they may have looked upon Zedekiah whom they had set in his place. This judgment seems to have been that of the Judahites as well, though the book of 2 Kings and Baruch's chronicle in the book of Jeremiah call Zedekiah "king." Seals of the royal official Eliakim, "servant of Jehoiachin," found at Tell Beit Mirsim and Beth-shemesh, and of Jaazaniah and Gedaliah (2 Kgs. 25:23), respectively "servant of the king" and "over the

house" (= royal steward), found at Tell en-Nasbeh (Mizpah) and
Tell ed-Duweir (Lachish), seem to support this [Abraham Mala-
mat, "Jeremiah and the Last Two Kings of Judah," *Palestine Ex-
ploration Quarterly* 83 (1951): 81-87; Karl Jaroš, *Hundert Inschrif-
ten,* nrs. 62, 76, 78].

Second and probably more important, "king" is not a term
that Ezekiel finds congenial to the description of an Israelite leader.
It may be appropriate for the rulers of the Gentiles, but not for
the ruler of Judah. Undoubtedly the prophet's theology motivated
this reticence. Ezekiel accepted the privileged status accorded the
Davidic dynasty by Jerusalemite tradition, and accordingly he
incorporated a Davidic ruler in his vision of the ideal Israel of the
future. Still he insists upon the neutral title "prince" (*nasi'*, "chief").
(In the modern State of Israel *nasi'* is the title given to the president
or chief of state who holds a mainly ceremonial position.) Ezekiel
seems to have shared the attitude reflected in the early chapters
of 1 Samuel and sporadically in the prophetic and other writings
of the OT. The kingship was, for Israel, in some ways a repudiation
of its unique character, an assimilation to the ways of the Gentiles,
and an affront to Yahweh who alone was Israel's king (cf. Isa.
6:5).

12:17-20 The other "action" that the prophet does is immediately explained. God instructs him to communicate its meaning.
The RSV has incorrectly translated the text of Ezek. 12:19 (or
has emended the text without noting it). This version has Ezekiel
speak "of" rather than "to the people of the land." Here "the land"
is not the land of Israel or Judah. It is, as in 33:2, the land
wherever a people dwells, which in this context is the land of
Babylon. As usual, the prophet is speaking to his fellow exiles
"concerning the inhabitants of Jerusalem in the land of Israel"
who will soon be joining them.

They are probably correct who see in this "action" of Ezekiel's
eating and drinking with palsied hand ("quaking" and "trembling") a condition that doubtless caused him to fumble about
and spill his drink. It was some natural infirmity that has become,
by the LORD'S inspiration, another prophetic sign. To the callous
observer such an affliction can be the occasion of disgust or of

ridicule, depending on the observer's humor at the time. At a much later date something of the same sort would occur in the career of Paul the Apostle, who had his share of physical infirmities. When the apostle appeared before the Corinthians "in weakness and in much fear and trembling," he exemplified how "God chose what is foolish in the world to shame the wise, God chose what is weak in the world to shame the strong" (1 Cor. 1:27; 2:3). Here the "wisdom" of the exiled house of Israel is strong in its illusory conviction of the impregnability of Jerusalem and of the land. A weakness that images the demoralization and devastation soon to descend upon both land and city confounds that wisdom.

12:21-25 Two oracles of the LORD take up the remaining verses of this chapter. The first mainly concerns the efficacy of the prophetic word. There was a saying that had long been common in Israel—and no doubt has been common in many other lands among many other peoples—expressing the popular cynicism that greeted Cassandra-like utterances: "The days grow long, and every vision comes to nought." Every passing day put between a predicted evil and its not coming to pass contributes to the *non sequitur* conclusion that it will never happen. Yahweh is guarantor that it will happen, and soon.

12:26-28 "Soonness" is the theme of the second oracle. There are many forms of disbelief, many forms of complacency. One need not entirely reject the validity of the prophetic word or be totally oblivious to the prophet's having correctly read the signs of the times, to deny its actual efficacy. "There will be peace in our time." Let there be no doubt about it, says the LORD; the word has been uttered about *you*. There will be no further delay in God's bringing it to fulfillment.

FALSE PROPHECY
Ezekiel 13:1–14:23

Most of the two following chapters of the book of Ezekiel has to do with the bad spiritual leadership that has contributed to Israel's downfall. In ch. 13 the emphasis is on the evils of this kind still rampant in Jerusalem in its dying days. On the other hand, 14:1-11 pertains to the exiles already in Babylon as it focuses on false worship. Ezekiel's prophetic mission was to the whole of the house of Israel. The appendix of 14:12-23 comes from later, after news of the final fall of Jerusalem had reached the prophet's fellow exiles, but probably before their fellow Judahites, newly expelled from the Holy City, joined them.

13:1-9   First comes a condemnation of "the prophets of Israel" (an expression found only in Ezekiel). What strikes the reader immediately is the paradox that the LORD has sent Ezekiel so the rebellious house of Israel may know "that there has been a prophet among them" (2:5). Still Ezekiel finds it his task to spurn the prophets of Israel as deceivers and liars. His concern, of course, is with those whom we have become accustomed to term "false prophets." (The LXX coined the word "pseudoprophet" for occasions like this, though it does not use it in this passage.) The Hebrew has only the one word, *nabi*, which—again following the LXX, the first translation of the Hebrew Bible into a Western language—we translate "prophet." This term refers indiscriminately to anyone who laid claim to be or was acclaimed to be one who gave voice to the mind of God. It is probable that a generation earlier Ezekiel would not have applied this term *nabi* to himself. The word originally referred to various categories of "holy men" or "men of God." For various reasons, prophets like Amos, Hosea, and Isaiah

82

distanced themselves from these prophets even as Ezekiel is distancing himself here, though not by name. The term *nabi*, in other words, underwent an evolution (cf. 1 Sam. 8:9) by which it became a catch-all expression for a common phenomenon that had once been subject to finer distinctions. (See Bruce Vawter, "Were the Prophets *nābî's?*" *Biblica* 66 [1985]: 206-220.)

The first "false" prophets that Ezekiel condemns are those who "have spoken falsehood and divined a lie." These prophets, whether in good faith but self-deluded or in bad faith and deliberately deceiving, have professed to speak the mind of the LORD when in reality no spirit other than their own moved them. They have been, he says, "like foxes among ruins." The simile is probably related to what the Song of Songs says of the "little foxes" (Cant. 2:15). Just as the "foxes" (Heb. *shu'alim*, often translated elsewhere "jackals," probably refers to some kind of garden rodent) eat away at the roots of a vineyard, so the prophets of Israel, rather than standing in the breaches of Jerusalem's walls and constituting a bulwark for its defense, have instead sapped these walls and undermined them. The metaphor is mixed and somewhat cumbersome, but that is not at all atypical of Ezekiel's metaphors.

Against these lying prophets the LORD will oppose the divine "hand" (recall Ezek. 4:7, where God commanded the prophet to shake his fist toward the city of Jerusalem). "They shall not be in the council of my people." The intimacy in which Yahweh and people together shared a common counsel is at an end as far as these false messengers are concerned. Their names shall disappear from the once proud "register of the house of Israel, nor shall they enter the land of Israel." Israel will rise again. The new Israel will occupy much of the prophet's attention in the second part of his ministry.

13:10-16   A second charge against the "false" prophets recalls the nemesis of Ezekiel's contemporary, Jeremiah: the prophets of "peace" whose lack of realism persuades them to promise a comfortable and tranquil future when all the signs of the time, for anyone who can read them rightly, portend only disaster and calamity. A graphic and homely image illustrates the effect of their soothing words that have lulled the people into an inauthentic existence. Just as an ill-built wall—of stone or brick poorly joined, not mortared, and held together only by precarious tension—can still give the impression of stability when a thin layer of plaster covers it (RSV "whitewash"), such has been the effect of these prophets who have produced a façade of impregnability that is totally illusory. Their preaching has been the plastering over of a defense that does not exist. It cannot withstand the elements of destruction that are surely coming, that will quickly crumble and bury in its rubble both those who have relied on it and those who pronounced it reliable.

13:17-23 Now the prophet is to prophesy against "the daughters of your people," women whom we would doubtless characterize as sorceresses or witches. We need not, as Georg Fohrer did for one, consider this passage to be a conflation of two separate condemnations, one of prophetesses, the female counterparts of the prophets of peace with whom Ezekiel has just dealt, the other of those women who pandered to the ineradicable superstitions of desperate people who seek a magical solution to insoluble problems (Georg Fohrer, *Ezechiel*. Handbuch zum Alten Testament 13 [Tübingen: J. C. B. Mohr, 1955], 73-74). Neither need we imagine, as other commentators would have it, some sarcastic sense given to the first use of the verb "prophesy" in 13:17. We have here a prime instance of the flexibility and ambiguity of the term *nabi* (which is not applied to these women) discussed above, with the associated verbs *hinnabe* and *hitnabe,* "prophesy," but also suggesting the performance of other actions closely or remotely connected with prophecy.

The following vv. 18-23 are somewhat obscure. We can only guess at what, precisely, were the magic wristbands and headveils created by the sorceresses. It seems to be obvious that they were fetishes of some kind that were accompanied by magical spells ("prophesying"). People bought these for a price and believed that they made the difference between life and death. Israel's traditional religion strictly forbade magical practices of this nature (cf. Deut. 18:10-11; 2 Kgs. 23:24), but not because people thought them to be ineffective or harmless! There is no reason to think that Ezekiel,

84

a child of his age, thought of these things as other than evil devices "putting to death persons who should not die and keeping alive persons who should not live." The women who made use of them were not, for this prophet, carnival gypsies whom one frequents for amusement; they were practitioners of the dark arts. When he says that they purveyed "lies," we must bear in mind the scriptural meaning of a lie, which is not that a thing is not factual but that it is pernicious. It is in this sense that Satan is "the father of lies" (John 8:44). The worst aspect of this whole grubby affair is that it has been done in the name of Yahweh. Thus the Israelite "holy women" profaned God among God's people.

In the final verses it is Yahweh who takes the initiative in bringing down retribution upon these women of Jerusalem. God will tear off the arm bands and the veils. God will deliver those who have been their prey. Finally God will end their shameful practices.

14:1-5   These verses seem to take up the theme of Yahweh's direct action just broached concerning "the daughters of your people." The circumstances are those of a delegation of "the elders of Israel." The elders came to Ezekiel and sat before him in the expectation of receiving through him "an oracle from the LORD." What they are asking for *(darash)* is a commentary on what they ought to do *(midrash)* — and this Yahweh refuses to give them through Ezekiel. They are unworthy of prophetical communication because of "the stumbling block of [their] iniquity" and "the multitude of [their] idols." There are no further determinations: we are left simply with the position that Yahweh will no longer talk to Judah through the prophets. Their circumstances are hopeless, and that is the end of it. We have no further information about where this episode fits into the ministry of Ezekiel. Also we have no idea about the crimes that the prophet condemned at this time. The passage, however, forms an appropriate redactional introduction to the verses that follow.

14:6-11   These verses are an instruction which God tells Ezekiel to deliver to the house of Israel. "Idols" is a charge that the prophet brings against this people. We probably should not think of these in

85

any crude sense of wooden or stone images but in spiritual terms of whatever has alienated this people from its LORD and rendered it inaccessible to God's ordinary communication. The language is "traditional" throughout. Witness the references in Ezek. 14:7 to the *ger,* the "stranger" in Israel, the protected alien or sojourner whose presence native Israelites tolerated as long as he offered no offense to the popular taboos and observed the minimum of Israelite proprieties. In Babylon there were no Israelite *gerim,* for the Israelites themselves in Babylon were all *gerim.* What the text says simply is that all Israelites, native and *ger,* have through their idolatry cut themselves off from Yahweh's prophetic communication. God will now deal with them directly.

The further point is made that there is an interaction between the prophets "deceived" by the LORD and those who have permitted such prophets to deceive them. (Here we have a connection established with the "false" prophets of the preceding chapter.) Both are equally guilty, and who can properly assess the blame? Wish fulfillment will always find those in authority who are anxious to fulfill wishes.

14:12-20 Again an element out of Ezekiel's collected prophecies confronts the reader. The text introduces it here only in view of some superficial verbal connections with the surrounding context. What it very much looks like is a word of justification delivered on behalf of Yahweh's justice. It serves to explain to the Israelites in exile why the Babylonians were able to destroy the Jerusalem of their hopes, the innocent perishing with the guilty. We are, in these verses, doubtless in the post–586 era.

Ezekiel offers no compromise. There are no mitigating circumstances that can call the judgment of the LORD into question. As a *reductio ad absurdum* he invokes from the distant and folkloric past three proverbial heroes of righteousness. Their hypothetical presence in Jerusalem would still not have sufficed to spare the city. Noah, of course, we know from Gen. 6–9. He was the one righteous man whom the LORD found in a world that was totally corrupt in God's sight (Gen. 6:11). For his sake God spared the world and perpetuated the humankind of whose destiny God had despaired. Noah, under other names, was also the hero of the many Mesopotamian legends of the Great Flood. These were current in the Babylonian ambient of Ezekiel and his fellow exiles. Job we know from the biblical book of Job. What this text alludes to is not the magnificent poetry of the biblical work but the prose folktale preserved in its prologue and epilogue that tells of an Edomite patriarch whose righteousness eventually prevailed over all obstacles and got final vindication. As for Daniel, the name is most familiar to us from the biblical book that bears this name, but to Ezekiel's fellow exiles and contemporaries (who lived, no doubt, long before the composition of that biblical work) the name of Daniel would have been well-known from Canaanite legend as a proverbially righteous ruler whose fulfillment of the Near Eastern ideal of kingship had merited for him the special solicitude of the gods (cf. *Near Eastern Religious Texts*, ed. Walter Beyerlin, 225-26). It may be interesting in passing—though no particular point is made of it by Ezekiel—that none of these three righteous persons was an Israelite: Noah was but a remote ancestor of Israel, to the extent that his children fathered the whole human race after the Flood; Job was an Edomite; and Daniel, a Canaanite.

More important to the thought of the passage is the assertion, which in some circles must have been disconcerting (cf. the contrary doctrine of Isa. 52:4-12), that there is no collective guilt. The righteous do not atone for the sins of the multitude, even as Noah's rectitude had guaranteed the preservation of the sinful human race and Job's intercession had atoned for the guilt of his "friends" (Job 42:8). No, says Ezekiel, from now on, it shall not be so. Were these three righteous men part of the people of that land on which the LORD has determined to bring doom, they themselves would be spared. Their presence, however, would not suffice to deliver even "sons [or] daughters" (as Noah's had), let alone anyone else. This is an assertion of personal and individual responsibility that runs athwart the old idea of communal virtue and vice in which all participated as a people, but is now proper to an age in which the LORD would deal with Israel less as a people than as a religion (even, in a sense, as a "church"). Habituated as we are to the notion of individual responsibility, we do not easily recognize what a revolution in thought it was to the idea of Ezekiel's contemporaries. The exile had done more than to transport them physically; it had also transported them spiritually and ideologically into a new religious realm. The old covenant with Israel was truly dead. The new covenant which Ezekiel, for one, would mediate was truly new and with new rules. The prophet himself did not always fully understand these rules. Some did come to understand the new rules, for example, Third Isaiah (though not Second Isaiah, apparently), some postexilic prophets, and authors of other postexilic works. Ezra and Nehemiah, whose views conditioned so much of postexilic Judaism, did not accept the new circumstances and their consequences. We can do no more here than to take note of the phenomenon.

Commentators often compare this passage of Ezekiel with Jer. 15:1-4. There are some obvious similarities and some equally obvious divergences. On the one hand, both passages evoke righteous men of the past, in Jeremiah's case the Israelite heroes Moses and Samuel. Both accounts also agree that the prayers of such worthies would not suffice to save the people from its just judgment. Jeremiah by no means dwells on the implications of this fact for the assignment of responsibility as does Ezekiel. Both passages talk of four kinds of destruction, though the four differ slightly in particulars. It would appear that while Walther Zimmerli regards the Jeremiah passage as the "prototype" of that in Ezekiel (*Ezekiel 1*, 314), they are parallel insights from the same or similar situation in which the one prophet has perceived implications that the other did not.

14:21-23 The three "acts of judgment" that the LORD has promised to bring down on Jerusalem—sword, famine, and pestilence—now rate a fourth: "evil beasts." It was a traditional theme to think of a devastated land as the habitat of wild beasts and unclean creatures (cf. Isa. 13:21-22). Also the progression from three to four plagues may be a symptom of proto-apocalyptic thought in the Bible. Apocalyptic loves to deal in fours.

The possible "survivors" of the Jerusalem debacle to come still do not form anything like a "faithful remnant," a nucleus of the Israel-to-be. That they will be "consoled for the evil that I have brought upon Jerusalem" means only that they will survive to testify "that I have not done without cause all that I have done in it," says Yahweh.

PART III
JUDGMENT ON THE PAST

Ezekiel 15:1–24:27

THE GREAT ALLEGORIES
Ezekiel 15:1–19:14

This chapter will be concerned with what is, in the main, a series of allegories (with prophetic commentary). Through these allegories the prophet describes the sins of Jerusalem and its kings and announces the consequent judgment of the LORD. In Ezek. 18 there is an intervening section on the possibility and conditions of repentance and thus of escaping future retribution. In substance these passages belong to the prophet Ezekiel. Still the allegories obviously predate the coming fall of Jerusalem. Chapter 18 just as obviously presupposes it and therefore must pertain to the second stage of Ezekiel's ministry to Israel.

15:1-8 The first words that we read appear to be less an allegory than they are a parable, a simple simile or metaphor. Their allegorical character, however, derives from the vine-figure that represents Israel. It is not a figure that the prophet chose at random, but it is rather one that has a history in Israelite symbolism. Following the sequence of passages assembled in Walther Zimmerli's commentary, we can note Num. 13:23, where the vine appears as a sign of the richness of Canaan; Jotham's fable of the noble vine in Judg. 9:12-13; Gen. 49:11, in which the vine represents the fullness of the blessing of the messianic age; the parable of the vineyard in Isa. 5:1-7; the lengthy comparison of Israel with a vine stock in Ps. 80:8-19; Israel the luxuriant vine in Hos. 10:1; and the imagery of Ezekiel himself in Ezek. 17:5-10 and 19:10-14. This is not the only time that Ezekiel takes a traditional figure connoting the "messianic" character of Israel as the repository of God's favor and turns it against itself in almost cynical fashion as a symbol of discarded worthlessness.

For what, he asks, is the value of a vine in comparison with
the sturdier wood out of which one can fashion furniture and
implements? It is useless except for fuel, and even for that its use
is ephemeral. The vine symbolizes Israel, as it has in the past.
Now its quick life in the fire suggests the suddenness and finality
with which Yahweh will get rid of this particularly worthless vine.
"Like the wood of the vine among the trees of the forest, which
I have given to the fire for fuel, so will I give up the inhabitants
of Jerusalem."

16:1-7 In setting the scene for the next allegory Ezekiel regis-
ters some striking departures from his prophetic predecessors.
Prophets like Amos and Hosea had pictured Israel's beginning in
Yahweh's liberating call to them out of the bondage of Egypt.
Also they had contrasted with Israel's later infidelity the relative
innocence of this people at the time of its summoning: only later
did Israel prove itself to have been unworthy of the LORD's
election. To the contrary, Ezekiel views Israel as a hopeless case
from the outset—no idyllic period of the past in which it had
been a faithful client or spouse covenanted with the LORD—and
the prophet sets Israel's origins not in Egypt or in the desert of
Sinai or Kadesh but in the land of Canaan itself. The latter note
is the more readily understandable since Ezekiel, like Isaiah, uses
Jerusalem as the epitome of the rejected Israel. Jerusalem, albeit
the City of David, was bone and flesh of the land of Canaan.
Even in Israelite times the city was more redolent of the traditions
and ways of Canaan than even an Isaiah, a Jeremiah, or an Ezekiel
would have willingly admitted or even have been aware of fully,
so much had they become the ways of Israel.

"Your father was an Amorite, and your mother a Hittite." It
is probably wrong to try to find in these terms any precise knowledge on Ezekiel's part about the ethnic composition of early
Jerusalem. As in Gen. 15:19-21, people remembered these and
other like names simply in the sense of "aborigines." What the
prophet stresses is, of course, this people's Canaanite origins, and
it is this theme that he pursues in the following verses. The
Jerusalem that the prophet pictures here as a girl child born of
non-Israelite parents came in for the type of treatment that female

infants experienced in the world at that time. Their parents abandoned them to die of exposure because they came into a world that did not want them. Not only did the child not receive the hygienic care normally given to newly born infants, its parents treated it as an obscene excretion. Its parents abandoned it to welter in the blood of its afterbirth to which its umbilical cord still bound it.

In this first scene of the allegory Yahweh appears simply as a "Good Samaritan." The allegory portrays God as a kindly passer-by who takes pity on this helpless object and ensures that it shall live. The prophet does not sustain the figure. He does not give his readers details but merely informs them that under the LORD's protection the child enjoyed its nourishment and came to the maturity of womanhood. "Yet you were naked and bare" reminds us that we are in the midst of an allegory that has a logic of its own. The castaway infant has survived and has arrived at puberty. The prophet asks us to keep in mind its original miserable state, which is now exchanged for one that far transcends mere physical life.

16:8-14   In the second scene of the allegory Yahweh again passes by. This time the allegory portrays God as sexually attracted by the sight of a nubile girl ripe for marriage. The imagery is bold. It is reminiscent of Hosea's metaphors. This allegory is particularly daring in view of Jerusalem's proclivity, as we know from Jeremiah's prophecy (not to mention what Ezekiel has already revealed in his temple vision), for the worship of the Canaanite Astarte, the "queen of heaven," the fertility goddess who was consort of the national god. Ezekiel, even less than Hosea, does not flinch at this imagery. Every detail proper to the description of a secular marriage comes into play—the bride-price, the festal gifts, and beyond, the special favors that a royal prince bestowed on this abandoned girl. This prince could bring her to an estate she could never have dreamed of otherwise. Such was the marriage of Yahweh with Israel.

16:15-34   But just as Hosea's imagery, bold as it was, became understandable by its denouement, the harlotry of Gomer, so it is with Ezekiel's. The figure of the wanton and faithless wife symbolizes several forms of Jerusalem's (and Judah's) apostasy: (1) unlawful worship on the "high places"; (2) idolatry; (3) the cult of "Moloch"; and (4) traffic with foreign nations and the adoption of foreign ways. The accusations come in a stream and the figures leap back and forth—as is not unusual with Ezekiel. There is a consistent theology to the passage, though its sequence may be confusing. The imagery derives from the Western Semitic mythological pattern that imagined a city to be the spouse of its patron deity. From this perspective it is natural to portray Jerusalem's faithlessness as marital infidelity.

The prophet portrays Jerusalem as a simple prostitute, offering herself to every passer-by. In Ezek. 16:30-34 in a piece of fine sarcasm Ezekiel portrays Israel literally as a nymphomaniac whose promiscuous lust has caused her to reverse the usual order involved in prostitution. She has hired rather than been hired by her clients. This refers, of course, particularly to the preceding vv. 26-29 regarding her seeking out alliance and commerce with Egypt, Assyria, and Babylon. (The prophet does not portray the Philistines of v. 27 in the same way. They are enemies. Ezekiel anticipates what he will say of them much more negatively in 25:15-17.)

In 16:20-21 Ezekiel lists as the worst of Jerusalem's religious harlotries the sacrifice of infants that took place in the valley of Ben-hinnom, probably under Assyrian influence. This is apparently the prophet's sole explicit reference (besides 23:37, 39) to this abominable practice, which is surprising in view of the extensive attention given it by both Jeremiah and 2 Kings.

16:35-43 In these verses, which require little comment, the prophet portrays Yahweh, the wronged husband, as bringing down public shame on his wayward spouse. Appropriately, it is Israel's "lovers" who will execute God's vengeance upon her. By that they add to the depth of her shame. They show how cheaply they had valued what she had to offer them and the real contempt in which they held her. This passage is one of inexorable doom without mitigation. Israel will cease to be the prostitute, but by external force and circumstances and not because of repentance. In turn, the LORD's fury will be sated and spent. God "will no

94

more be angry"—here there is no hint that God will again turn to Israel. Israel is an episode in the divine dealing with humankind that now belongs to the past, with no intimation of any other episodes to come.

16:44-58   This chapter of Ezekiel continues and concludes for the moment the representation of Israel's doom as that of the punishment of a faithless spouse. The prophet adds some curious twists to the allegory. One may aptly call this passage "the allegory of the three sisters," anticipating the allegory of Oholah and Oholibah in ch. 23. It builds in **16:45** on the same theme that the prophet enunciated at the beginning of this chapter: "Your mother was a Hittite and your father an Amorite." Here the emphasis is on the depravity of the mother, who serves as a paradigm for the performance of her daughters. They imitate the example she has set for them: "Like mother, like daughter" (or, in its more familiar form, "Like father, like son") is probably one of the primordial proverbs that occurred to the human race once it began to observe the patterns of its conduct. It is probably pointless to ask what precisely Ezekiel had in mind when he accused the mother in the allegory as one "who loathed her husband and her children." The prophet set up the allegory not to delineate the historical crimes of the Hittite. He wanted to catalogue those of her "daughter." Ezekiel assumes that both "Hittite" and "Amorite"—who are mere ciphers and stand for the aborigines whom Yahweh removed to make way for Israel to inherit the land—sinned and deserved their fate. What the prophet is saying is that his people's history in this land testifies more to its Canaanite origins that it was supposed to surpass. There is little that remains of the Yahwistic ethos that created a new people on the soil of Canaan.

The three sisters are Jerusalem (and Judah), Samaria (i.e., the northern kingdom of Israel whose fall had come in 721 B.C.E.), and Sodom. Ezekiel calls Samaria the "elder sister" and Sodom the "younger sister" not out of any chronological interest (the Hebrew terms are, literally, "big" and "small," respectively). Ezekiel has in view their historical importance to those whom the prophet addressed. The fate of the kingdom of the north, far greater in political importance than the lesser kingdom of Judah, remained in living memory as an object lesson for the surviving house of Israel. It was testimony to the disaster that the LORD could bring down upon a faithless people. Sodom was one of the legendary "cities of the plain" to the south. It was simply a piece of folklore, proverbial of the inexorable anger of God that would strike down wickedness (cf. Hos. 11:8; Jer. 23:14; Deut. 29:23; Wisd. 10:6-8). The particular wickedness for which Sodom had become proverbial was by no means specified in the folklore with the precision of the stories of Gen. 18–19. The stories there have contributed to our language terms like "sodomy" and "sodomite." Ezekiel charges Sodom and her daughters (dependent villages) with "pride, surfeit of food, and prosperous ease," who "did not aid the poor and needy"—in the best prophetic tradition. Also in the best prophetic tradition, and with perhaps a bit of prophetic exaggeration, Ezekiel drives home the point of the allegory. Jerusalem has proven to be much worse than either Samaria or Sodom. Jerusalem has made these two wicked cities "look good"—"you . . . have made your sisters appear righteous," the prophet says in Ezek. 16:52. This is reminiscent of the sarcasm of Amos 3:9-10, where Egypt and Assyria, those models of depravity, come to Samaria to observe sinfulness as "professionals" can practice it.

It is doubtless in this spirit that we should understand Ezek. 16:53-58. The text speaks of "restoring the fortunes" of Samaria, Sodom, and Jerusalem and of their "returning to their former estate." Obviously there is no intention of saying that they shall resume their sinful ways, but neither does the prophet mean any "restoration" in the sense of redemption. The prophet asks us to picture the three as contemporaries, in which situation Jerusalem would be a consolation to her less wayward sisters and Sodom could no longer be a byword of iniquity for the sinful city (v. 56).

16:59-63 These concluding verses of ch. 16 are somewhat difficult to interpret in context. In part they continue the preceding theme of the three sisters, but also they reach back to the marriage theme of 16:8-14 ("the covenant" of vv. 59-60a). Then they speak of a new covenant that the LORD will effect with a new Israel (vv. 60b, 62), when Samaria (and Sodom) will become its daughters. ("But not on account of the covenant with you" in v. 61 probably means that the LORD will do these things not in virtue of Israel's marital fidelity, which was entirely lacking, but simply out of God's mercy.) None of this thought is foreign to Ezekiel, but some of it seems out of place here. The passage is probably best seen as a redactional supplement anticipating thoughts that the prophet only later unfolded. Moshe Greenberg aptly observes that in v. 63 "the usual sequence of shame leading to repentance and expunging of sin by God is reversed" (*Ezekiel 1-20*, 292). This is a precious insight into the gratuity of God's mercy and of the quality of mercy itself ("blessing both him that giveth and him that taketh").

17:1-10   Now comes the allegory of the eagle(s) and the vine. It is for the most part pure poetry, though the RSV has set it as prose. The imagery is lucid, hardly requiring the prophetic interpretation that follows v. 11. The "great eagle" is the Babylonian army that had descended already upon Jerusalem. It had come to the "Lebanon," which was also the route of conquest into Israel and its northernmost border. There flourished the great cedars that were proverbial in their royal majesty (Cant. 5:15), the very "cedars of God" (Ps. 80:11 MT). From its branches the eagle broke off "the topmost of its young twigs"—an allusion to King Jehoiachin, the exilic monarch whose deportations date Ezekiel's prophecies. He was taken "to a land of trade" ("Canaan" is the word used, as in Prov. 31:24, but the term is occupational rather than geographical), to "a city of merchants," that is, Babylon. There the twig became a seedling and finally a transplanted "vine"—an ancient symbol for Israel (cf., e.g., Isa. 5:1-7); it took root and flourished, as Ezekiel and the house of Israel who heard him in Babylon could testify.

The allegory moves beyond recent history. This follows in the second part of the allegory. For there is "another great eagle"— Egypt—which purports to do precisely what Babylon has done to allow the residual Israel to survive and thrive. Ezekiel is doubtless thinking primarily of the muddled politics of Zedekiah. He was the regent whom the Babylonians had left behind in Jerusalem in Jehoiachin's place, and who was now scheming at ways of circumventing the inevitable. Egypt will provide no more solace for Judah than had Assyria. The great politicians of Judah, the "wise" men of Isaiah's and Jeremiah's diatribes, the "statesmen" of the land, had guessed wrong. Invariably they backed the losing side at every opportunity. The "idealism" of the prophets matched against such "realism" leaves the prophets in possession of the field: *Realpolitik* was a craft that the leaders of Judah did not know how to pursue.

17:11-21 These verses, an almost redundant interpretation of the preceding parable, drive home the lesson of this allegory and make its moral point. Faith is faith, and treaty is treaty (covenant), even when made with an infidel. Ezekiel's disciples may have added these verses after the event. Their message is clear: broken promises, no matter to whom directed, contain their own sanction of disaster.

17:22-24 These verses are not foreign to the thought of Ezekiel, but they are out of place in this context. Redactors are at work again. As we shall see, Ezekiel believed—but only in his fashion—in a restoration of the Davidic dynasty. The prophet hoped that the dynasty would rule over a new and renewed Israel in the times to come. Still he had no mystical ideas of this kingship. When he speaks of the Davidic restoration he refers only to a "sprig" from the top of the cedar. If properly tended this sprig could become a luxuriant vine bearing all kinds of fruits and providing shade for every animal. But all this lies in the potential future.

18:1-32 This is a curious chapter in the book of Ezekiel. It is so not because of its content, which is perfectly compatible with the prophet's understanding of the divine will as God had revealed it to him. The problem lies with the positioning of this chapter by the disciples/redactors who are responsible for the book as we have it. This text pertains to a period of Ezekiel's prophetic career that followed the Jerusalem debacle of 597/6. It is an answer to quandaries that then presented themselves to puzzled Israelites who were trying to sort their way through the course of events that had overtaken and overwhelmed them.

First there is the question of responsibility. "The fathers have eaten sour grapes, and the children's teeth are set on edge." Similar proverbs probably have arisen in every culture of any time. It asserts, "we are suffering not for our own faults but for what our ancestors did before us." (Jer. 31:27-30 cites the same proverb. In Jeremiah the citation is probably secondary and dependent on the collected prophecies of Ezekiel.) To this charge the LORD replies: "Not so!" Individuals shall be responsible for their conduct and for no other person's. They shall perish or prosper in that measure and by no other, either for good or for bad. We have to reflect that, however reasonable it may appear to us, habituated as we are to the sense of personal responsibility, it was a revolutionary idea to present to Ezekiel's contemporaries. They were more at home with the idea of collective righteousness and blame. The prophetic ancestors of Ezekiel had encouraged this idea. For example, Amos saw Israel as a hopeless case that was beyond remedy. For Hosea, hope was present, but only through a national regeneration. Here, for the first time, prophetic speech suggests a one-for-one relationship between God and human beings. It is questionable, of course, who has the better of it, Ezekiel or his predecessors. All of us must declare ourselves responsible for the sins of our society. If society is evil, unjust, racist, oppressive, we cannot exculpate ourselves from its collective stigma by dissociating ourselves from its bad features. That we have remained in this society testifies to our adherence to it. On the other hand, there is sometimes no other escape for the righteous person in an evil society than a disclaimer and (generally ineffectual) protest. It is to these circumstances that the prophet addresses himself, with an emphasis that pertains more to the postexilic Israel of "the restoration" than it does to the Israel of the past, first a United Kingdom and then the divided kingdoms of Israel and Judah.

The rest of this chapter merely explains in detail the principle of individual responsibility that the prophet has already stated. Parents are not responsible for their children's sins, nor are the children responsible for their parents'—the one who sins shall bear the guilt, shall "die." What is interesting about this chapter is the determination of the constitution of "righteousness" versus that of "wickedness." On one and the other side we have mingled here ethical, moral, and purely tribal/traditional practices blended indiscriminately. This, too, is characteristic of the Judaism that came out of the Babylonian Exile, which had to seek its identity in its "differentness" from all other peoples. Nobody could deny that robbery, murder, and the oppression of the poor and the defenseless would be accounted great evils in the parliament of the human race. Mixed in with these "obvious" sins are others that are peculiar to the postexilic community of Israel and give it some of those characteristic stamps that have become the heritage of Judaism forever afterward. Taking no interest from a fellow Israelite, having no intercourse with a woman in her menstrual cycle—such are tribal imperatives. While they derive, no doubt, from sound experience, they are not the property of a universal human experience.

19:1-9   The whole of Ezek. 19 appears in the so-called poetic *qina* or "lamentation" mode (cf. v. 14) made up of a line of three tonic accents interrupted by a caesura and then followed by another two tonic accents. This pattern apparently attempted to imitate the drumbeat (or its equivalent) of a funeral dirge: BOOM BOOM BOOM-pause-BOOM BOOM. Besides the question of its meter, this chapter deals with two different, though parallel, allegories about the fate of Jerusalem.

First is the allegory of the lion/lioness. "The lion of Judah" was probably as proverbial a term in Ezekiel's days as "the Russian bear" or "the American eagle" is in our own times. The nation of Judah was the lioness, and her "whelps" were Judah's kings. There seems no doubt which two "whelps" the prophet intends to celebrate in this dirge. The first, though "a young lion" who "learned to catch prey" and "devoured men," must be Jehoahaz, the luckless son of Josiah. He paid for his father's rebellion against Pharaoh Neco, and the Egyptians took him by hook into captivity. He never reigned in Judah (cf. 2 Kgs. 23:33-34). The other king, to whom the text assigns the same lionesque qualities, and who was brought "with hook" in a cage to the king of Babylon, can be either Jehoiachin (more likely) or Zedekiah (less likely). It is probably Jehoiachin because, for Ezekiel, he was a Judahite king, while Zedekiah was not. Therefore the prophecy, which is totally negative, undoubtedly pertains to the first stage of the prophet's career, before the fall of Jerusalem in 587. One should note that there is no mention of Jehoiakim, the first nemesis of the prophet Jeremiah. This king doubtless perished in the first phase of the Babylonian conquest that was responsible for Ezekiel's presence with the exiles.

19:10-14   The second part of this lamentation allegory adopts another figure: that of the vine. As we have seen before in this chapter, the vine traditionally symbolized Israel itself (cf., e.g., Isa. 5:1-7; Zech. 8:12-13), especially as it was destined for resurgence. For Ezekiel at this point, there is no resurgence in sight. Again this oracle is entirely negative. Israel is a vine from which came a royal "stem," to a "ruler's scepter" (cf. Isa. 14:5)—obviously, the prophet is talking about the Davidic dynasty, the pride of Judah. Alas, the "east wind" (Babylon) has withered it and transported the vine itself into "a dry and thirsty land" (the same Babylon) where "no strong stem" can again prosper as a "scepter for a ruler."

What is obvious is that Ezekiel is writing the *finis* to the Davidic dynasty. It is not necessary to think that this prophecy presupposes the transportation to Babylon of the wretched Zedekiah. Ezekiel probably never considered Zedekiah to be a Davidic king in the first place. The transportation of Jehoiachin would have been sufficient to provoke this outburst. The prophet may have thought that Jehoiachin was a legitimate Davidic king—but he was the last legitimate Davidic king. With him the dynasty ended. As we shall see, in the ideal Israel of the future Ezekiel makes room, as a matter of protocol, for a Davidic "ruler." In the prophet's vision, such a "ruler" was doubtless as inevitable as the presence of a "temple" (also radically revised). Still there is absolutely no hint of the royal mystique that had characterized both the United Monarchy and the divided kingdoms of Israel and Judah. All this will be gone, part of the unrecoverable and not-to-be-recovered past, a vanished age with no relevance for the future.

THE SWORD OF THE LORD
Ezekiel 20:1–21:32

These two chapters of the book of Ezekiel deal with Israel's sins of the past. The same is true of the preceding chapters and the ones that are to follow. They pass what amounts to a final and definitive verdict on this people. There is no hope for redemption from all Israel's transgressions, unless—and this is hardly expressed—there be an extraordinary mercy of the LORD, who can restore the unrestorable. The text develops this motif in several stages.

20:1-31 First there is a series of oracles repudiating Israel, bound together by the reiterated "As I live, says the Lord GOD." This represents the God of Israel swearing an oath, and, in default of anything higher, perforce swearing by God's own name. The occasion, or at least the initial occasion, is the request of "certain of the elders" "to inquire" (*darash,* the root of the word midrash, "interpretation") of the LORD. Use of this term signifies that the exiles recognized in Ezekiel the source of oracles, of enlightenment into what were the intentions of the LORD. On what did they seek enlightenment? Of this we are not told—we may guess, but guesswork is pointless in view of Yahweh's total repudiation of any right or privilege for the house of Israel to inquire of him about his designs.

Instead we have a familiar rehearsal of all the deeds of mercy that Yahweh has bestowed on this people in the past, through the several stages of its development. The text also describes the miserable and contemptuous response that they have made to these acts at every possible stage. In a much more wordy and extensive fashion—typical of Ezekiel's style—what the prophet

102

says is what Amos had said long before: "You only have I known of all the families of the earth; therefore I will punish you for all your iniquities" (Amos 3:2). And "Are you not like the Ethiopians to me, O people of Israel? says the LORD. Did I not bring up Israel from the land of Egypt [—but also] the Philistines from Caphtor and the Syrians from Kir?" (Amos 9:7). Yahweh now repudiates Israel's election—that marvelous grace in which the people put their blind trust. Yahweh does this because the Israelites themselves have repudiated it by spurning their reciprocal obligations under the covenant. Therefore Yahweh is equally contemptuous in return. The Exodus from Egypt? The action of a liberating God who had by that action constituted this people? Their actions have shown that they have held this at such little price that it means nothing more than the migrations of other peoples from west to east or east to west—for these too, of course, are under the dominion of a sovereign LORD. The Exodus has become nothing more than a "secular" affair. And therefore, "Shall I be inquired of by you, O house of Israel? As I live, says the Lord GOD, I will not be inquired of by you."

20:32-44   Some commentators take this passage to be an expansion on the preceding one. Here Ezekiel's later disciples tempered Yahweh's repudiation of Israel as set forth in the previous verses with thoughts drawn from the latter period of the prophet's career. At that time he began to speak about an eventual salvation. A little closer attention paid to the text may convince us that the circumstances are not that simple. There is very little in these verses that is not compatible with what has immediately gone before: the theme of Israel's rejection continues. It is true, in Ezek. 20:40-42 there is talk of restoration, of an Israel that the LORD will accept. We shall see that in a moment.

This oracle follows in the spirit of the preceding. "I will be king over you," says the Lord GOD (v. 33). This is no salvation promise. "King," in prophetic language (aside, perhaps from Isa. 6:5, which may or may not be an exception), is not a salvific title. It is one of doom. (The opposite is true, of course, of the so-called "royal psalms." These psalms were the product of court- and temple-prophets whom the common Near Eastern mystique and mythology of kingship imbued. The prophet spurns this notion of kingship in Ezek. 20:32 when he says that it shall never happen that Israel shall be like the nations.) 1 Sam. 8:11-18 reveals what "king" meant to the prophets. (We must acknowledge too that the prophet Isaiah, who almost alone among the preexilic prophets of Israel put his reliance not in the Mosaic traditions of his people but in those of a Davidized Jerusalem, had a positive view of kingship — but that is another story.)

The point is, if one reads these verses dispassionately, that they proffer not salvation to the existing Israel but the opposite. The only "mercy" that Yahweh promises, the only surcease of exile where Israel finds itself, is that it may be confronted by its Master. The result of this confrontation is that Israel will come to realize the enormity of its guilt. The people will loathe the evil that they have done. The nation will acknowledge its role in the profanation of God's holy name. Yahweh offers no solace to this existing Israel, only the exaction of vengeance. It will be the bringing home to a faithless partner the terrible consequences of its infidelity.

Yet we do have in Ezek. 20:40-42 (and perhaps part of v. 44) the promise of salvation. Here we probably have to recognize the presence of a redactor. The redactor depends not only on the words of the later Ezekiel (though in a different context) but also on other prophecy as well. For example, "my holy mountain" of v. 40 is hardly an expression characteristic of Ezekiel. It is distinctively Isaianic. The redactor, therefore, looks forward to the eventual significance of the prophet's message rather than to its contemporary and existential meaning. He has tempered and modified the message because of what a later providence had decreed.

20:45–21:7 (In the MT this section is 21:1-12. Here the RSV follows the verse enumeration of the "English Bible"—an enumeration that most other versions of the Bible used throughout the world do not employ.) "The sword of the LORD" or its equivalent connects these verses with the rest of ch. 21. Together they represent a series of doom-oracles that a redactor gathered to continue the theme already set: the inevitable destruction of Jerusalem and the dashing of any hope for relief from the threat of a total conquest at the hands of the Babylonians and their allies.

First is an oracle that raises several problems. "Preach against the south" (RSV) is a pallid equivalent of the Hebrew, which is more actually "spit toward the south"—the word occurs in Ezekiel only in this passage. Probably it draws on the vocabulary associated with the ecstatic prophet, whose modes of communication and gesturing were never precisely "normal." It may be surprising to hear that text describe the southland of Judah as "the forest of the Negeb." The Negeb is now, was in Ezekiel's time, and perhaps always had been, a desert. What we are reading here is doubtless idealized language without much attention paid to mundane realities. The point is that devastation will come to Jerusalem and Judah—the figure of a burning forest serves the purpose of describing total destruction. (In 20:49 we have a prophetic aside, where the prophet acknowledges the incredulity of those to whom he is predicting this disaster.)

These verses direct their attention to Jerusalem itself, in terms with which we are already familiar: a doom that is inexorable and without recall. Ezek. 21:6-7 should not go unnoticed, though they express the anguish of the situation and the prophetic sign that God directs Ezekiel to display frankly and even crudely. God enjoins the prophet not so much to "sigh," as the RSV would have it, but to "groan" in agony, as not his "heart" but his *loins break* in the presence of his fellow Israelites. This is a presage of what is to come when "all knees will run with (RSV "be weak as") water." Fear, terrible fear, reduces people to their basic animal condition, when the rational can no longer control the purely physical.

21:8-17 These verses, this "song of the sword," personify the sword of the LORD as in Gen. 3:24. They present it not so much as a sword of battle (though there can be no doubt that the "slayer" for whom it has been sharpened and burnished is the dread Nebuchadnezzar, whom the ensuing verses will feature). It is a sword of execution, of "slaughter." The text uses the word *tebah,* usually a term for the slaughter of animals.

Ezekiel appears almost in two characters here, both of which are compatible with his mission as a prophet. On the one hand, God enjoins him to "cry and wail," to lament, for the judgment of execution is coming against God's people, to which he belongs and with which he must empathize. It is true that these oracles of judgment do not stress this aspect of the prophetic (and therefore the divine) pathos over the destruction of Israel. In the same way, however, when God tells the prophet to "smite upon your thigh," we hear another sound of sorrow (cf. Jer. 31:19). Still Ezekiel is above all the messenger of Israel's doom, and not only that but also of the LORD'S fury (cf. Ezek. 5:13; 16:42; 24:13) about to be unleashed upon God's faithless people—God's vengeance, if you will. Therefore, the injunction to "clap your hands," a gesture in which God even joins, with the stamping of the feet (cf. 6:11; 25:6) is a sign of defiance. It encourages the murderous work of the sword and exults over the inglorious end of this callous people.

21:18-23   These verses record not only a prophecy of Ezekiel but also a symbolic act that he must have performed before his fellow exiles sometime around 589. The redactor placed it here in a proper context to clarify what has gone before and what will follow.

The LORD tells Ezekiel to "mark two ways (on a clay tablet, as before?) for the sword of the king of Babylon (no longer, precisely, the "sword of the LORD") to come; both of them shall come forth from the same land." This land is Babylon, where the prophet and his fellow exiles were now living. The text pictures Nebuchadnezzar as faced with a dilemma, or with two equally palatable options. The only question is which should take precedence. Shall he follow the route that will take him to "Rabbah of the Ammonites" to humble those rebels? Or shall he take the alternate route to "Jerusalem the fortified"?

Nebuchadnezzar falls back on divination as the means of arriving as a decision. The text mentions three methods of divination. First "he shakes the arrows," probably attempting to "read" their message from their chance pattern as they fall to the ground. Second "he consults the teraphim." These were doubtless "yes"

106

and "no" counters taken at random from a container. Third "he
looks at the liver." Here we have a truly authentic Babylonian
divinatory process, which had come into Canaan. A "science" had
grown up around this divinatory technique. It also spawned a
professional priesthood that confidently predicted a proper course
of action by examining the color and the internal segmentation
of the livers of newly slaughtered animals. By whatever method,
into Nebuchadnezzar's right hand—the hand of destiny—comes
the decision: On to Jerusalem! Set siege to it and destroy it! It
matters little that this people against whom he throws himself
count his divination, and his confidence of victory, for nothing.
They will, for their own sins, suffer the retribution that he promises.

21:24-27 This little paragraph may originally have been part
of the preceding or a redactor may have added it. What is sure is
that it singles out for special attention "the prince of Israel," reven
as 21:12 above featured the "princes of Israel" in the general
condemnation. Here there can be no doubt that the prince in
question is Zedekiah, the uncle of Jehoiachin and the creature of
the Babylonians. He was the puppet whom Nebuchadnezzar had
put in place as king of Judah after the initial conquest that had
taken Ezekiel and so many others into exile. The text characterizes
him as an "unhallowed wicked one . . . whose day has come."
While the prophet makes no specification of the crimes of which
Zedekiah was guilty to merit such special attention, it is probable
that Ezekiel has in mind Zedekiah's breaking his oath to Nebuchadnezzar, his liege. Both Jeremiah and Ezekiel doubtless
belonged to what the politicians of Judah would have considered
the "pro-Babylonian faction"—in the sense that they look forward
to a restoration of Israel that would come about in the LORD'S
time but independently of the residual Israelite statecraft. Meanwhile, it was the will of Yahweh that the Israelites in Babylon
reconcile themselves to life there. They were to give up the possibility of home-style maneuvering against the Babylonian domination as a hopeless job, and wait for what the future held for them.
Zedekiah and his bumbling coconspirators could only delay the
working out of what Providence had in store. Zedekiah was guilty

of criminal behavior. It was because of his broken oath and complicity in a doomed rebellion against Babylon that he was directly responsible for the final devastation about which Ezekiel has been preaching in the previous twenty chapters.

Thus we probably should understand Ezekiel's verdict on Zedekiah, which reads better in the NAB version than it does in the RSV:

> Off with the turban and away with the crown!
>   Nothing shall be as it was!
> Up with the low and down with the high!
>   Twisted, twisted, twisted will I leave it!
> It shall not be the same until he comes who has the claim against
>   the city;
>   and to him I will hand it over.

What is twisted? What is that which shall never be as it was before? There is a consensus that what Ezekiel had in mind was the "messianic prophecy" of Gen. 49:10 that promised the tribe of Judah (and in Judahite tradition, the house of David) an unending succession of eventually salvific rulers who would fulfill the divine designs: "The scepter shall not depart from Judah, nor the ruler's staff from between his feet, until he comes to whom it belongs; and to him shall be the obedience of the peoples."

Is Ezekiel saying that the "prophecy" is now twisted, reversed, void, as far as "the prince of Israel" (= the Davidic ruler) is concerned? It is not unlikely, as we shall see from our later consideration of the prerogatives he assigns to this traditional ruler. Ezekiel, as we have seen and shall see, lacks messianic vision for the Davidic house. Like prophets before and after him, he was able to dispense entirely with the idea of a personal messianism — which is a later Jewish rather than a biblical notion, though its roots are in the OT, not only in Gen. 49:10 but also particularly in the prophet Isaiah.

If the prophet is consciously parodying Gen. 49:10, who, instead of the Davidic scion, is "he [who] comes who has the claim against the city"? It can only be Nebuchadnezzar. This is a twist, but a twist no greater than that expressed by Second Isaiah. That prophet used the word *messiah* (possibly the only time that it occurs in the OT in this technical sense) concerning the pagan Cyrus, king of the Persians (Isa. 45:1). Cyrus presided over a second exodus for God's people that was the result of no messianic kingly power but of other, incredible means (William L. Moran, "Gen 49,10 and Its Use in Ez. 21,32," *Biblica* 39 [1958]: 405-425).

21:28-32   It is a moot question whether these concluding verses belong to Ezekiel or are someone else's idea of the proper way of rounding out this chapter. On the one hand, the prophet has words to say against Ammon (cf. Ezek. 25:1-7). There is strong motivation behind Ezekiel's later words, but here the motivation is vague and the consequences of the condemnation are stereotypical. Also this looks very much like the tying up of the "sword of the LORD" motif with a tidying up of the unfinished business of Nebuchadnezzar. The Babylonian king had passed up Ammon in favor of Jerusalem. The passage is a good imitation of Ezekiel. It is not alien to his spirit, but also it is not his.

THE BLOODY CITY

Ezekiel 22:1–24:27

These chapters contain what amounts to Ezekiel's final words on the doom of Jerusalem (and Judah): a series of oracles, allegories, and prophetic symbols, active and passive. We begin with what Peter Craigie has called a "catalogue of crime" (*Ezekiel*, 164).

22:1-16 These verses read very much like a "checklist" of sins against which one can measure Jerusalem's performance. It is similar to the handy little cards that were once in use by Roman Catholics to aid them in the "examination of conscience" before approaching the confessional. Nor is the similarity all that superficial. There are two types of "sins" in both Ezekiel's "catalogue" and in the Catholic "examination of conscience." The first includes transgression against morality that the common consent of humankind regards as wrongdoing. The second comprises crimes that were such only in respect to the respective religion that was involved. The latter include violations of the respective religion's sense of propriety and of its taboos. We have here, in other words, a checklist which embraces both the "commandments" and the "precepts of the Church." That this is so is doubtless due to Ezekiel's priestly and prophetic character. This is a feature of the prophet's person that we have considered before this.

Concerning the catalogue of Jerusalem's sins, we have already heard from Ezekiel the greater part of it. It echoes not only the ancient covenant law of Israel (cf. Exod. 23, e.g., part of the Book of the Covenant) but also, especially in matters sexual, the "priestly" legislation of Leviticus (cf. esp. Lev. 18). Both contained equally ancient proscriptions. Even as Ezekiel was speaking, these were being elaborated and codified in much the same form that we now find them in the Pentateuch and that would eventually serve the postexilic Jewish community in its search for cohesion and identity. The precise transgressions that are listed are less important than their cumulative effect that is the burden of Ezekiel's charge. The prophet stated that Jerusalem, by its turning away from all that had made it distinctive as the LORD'S people, had already cast itself adrift as merely one of the many nations of the earth, among which it was now to be destined to dwell. The LORD'S sentence of exile, therefore, was but the ratification of a decision made by a people that had refused to honor its own heritage.

22:17-22 A redactor has inserted a short oracle of Ezekiel here. It briefly interrupts the prophet's renewed indictment of the sins of the house of Israel, epitomized by Jerusalem. The figure is a familiar one. The smelting of ore of crude metal in a blast furnace to separate slag or dross from the refined product was a technique well-known in antiquity. The OT references to fire or furnace (e.g., Deut. 4:20) are symbols for excruciating pain and suffering. These also evoke the notion of fire as a purifying agent and of "smelting" as a way to spiritual regeneration (cf. Isa. 1:25).

Ezekiel chooses, as he does so often, to turn this familiar figure topsy-turvy: the fire produces dross—not refined metal. The image of the furnace remains with the breath of Yahweh's wrath providing the blast. From this metallurgical process nothing that is pure emerges. Everything that is poured into the furnace—all Israel—turns out to be dross. One can hardly imagine a more thoroughgoing repudiation of this people.

22:23-31 Ezekiel's instruction (so Ezek. 22:23-24) to excoriate the city and the land now continues and concludes with the further refinement of the assignment of separate guilt. First, "her princes"—the civil authorities, the kings and their minions—are charged with having betrayed their sacred trust. The Near Eastern ideal—not merely the Israelite ideal—of the king, the judge, the ruler was of the one who would make justice prevail. It was the king who would protect the defenseless, the last mentioned often epitomized as "the widow and the orphan." Instead, the princes of Israel have devoured their people, creating widows and orphans (cf. Isa. 1:23 for a similar indictment).

Second, "her priests," whose duty it was to inculcate the *torah,* the law or instruction of the LORD, instead have profaned it. It is perhaps typical of Ezekiel the priest-prophet that in this present context he makes reference only to priestly dereliction regarding the cult, but we already know from the preceding how much in his mind cultic and moral offenses became as one.

Finally, "her prophets" (by which term we must understand, of course, those whom the contemporary Jeremiah would call "the prophets of peace"), whose office—in the temple or at the court— was purportedly to act as Ezekiel had been instructed to do, to act as watchmen for what were God's designs, had instead been suborned by vain hope, nationalist prejudice, or simply their interest in "the establishment" to utter consoling words of false confidence in the face of every sign of the time that argued against such hope. These prophets were not unlike the "wise" counsellors of Judah's kings whom Isaiah had opposed a generation before. They were, in their religious society, those whose counsel people identified as the LORD'S will when it was a lie (cf. Zeph. 3:4). They have "daubed with whitewash" the crimes of Israel that cry for punishment, and therefore have been "seeing false visions and divining lies" of future peace and tranquillity for a people whose destiny it is to have neither of these since there is a just God in heaven.

Ezek. 22:25-28 is remarkably similar to Zeph. 3:3-4. The latter is the prototype for the former. In his text Ezekiel uses homiletical embellishments to specify the more general accusations of Zephaniah. Ezekiel here uses what must have been a fixed form and traditional phraseology to speak against the sins of his time.

"I sought for a man among them who should build up the wall and stand in the breach before me for the land, that I should not destroy it; but I found none." Like Abraham in Gen. 18:22-33 who had "bargained" with the LORD to spare the cities of the valley in favor of the just who might be found there amidst a sea of corruption—and who failed in his pleas because not even his most minimal reduction of guilt could be verified—so is Ezekiel's melancholy verdict: the people, whole and entire, deserves to be destroyed, without any qualification.

23:1-49   This section concludes with an allegory, a prophetic action that also is an allegory, and a prophetic experience that becomes an allegory. First comes the allegory. It is the case of Oholah and Oholibah. It is obvious, in the first place, that Oholah stands for the now defunct northern kingdom, whose capital was Samaria. She is the "elder sister" both in point of time and of political priority to the Oholibah of Judah, whose capital was in Jerusalem. Ezekiel, though a loyal Judahite, had to bow to the facts of remembered history. The "schism" of north and south following on the stupidity of Solomon's son Rehoboam (recorded in 1 Kgs. 12:1-20), though represented by the (Judahite) authors of the Hebrew Bible as we now have it as provoking a secession of the north from the south, had been in reality a casting off of Judah—a late arrival into the Israelite tribal federation and nation—by those who had first formed the people Israel. Oholah, therefore, is the "elder daughter," and Oholibah—Jerusalem—is "her sister," a later arrival. Is it necessary to ask about the etymology of these names? *Ohel* ("tent" = "tabernacle") has often been suggested in this direction, but without much resolution. It is sufficient to note that for Ezekiel it remained as a vivid memory that there were *two* Israels. Each of these had rivalled the other in promiscuous harlotry—the image that remains throughout to signify religious apostasy.

Ezekiel's real target is, of course, Oholibah: Jerusalem. Therefore Oholibah and her fate at the hands of the Assyrians, her "lovers," appear in the past tense. These should have been cautionary examples for her younger sister, but had not been. Far from profiting from the lesson of Samaria's downfall, Jerusalem has outdone her elder sister in lewdness and now must face the consequences. From Ezek. 23:22 onward the passage contains a mingling of words addressed directly to Oholibah and to Ezekiel as the messenger of God's wrath against her. The purpose is the same anyhow. Her "lovers," too, shall invade and overwhelm her "from the north" (the traditional route of incursions from Mesopotamia; cf. the "boiling pot, facing away from the north," in Jer. 1:13). That Ezekiel mentions "Babylonians" with "all the Chaldeans" in Ezek. 23:23 would, if one would press the distinction, seem to set the original Amorite Babylonians alongside the recent

Neo-Babylonian Empire—but with "Pekod and Shoa and Koa, and all the Assyrians with them" (the Assyrians, for one, were no longer a threat since the Babylonian conquest), the intention seems merely to accumulate familiar inimical names to designate the "host" (v. 46) that will be summoned up to execute the LORD'S vengeance. There is considerable repetition in these verses. One suspects that the later redactors of Ezekiel's prophecies have felt free to amplify and enlarge upon his original words.

24:1-14 The final allegory in this record of the first period of Ezekiel's prophetic career now follows. The prophecy dates (see the Introduction) to the beginning day of the final siege of Jerusalem by Nebuchadnezzar. How did Ezekiel, in Babylon, know what was happening in Jerusalem to attach it with such precision to this "allegory of the seething pot"? We need not invoke the presence of extrasensory powers—though these, of course, are always a possibility—to explain this text. We need to remind ourselves, as we have had to do more than once, that the book of Ezekiel is a work of later redaction. The redactors benefited from the realization of later history of prophesied events that were not very determined in their original utterance.

The allegory of the seething pot continues and in a way completes Ezekiel's entirely negative view of the effect on Israel of purificatory fire (ch. 22) that, instead, had led only to greater enormities. The pot in this figure is Israel. The fire set beneath it is the visitation on it. The allegory begins with the initial deportation by the Babylonians of which Ezekiel and his companions in Babylon had been a part. Then a potentially tasty "stew" had been prepared: the choicest parts of the people had been assembled in this crucible with the possibility of a true regeneration, a new creation through purification. What had happened? The pot—both the Israel of the Exile and the Israel that had remained in Palestine—had proved to be altogether polluted with "rust." It was a contaminant rather than a vessel of health and wholeness. The great opportunity had passed by. And therefore, says the LORD, the fire will be an agent of destruction with no purificatory features whatever. So 24:10-14. The fire—now the final destruction of Jerusalem by the Babylonians—will be heaped up, and the pot will be reduced to molten metal. There will be no regeneration, only total destruction.

24:15-27 The final section concludes Ezekiel's prophecies of doom for the "rebellious houses of Israel." Still the redactional character of the book makes the sequence of events somewhat difficult to understand. Verse 26 says that "a fugitive" (literally, *the* fugitive, the proverbial messenger of bad news, of defeat) will come to report about the destruction of the temple (i.e., a couple of years following the preceding verses, which date to the beginning of Nebuchadnezzar's final siege). This reference corresponds with 33:21-22, according to which date (also see the Introduction) Ezekiel's dumbness ceased. On this "dumbness," see the Commentary on 3:22-27 above. Evidently the prophet could not speak for some reason and for an indeterminate time till his final "release" in the definitive end of the old Israel and its proclamation to those in exile.

This final prophecy comes with a prophetic "sign," and a sad one. "I am about to take the delight of your eyes away from you at a stroke," says the LORD. Yet no mourning is to take place, for this is a judgment that calls not for mutual consolation but for mutual shame and recrimination. This refers to the desecration of the temple, of course. The Israelites could not plead sorrow or mourning for its desecration. It was their conduct and apostasy that had made this final obloquy inevitable. It is with a final twist of tragedy that the lesson comes home to Ezekiel. The prophet—any prophet—was never a person who could divorce himself from the people to whom the LORD sent him both as a messenger and as a representative. Not even Amos (cf. Amos 7:1-6) could do this. It was part of the prophetic vocation and its burden that it had to share in the destiny of its people. Such was the "unjust" charge that a jealous God laid upon God's chosen. So as Ezekiel records, "I spoke to the people in the morning, and at evening my wife died." Apparently he was simply a casualty to divine providence, a sign, a symbol. Some faith is necessary. "And on the next morning I did as I was commanded."

PART IV
ORACLES
AGAINST THE NATIONS

Ezekiel 25:1–32:32

Oracles against foreign nations as a prophetic speech form go back to the 8th-cent. prophets Amos (Amos 1:3–2:16) and Isaiah (Isa. 7:7-8; 10:5-15). Although they are similar in form to the oracles of judgment against Israel, the oracles against the nations have a different function. In effect, they serve to announce Israel's impending salvation because prophets usually direct these oracles against the nations that have profited from Israel's fall. In Ezekiel they function as a kind of transition between the first major section of the book (Ezek. 1–24), which contains the prophet's words of judgment against Israel, and the last section of the book (chs. 33–48), which speaks of Israel's restoration. The fall of the nations is a harbinger of better times for Judah.

In these oracles the prophet condemns foreign nations because of their treatment of Israel. The Egyptian Execration Texts that date from the 19th-18th cents. B.C.E. are examples of a similar phenomenon from an earlier time. The Egyptians would write curses against their enemies on a clay tablet and then dash that tablet to the ground. Its destruction signaled that the curse was taking effect (*ANET*, 328-29).

The arrangement of this collection of oracles against the nations and their placement in their present position in the book of Ezekiel are probably the work of an editor. This is clear from the artificial separation between the prophet's proclamation of Jerusalem's imminent fall (24:25-27) and the report of the fulfillment of that prophecy (33:21-22). Another clue that an editor placed these oracles here is the artificial ordering of the material in these chapters. There seems to be a fascination with the number seven. There are seven nations that the prophet addresses. The seventh nation is Egypt, which has seven prophecies devoted to it. In the seventh of these, the text surveys seven nations. According to Deut. 7:1, before Israel could take possession of the land, the seven nations of Canaan had to fall. Perhaps this fascination with seven in Ezekiel is an allusion to this tradition. It may suggest a hope for a new exodus and a new settlement in the land.

AGAINST ISRAEL'S
CLOSE NEIGHBORS
Ezekiel 25:1-17

The oracles against the nations that the editor assembled in this chapter presuppose the fall of Jerusalem in 587. The prophet directs his words against neighboring countries that had the most to benefit from Jerusalem's catastrophe. The lack of any topographical details in these oracles may be evidence that the prophet delivered them while far from Jerusalem.

25:1-7 The prophet directs two oracles against one of Israel's Transjordanian neighbors: Ammon. In spite of its limited territory between the mountainous area of southern Gilead and the eastern desert, Ammon's importance and wealth were significant. It enjoyed unrivalled domination of the King's Highway. This important commercial artery ran the length of the Transjordanian highlands from the Gulf of Aqabah to Damascus. The Edomites refused to allow the Israelite tribes travel on the portion of this road that they controlled (Num. 20:17; 21:22). The highway was of special importance because it made possible the export of precious perfumes from the countries of South Arabia. The highway ran near desert and passed through regions in which the population and government were not always permanent. It served primarily as a trail for nomadic caravans.

Ammon occupied the east bank of the Jordan River in what is now the modern state of Jordan. Its capital city Amman reflects the ancient name of this region. The Ammonites called their capital Rabbah (Ezek. 25:5). In certain periods the Ammonites organized and fortified the region. They tried to enlarge their domain by annexing various parts of Gilead. The kingdom of Ammon arose toward the end of the Late Bronze Age (13th cent.) when several small states came into being within the region.

According to Gen. 19:30-38 the Ammonites were kin to the Israelites through Lot, Abraham's nephew. The Bible refers to several conflicts between Ammon and Israel (Judg. 10:6-7). At first the Ammonites had the upper hand until Israel attained dominance under the leadership first of Saul (1 Sam. 11) and then of David (2 Sam. 12:26-31). David incorporated Ammon into his empire. With the waning of Israelite power after the breakup of the united kingdom following Solomon's death, the Ammonites were able to choose their destiny.

There are two oracles against Ammon in this chapter. The first (Ezek. 25:1-5) asserts that the Ammonites will fall to the nomadic incursions that will come from the east. These nomads were probably the Nabateans who established their kingdom in the territory of Ammon. Their rule continued into the 2nd cent. C.E. The Transjordanian highlands gradually blend into the Syrian-Arabian desert to the east. There exists no natural border but the wilderness itself. This is the reason that the fate of Transjordan is so closely intertwined with the desert. Nomads sweep over Transjordan whenever central authority in the highlands is weak. This explains the long intervals between periods of permanent occupation in the history of this region, most strongly observable in the south. The prophet asserts that again the desert will claim Transjordan. This will happen because of divine judgment on the Ammonites for their reaction to the fall of Jerusalem. The second oracle (vv. 6-7) is more generic in content and simply promises defeat for the Ammonites.

25:8-11   Moab is the next object of prophetic invective. Also located in the Transjordan, Moab was just to the south of the Ammonite kingdom. Several biblical traditions show that relationships between Moab and Israel were never friendly (Num. 22–24; Judg. 3:12-30; 1 Sam. 14:47; 2 Sam. 8:2). The Bible does not mention that Moab fell to Israel under Omri. We know this from the Moabite Stone, which describes how Moab secured its freedom (see *ANET,* 320-21).

Ezekiel promises that Moab will fall to the same invading Arab

tribes as Ammon. The prophet singles out three cities for special
mention because of their importance to Moab (Ezek. 25:9).
Walther Zimmerli holds that these cities did not belong to Moab
proper but were in an area under dispute with Israel (*Ezekiel 2,*
16). Were that the case, it seems likely that there would be some
hint that they would revert to Israelite control in the future. There
is no such promise. It is likely that the Babylonian conquest ended
Moab as a political state and this opened the region to conquest
from the east—the same fate that awaited Ammon (v. 10).

The Hebrew text adds Seir to Moab in v. 8. Seir is another
name for Edom, and most commentators believe this addition is
secondary. It is missing from ancient Greek versions. Edom comes
in for its own judgment beginning with v. 12. Its presence in v. 8
may be the result of an overzealous editor.

25:12-14   The Edomites were the southern neighbors of Israel.
They were of Semitic stock and entered the region in the 14th
century. According to Israelite tradition they were descendants of
Esau, the brother of Jacob who was Israel's ancestor (Gen. 36:8).
Traditions about Israel's entrance into Canaan assert that Edom
was a problem to the incoming Israelite tribes (Num. 20:14-21).
During the early Monarchy, Edom came under Israelite control
(1 Sam. 21:7; 22:9, 18, 22; 2 Sam. 8:12-14). After the time of
David, Judah's domination over Edom was intermittent until the
time of Ahaz (8th cent.) when Judah was unable to hold effective
power any longer.

The basis of Edom's economy was its control of that portion
of the King's Highway that passed through its territory. Once the
Babylonians ended this control in the 6th cent., the Edomites
were in serious economic trouble. By the 4th cent. the Nabateans
replaced the Edomites, and the latter moved into southern Judah.
The name of the area "Idumea" reflects their presence.

The prophet accuses Edom of doing more than simply scoffing
at Israel's fall. He accuses the Edomites of complicity in that fall.
Still this oracle is not very specific in either its accusation or
judgment against Edom. The prophet asserts that since Edom
took vengeance on Israel, God would take vengeance on it. Again
Ezekiel singles out individual cities for special mention (Ezek.

25:13). One unique feature of this oracle is the detail that Israel will participate in Edom's judgment (v. 14). This led J. Herrmann to suggest that this verse is a gloss from the Hasmonean period. At that time John Hyrcanus (135-130 B.C.E.) forced the Idumeans to accept Judaism (*Ezechielstudien.* Beiträge zur Wissenschaft vom Alten Testament 2 [Leipzig: J. C. Hinrichs, 1908], 28). Invaders from the desert were instruments of divine judgment directed at Moab and Ammon according to Ezekiel. From a historical perspective, Edom too felt the pressure from the nomadic tribes. The other Transjordanian states felt the same pressure when the Babylonian invasion weakened them militarily, politically, and economically.

25:15-17 The prophet passes to an oracle against the Philistines. The Philistines were part of the Sea Peoples who invaded the Eastern Mediterranean from the Aegean Basin at the end of the Late Bronze Age. They became Israel's main rivals for the control of Canaan. This rivalry erupted into a war. The balance of power favored the Philistines until the establishment of the Israelite national state. Though Saul was not very successful, David was able to break Philistine military superiority. After David's victories, the Philistines were no longer a serious threat to the Israelite hegemony in Palestine, though hostility between the Israelites and Philistines continued for some time.

The Philistines concentrated their population in several city-states along the Mediterranean toward the south (v. 16). In the 8th cent. these cities came under the control first of Assyria and then of Egypt. In the 6th cent. the Babylonians deported the rulers and the populace of Philistia (Jer. 25:20; 47:2-7; Zech. 9:5-6). Philistia was no longer an independent political unit.

The prophet accuses the Philistines of acting like Edom in taking an active part in Israel's destruction so God will destroy them. A key word in this oracle and the one against Edom is "vengeance." Because both nations took what belonged to God, they should anticipate divine retribution.

For Ammon and Moab, nomadic tribes from the East were to be instruments of divine judgment. For Edom, Israel itself was to serve as God's judgment. Philistia has to face the most severe form of judgment since the prophet does not mention any human agent of punishment. God will pass judgment on the Philistines directly.

Ammon, Moab, Edom, and Philistia come under divine judgment because they did not recognize in Israel's fall their precarious position. Instead of recognizing God's hand in Israel's fall, they either sneered at Israel's fate or, worse, used Israel's problems to advance their cause. Ezekiel promises that Israel's closest neighbors will soon experience divine judgment.

AGAINST TYRE AND SIDON
Ezekiel 26:1–28:26

Ezekiel, like Jeremiah, believed that Babylon was God's instrument of judgment against an unfaithful Israel. To resist Babylon was to resist the divine will. That is why Jeremiah counseled submission to Babylon and why Ezekiel did not include Babylon among the nations he condemned. At the time Judah was under Nebuchadnezzar's siege, only two other nations were still holding out against Babylon: Egypt and Tyre. Both nations came under intense criticism from the prophet. Ezekiel begins with four oracles against Tyre. This city-state controlled no vast territories or large populations. Its importance was its economic power. Its territory was no more than an island off the coast of southern Lebanon plus a small area on the mainland. Each of these contained a port through which passed much of the maritime commerce of the eastern Mediterranean region. The prophet's oracles against Tyre reflect its unique position among the nations of Ezekiel's world.

26:1 The first oracle against Tyre dates from the first day of an unnamed month in the eleventh year of Jehoiachin. The beginning of this year fell on 23 April 587. Since the oracle reflects the recent fall of Jerusalem, it must date from sometime after the exiles heard of the fall of Jerusalem. The most likely date is 13 February or 15 March 586.

26:2-6 While Tyre saw Judah as a political ally against Babylon, it likely considered Judah as a competitor in the economic sphere. Jerusalem's fall enhanced Tyre's control over commerce in the eastern Mediterranean. That is precisely how Tyre reacted to the

Babylonian devastation of Jerusalem (Ezek. 26:2). This callous venality prompted Ezekiel's words of judgment. The prophet envisioned the devastation of the island that was to make it fit for nothing except as a place for fishermen to dry their nets (vv. 4-5). The "daughters on the mainland" (v. 6) are the villages dependent on Tyre. They too will suffer great destruction. Tyre should have sympathized with a political and military ally when it fell. Instead Tyre saw the fall of Jerusalem as an economic advantage. Divine judgment decrees that Tyre too will fall. Tyre did fall to the Babylonians after a very long siege. By 570 there was a Babylonian commissioner "advising" the native Tyrian king.

26:7-14 The preceding oracle was not very specific in identifying those that will be responsible for Tyre's fall. It names "many nations" (v. 3). This passage names Nebuchadnezzar of Babylon as the instrument of divine judgment on Tyre, just as he was for Judah. It may be a later expansion of the prophet's original oracle. Verses 8-11 describe the battle that will precede the city's fall. The effect of this is to negate any economic advantage that Tyre may experience with Jerusalem's fall. The oracle ends with a description of the desolation that will accompany the fall of Tyre. These verses function to specify and amplify the prophet's words in the preceding section. Babylon did encircle Tyre, but the siege ended differently than the prophet foresaw. Though the city escaped the kind of total destruction that this text describes, it lost its economic power since it became just another Babylonian satellite state. While a native continued to sit on Tyre's throne, the Babylonian commissioner held real political and economic power.

26:15-18 The prophet appends a lament over the fallen city of Tyre to his oracles of judgment against it. This lament underscores the prophet's conviction about the inevitability of Tyre's fall. The rulers of other maritime powers take part in Tyre's funerary rites. They put off their royal raiment and wail over not only the passing of the preeminent seagoing power but also the inevitability of their own end. If Tyre has fallen, how long can they withstand the pressure that Babylon will bring to bear upon them.

26:19-21   The first oracle against Tyre ends with a description of the city's fall in mythic terms. The "deep" into which Tyre falls is not the Mediterranean, but the primeval sea. The city will sink into the "nether world" from which there is no arising. The prophet uses this imagery to assert that Tyre will never recover from its destruction at the hands of the Babylonians. While he envisioned a great act of salvation for Israel, Ezekiel foresaw nothing similar for Tyre (v. 21).

After a thirteen-year siege Tyre did fall to the Babylonians, although the destruction was not as complete as Ezekiel believed it would be. Eventually Tyre did recover from the effects of the Babylonian hegemony, only to fall to Alexander the Great little more than two hundred years later. It became just one in a series of economic powers that rose and fell along the northern end of the eastern Mediterranean shore. Before Tyre there was Ugarit that flourished and fell centuries before Israel came into existence. A similar cycle has been repeated in our own day. At one time Beirut enjoyed the type of financial position in the region as Tyre once did. It too fell like its predecessors from antiquity.

The prophet was able to see the destructive power of the avarice that led Tyre to rejoice at the fall of its former ally, Judah. Tyre's cupidity prevented it from realizing the real significance of Judah's fall. The point was not a matter of profit and loss at all. God was speaking through the destruction that fell upon Judah. Tyre's obsession with its commercial ventures made it impossible for the city to recognize the hand of God in judgment on the infidelity and corruption of Judah. Tyre did not learn from this object lesson and did not recognize the precarious nature of its own position. That God's judgment fell upon Tyre was inevitable.

Tyre could not guarantee its own position by strengthening its economic base. The prophet implies that the city could have secured its own future by submitting to the judgment of God. This Tyre did not do because it misread God's movement in Judah's experience and so did the same in the difficult circumstances that eventually it had to face. According to the prophet it was Tyre's greed that blinded the city. Tyre did not recognize the significance of what had just happened in Judah's life and what was about to happen in its own.

27:1-3a   The second oracle against Tyre takes the form of a lament over the city's fall. This introduction to the lament contains two messenger formulae (27:1 and 3) that identify what follows as "the word of the LORD," though the lament itself is without divine judgment. It is simply an expression of grief over the fall of what had been such an important city. The lament itself contains no hint of any reproach of Tyre's conduct. Except for the assertions of vv. 1 and 3, this chapter is without any overt theological content.

The lament form has two basic components: a description of former grandeur and an account of present misery. This lament describes Tyre as a great merchant ship, built of the finest materials. The best crews manned it. It held the city's varied wares. Still a great storm from the east has wrecked it and the ship has sunk in the depths of the sea. This elaborately developed metaphor explores the significance of Tyre's role in the ancient world. Most of the oracle against Tyre takes the form of metaphors that the prophet chooses to express his belief in God's control over the city's destiny (Carol A. Newsom, "A Maker of Metaphors—Ezekiel's Oracles Against Tyre").

The shipwreck of a grand vessel fits the needs of this lament very well. In addition, the poet's decision to depict Tyre as a great ship is an obvious one given the city's renown as a commercial center. This poem suggests that either the city has already fallen or that its fate is beyond doubt. The lament does not rejoice over Tyre's fall, nor does it attach any blame to the city for its fate. The poem is a remarkable expression of grief over what befell Tyre. Any negative inference comes not from the lament itself but through its position in the book of Ezekiel. Placing this lament between two texts that are highly critical of Tyre results in a reinterpretation of the poem's original intent. The poem expresses sympathy for what happened to a great city. It grieves over the sudden loss of such great splendor, achievement, and power. It expresses its marvel over the catastrophe without delving into what caused such a disaster.

27:3b-9   The lament begins with a description of the beauty of the great ship "Tyre." Verses 5 and 6 give a detailed account of how the best materials went into the construction of the ship. Its hull, masts, oars, and sails were the finest. Its crew (vv. 8-9) also augmented the magnificence of the great ship.

27:10-11 With a slight departure from the metaphor that weaves its way through the lament, the poet moves into prose. He lists some mercenaries employed by Tyre in its defense. Replacing the image of Tyre as a great ship, these verses describe the city as a great fortress manned by the best soldiers available for hire in the ancient world.

27:12-25a Following the prose listing of Tyre's military defenders, the poet appends a second and somewhat longer list of Tyre's commercial contacts and their wares. The vocabulary of commerce dominates this section: "traded"/"trafficked" (vv. 12, 15, 16, 18, 21); "merchandise" (vv. 13, 17, 19); "wares" (vv. 12, 14, 16, 19, 22); "exchange" (vv. 13, 17, 19). The poet wishes to underscore Tyre's commercial wealth, based as it was on contacts around the then known world.

Although a modern Western aesthetic may deem this section intrusive, its inclusion did not affect ancient sensibilities. Poetry was, after all, the product of wisdom circles that relished making such lists. The introduction of this list of Tyre's worldwide contacts provided a prosaic background for the metaphor that was the heart of the lament. It amplified the poetic description of Tyre's achievements above. It also served to intensify the sense of disaster that follows as the poem resumes to describe Tyre's fall.

The Hebrew text has not preserved some place names correctly. For example, the RSV notes that one should read Dedan *(dedan)* for Rhodes *(rodan)* in v. 15. (The *r* and *d* in Hebrew are very similar. A scribe who was not proficient in geography as were those who composed this list could have easily confused the two.) In the following verse a similar problem occurs: the text confuses Edom and Aram. Aram is probably the correct reading.

The intent of this list of Tyre's trading partners is to show how successful the city was in its commercial activities. It maintained contact with all the significant producers of raw materials. Through it passed the most desirable commodities in the ancient world. Tyre was very successful. Its position seemed unchallenged, its splendor unrivaled, its future secure.

27:25b-36 Tyre's achievements make its downfall unexpected, and the response to the city's end is surprise and grief at such a great loss. It comes because of the "east wind" (v. 26), which the people of the eastern Mediterranean recognize as the paradigm of the destructive forces of nature. The poet is terse in the report of how the great ship foundered. The great ship is brimming with precious cargo. A storm of immense power overwhelms the ship, and it goes down with its crew and treasures (vv. 26-27).

The bulk of the lament concentrates on the reaction to this unexpected event (vv. 28-36). Those who grieve over the lost ship are the sailors who know from experience what dangers the sea holds for all who venture on it. Verses 30 and 31 detail some conventional patterns of mourning that these sailors follow to express their grief for the loss of the great ship.

Verses 32-36 are a lament within a lament that intends to express the universal sense of shock at Tyre's end. Kings and subjects alike express dismay and horror in view of what happened to Tyre.

The lament proper contains no explicit reference to God. This occurs only in the introduction (vv. 1-3). The original poet chose to avoid characterizing the storm from the east as an instrument of God's judgment on Tyre. The placement of this lament in its present context within the book of Ezekiel implies that there is a message from God in this unexpected and catastrophic event. The greatest commercial sea power in the world is utterly defenseless before the power of God. The great ship's superior fittings and experienced crew could not save it from the destructive forces of nature. Similarly, Tyre's success and wealth will prove equally ineffective in avoiding disaster.

Tyre's sin, according to the previous oracle, was its rejoicing over Judah's fall because of the economic benefits that this would bring for Tyre (26:2-3). The Israelite poet learned a lesson from that word of divine judgment. There is no gloating over Tyre's fall here. The fall of Tyre was a forceful reminder to Judah of its own precarious position before God. It is similar to the loss of any ship at sea as a reminder to all sailors of what can happen to them. In the face of this, there is no room for gloating but only for grieving.

28:1-10 The messenger formula in 28:1 signals the beginning of a third oracle against Tyre. The commission in v. 2 directs the prophet to announce an oracle of divine judgment to the "prince of Tyre." Ithbaal II was the king of Tyre during Ezekiel's ministry. The oracle fails to name him, nor does it describe the king with individual characteristics but rather with typical ones. The king here stands not as an individual but as the representative of the city of Tyre itself. The city is the real object of divine judgment.

Verses 2b-5 comprise the accusation. Here the prophet details the offense that evokes divine judgment. The sin provoking judgment is pride. The city of Tyre achieved much. It enjoyed the success and prosperity that the people of the ancient Near East attributed to its wisdom. That is why the prophet remarks that the king of Tyre is wiser even than Daniel the ideal sage (see 14:14). The prophet asserts this with sarcasm because he does not believe that Tyre was very wise at all. Tyre was wise enough to grow and prosper, but not wise enough to know how to live with its achievements. Tyre should have been proud of its success, but there are limits to that pride — limits which Tyre exceeded.

Following a second messenger formula in 28:6a, the prophet states the judgment of God on Tyre's sin of pride in vv. 6b-10. Because the king of Tyre uses language of himself that is appropriate to God alone, the king must become reacquainted with his humanity. There is no better teacher than death. Gods do not die; humans do. This is a commonplace in ancient Near Eastern mythology. The king's death confirms his folly. Verse 8 states that the king will die "in the heart of the seas." This may be an instance of a *double entendre* on the prophet's part. Tyre was, of course, an island. On the other hand, according to the mythology of Tyre's religion, it was the sea (Yam) that killed the god Baal (the king's namesake). Ezekiel does not hesitate to adapt mythological language and imagery to make his message clear.

Tyre's wisdom led to remarkable achievements and great success for the island kingdom. Unfortunately it did not have the wisdom to be able to live with that success. Tyre forgot that, despite all its efforts, its prosperity was a gift from God.

28:11-19   As in ch. 26 where a lament (vv. 15-18) followed an oracle of judgment (vv. 1-14), this lament over the king of Tyre immediately follows the preceding judgment speech (28:1-10). Although the introduction to this unit (vv. 11-12) identifies it as a "lamentation," it does not follow the usual metric pattern for laments. The content of the unit is also a departure from what is usual in such poems. It is more like an oracle of judgment, in which an accusation (vv. 12b-18a) precedes the pronouncement of sentence (vv. 18b-19). By labelling this poem a lament, the prophet implies that the execution of the sentence has occurred. The one component of the lament form that is evident here is the contrast between the king's former state in paradise and his wretched state after his fall. As in the preceding oracle, the person of the king stands for Tyre, the real subject of the prophet's lament.

Appreciating this "lament" is not a simple matter. Here the prophet alludes to several ancient traditions and fuses those allusions into a new entity that appears jumbled and confusing. The over-arching motif is that of the primeval human being whose achievements and the divine response to them decide the destiny of the human race. In vv. 13a and 14a are allusions to the version of this motif as found in Gen. 2–3. The list of precious stones in Ezek. 28:13 may betray the hand of a sage.

The "holy mountain of God" in v. 14 suggests the Canaanite myth that identifies Mt. Saphon north of Ugarit as the dwelling place of the gods (cf. Ps. 48). The theme of innocence followed by a fall is a common one in ancient Near Eastern mythological literature (e.g., the Gilgamesh Epic, *ANET,* 75-77; the story of Adapa, *ANET,* 101-3; Gen. 2:4b–3:24). In addition, there may be allusions to other traditions that escape us today. The prophet blends all this material into this lament over the king of Tyre. While it may not be possible to appreciate his literary efforts, his theological concern is clear. Ezekiel is certain that the fate of Tyre is the result of its fall from innocence.

In the previous oracle the prophet praised the wisdom of Tyre that brought it success and prosperity. Here Ezekiel laments the corruption of that wisdom for the sake of increased profits (Ezek. 28:17). Apparently he believed that Tyre's desire for profit went beyond acceptable bounds. Evidence of this is the city's reaction to the fall of Jerusalem, its former ally (26:2). Here the prophet's criticism is more serious. Tyre is not content with counting its profit from Jerusalem's fall. The city "is filled with violence" (28:16) in pursuit of more profit. It is this greed that led to Tyre's loss of innocence and fall. The irony is that, because of its mad pursuit of greater achievement, greater glory, and greater profits, Tyre lost everything.

28:20-24 In comparison with the other oracles against the nations in chs. 25–28, the oracle against Sidon is bland and trite. Ezekiel makes no accusations against Sidon here. There is only the pronouncement of judgment. At one time Sidon had been an ally of Judah in an anti-Babylonian coalition (Jer. 27:3). Evidently Sidon abandoned Judah when Nebuchadnezzar struck his fatal blows against Jerusalem. In Ezekiel's day, Sidon was not a very important state. In comparison with Tyre, its neighbor 40 km. (15 mi.) to the south, Sidon was insignificant though once it had been a formidable power. The author of this passage needed to include another nation because of his preoccupation with the number seven. With Sidon and Egypt there were seven nations against whom the prophet pronounces oracles of judgment. He chooses Sidon probably because of its association with Tyre (see Jer. 47:4; Joel 3:4; Zech. 9:2).

The oracle itself is a type of rehearsal of preceding judgments on the nations who were the immediate neighbors of Judah. What the prophet says about Sidon here is nothing more than he says about the other nations. In particular Ezek. 28:24 recapitulates the prophet's view of the nations. They are "briers" and "thorns" that make Judah's life miserable. The time is coming when these circumstances will change. The humbling of the nations is a feat that only God can do. When it happens, Judah and these nations will know that God has acted.

28:25-26 These two verses are an appendix to the preceding oracles against Judah's neighbors. They serve to explain Judah's exile and suffering as part of a larger plan that has as its goal the disclosure of God's "holiness" (v. 25). If Judah could not witness to God's holiness through its obedience and consequent prosperity, it would do so through its disobedience and exile. In any case, Judah must manifest God's holiness to the nations. There is an irreversible divine plan in the process of working itself out. Once the process is complete Judah will find itself restored to the land, dwelling there in security and enjoying its fruits. Once Judah witnesses God's judgment executed against the nations and experiences its own restoration, it will know that the LORD is God (v. 26).

AGAINST EGYPT
Ezekiel 29:1–32:32

Egypt is the seventh and last nation to hear the words of divine judgment addressed to it through the prophet. Seven oracles proclaim Egypt's end as a world power. Apparently this interest in the number seven is one way to emphasize the importance of these oracles. All the preceding words that the prophet spoke against Judah's neighbors are not as significant as the ones he has spoken against Egypt.

Ezekiel's concentration on Egypt is understandable. He believed that God had granted universal sovereignty to Nebuchadnezzar so that Babylon might serve as the instrument of divine judgment on Judah. Babylon's principal political and military rival in the 6th cent. was Egypt. While the other nations that the prophet condemned were little more than minor irritations to Nebuchadnezzar, Egypt alone could present serious obstacles in the way of his plans for a Neo-Babylonian Empire. What distressed the prophet was that Egypt was pulling Judah into its orbit. The only effect this could have was the prolonging of Judah's agony. The sooner Judah submitted to divine judgment effected through Babylon, the sooner its restoration would occur. In effect, Egypt was tempting Judah to avoid accepting God's will.

Egypt preferred to have an "independent" Judah on its northeastern border to serve as a buffer against the expanding Neo-Babylonian Empire. Since the rise of the Neo-Assyrian Empire in the 8th cent., the small states in the Syro-Palestinian land bridge between Egypt and Mesopotamia were part of the conflicts between these two powers. Judah's political circumstances were similar to that of today's smaller nations that must choose alignment with either East or West. During the siege of Jerusalem in

135

the spring of 588, the army of Pharaoh Hophra did provide Jerusalem with relief (Jer. 37:5). Egypt, of course, came to Judah's aid for its own purposes. Both Jeremiah (Jer. 37:6-10) and Ezekiel disdained this help from Egypt. The oracles against Egypt show how strongly Ezekiel felt.

All but one of the oracles have dates, and these cluster around the fall of Jerusalem in 587 except for Ezek. 29:17-21, which comes from some years later (571). Just before Jerusalem's fall, some factions in Judah were looking to Egypt for relief from Babylon. The prophet asserts here that God has decreed Egypt's downfall. Further reliance on Egypt was futile. Though the prophet was anti-Egyptian, this did not mean that he was pro-Babylonian. What Ezekiel affirmed was God's sovereignty—not Babylon's.

29:1-16 The first oracle against Egypt is a composite of three separate oracles. After an introduction (29:1-2), the first oracle (vv. 3-6a) condemns Egypt's pride, and the second (vv. 6b-9a) chastises Egypt as a false friend to Judah. The third oracle (vv. 9b-16) is unique in the book of Ezekiel. Not only does it see defeat and exile in Egypt's future, but also it promises its eventual restoration.

29:1-2 The date in v. 1 is equivalent to 7 January 587—just six months before the fall of Jerusalem. As he did with Tyre, the prophet speaks words of judgment against Egypt as represented by its pharaoh. Although the prophet does not mention him by name, the pharaoh at the time was Hophra who attacked Nebuchadnezzar in the spring of 588. This forced the Babylonians to lift their siege of Jerusalem.

29:3-6a The exiles who went to Babylon in 597 may have thought that Jerusalem could avoid its final humiliation at the hands of the Babylonians because of the intervention of Hophra. The prophet disabuses them of what he considers a false hope (v. 3a). Pharaoh too will experience God's judgment because of his pride (v. 3b). In the ancient world, kings presented themselves to their people as the source of their prosperity and well-being.

In Egypt the pharaohs made even greater claims by professing to be the god Horus incarnate. This is what may have led Pharaoh to make the outrageous assertion, "My Nile is my own; I made it" (v. 3b). The Nile was the source of Egypt's greatness. It provided rich alluvial soil along its banks, beyond which was desert. It provided a continuous supply of water to irrigate the land and to slake the thirst of the Egyptians and their animals. It provided a means of transportation that made it possible for Egypt to bring its bountiful harvests to market. There would be no Egypt without the Nile. Egypt, in the person of the pharaoh, was claiming that it was the source of its own greatness. This assertion, once made, sealed Egypt's downfall.

The Hebrew word that the RSV translates as "dragon" in v. 3 is rich in mythological allusions. It exhibits the irony of Pharaoh's claim. How can the dragon that in ancient mythology was the god of chaos take credit for creation and order? The word can also mean "crocodile." Egyptian prayers encouraged the pharaoh to be a crocodile to his enemies. The prophet promises that God will treat Pharaoh like a crocodile. Sometimes hunters take that reptile from the Nile and throw it on the shore to feed the birds (vv. 4-5). The prophet wants the exiles to realize that any hopes they may have for Judah based on any alliance with Egypt will come to nothing. Like Judah, Egypt too stands under divine judgment. Execution of this judgment will reveal God's holiness to Egypt (v. 6a).

29:6b-9a This belief in Egypt's fall moves the prophet to state explicitly that Judah cannot rely on Egypt for its deliverance. In doing so, Ezekiel uses the metaphor of the broken reed, which Isaiah used to warn Judah about Egypt's fickleness in the Assyrian crises two hundred years earlier (Isa. 36:6). Judah should have learned that Egypt's first concern is Egypt. The prophet condemns Egypt as a false friend to Judah. Hophra did eventually withdraw his army to Egypt. This allowed Nebuchadnezzar to reinstate his siege. Jerusalem fell a short time later. Ezekiel promises that Egypt too will fall (Ezek. 29:8-9).

29:9b-16 This final prophecy of the three that comprise the first oracle begins in a familiar enough way. The prophet sees

137

death and destruction from the north of Egypt (Migdol) to the south (Syene). God's decree will lead to the depopulation of Egyptian cities and the exile of their citizens (vv. 9b-12). Unexpectedly the prophet also envisions Egypt's restoration (vv. 13-16). In the future Egypt will be an unimportant kingdom located in Upper (southern) Egypt (v. 14). Presumably both these circumstances will make it possible for Judah to be free of Egypt's political meddling. This is the only instance in the book where the prophet speaks of the restoration of a nation other than Israel and Judah.

This final prophecy reflects the remarkable ambivalence of some traditions regarding Egypt. Biblical tradition remembers Egypt as the oppressor of the Hebrews but also as the nation that welcomed the families of Abraham and Jacob in times of famine. Deuteronomy, which is not known for its universalism, advises its readers: ". . . you shall not abhor an Egyptian, because you were a sojourner in his land" (Deut. 23:7b). Here Ezekiel affirms that divine judgment on Egypt means not only its destruction but also its restoration and reordering. This is an exceptional text in the book of Ezekiel.

29:17-21 The date of this oracle is 26 April 571. Of the dated oracles in Ezekiel this is the latest. What this text attempts to do is to restore the prophet's credibility after the prophecies that he uttered against Tyre (see Ezek. 26:1–28:19) did not come true. The 1st-cent. A.D. Jewish historian and apologist Flavius Josephus stated that the Babylonian siege of Tyre lasted for thirteen years (*Antiquities* x.11.1). Tyre consumed its treasures in its own defense or otherwise made them unavailable to the Babylonians. The prophet admits that all this siege did was to make the Babylonian army old and spent (Ezek. 29:18).

Although Nebuchadnezzar was successful against the dependencies of Tyre on shore, he could not conquer the island. Some two hundred years later Alexander the Great accomplished this feat by building a causeway between the mainland and the island. The Babylonian siege of Tyre began in 585 and ended in 572 with some compromise that allowed Tyre to maintain a modicum of independence under a native king. This is not the picture the prophet had painted of Tyre's fall. The prophet salvages his credibility by asserting that God had allowed Tyre to survive in order to lead Nebuchadnezzar to Egypt that he might plunder it. This is just what happened. The Babylonians invaded Egypt in 568, and Pharaoh Amasis had to pay Nebuchadnezzar substantial tribute after the Babylonian victory. One way to deal with unfulfilled prophecy is to reinterpret it. This is what the text does here.

The biblical tradition had to deal with the failure of prophecy. Other examples of reinterpretation are the words of Haggai and Zechariah, who reinterpret the exilic prophecies of salvation by asserting that the community's failure to rebuild the temple was the cause for their nonfulfillment. Surprisingly, the failure of prophecy often resulted in stronger faith in the prophecy among believers. (For an explanation of this phenomenon, see Robert P. Carroll, *When Prophecy Failed: Cognitive Dissonance in the Prophetic Traditions of the Old Testament* [New York: Seabury and London: SCM, 1979].)

The last verse is a separate unit. While it presupposes the oracle against Egypt that precedes it, there is no explicit reference to the oracle in v. 21. The reinterpretation of the prophet's oracles against Tyre is a convenient opportunity to affirm that whatever decisions God makes regarding the rise and fall of nations always redound to Israel's benefit. It may appear that God is repaying Nebuchadnezzar for the frustrations he experienced at Tyre by giving him Egypt (v. 20). Still God's final purpose is the salvation of Israel. The expression "make a horn sprout" (v. 21) is found elsewhere only in Ps. 132:17 in reference to the restoration to the Davidic dynasty. The reference here appears to be more general. It alludes to the coming deliverance of Israel. The expression "I shall open your lips," which occurs also in Ezek. 16:63, implies that God will stand behind the prophet by making his oracles against the nations come to pass.

30:1-19 The messenger formulae in 30:1 and 20 mark this undated oracle as a unit; however, like many of Ezekiel's oracles, the unity here is only apparent. This oracle is a cluster of three subunits describing the prophet's vision of Egypt's eventual fall. There is little specific reference to historical events here. Ezekiel uses language that is typical of prophecies against foreign nations. What makes this text so extraordinary is the faith that prompted it.

It is hard for the prophet's words to have the impact on readers today like the impression they must have had on those who first heard or read them. Imagine an exile from Judah, a third-rate Palestinian state whose future was very much in doubt, asserting that Judah's national deity is about to bring an end to Egypt! When Ezekiel spoke these words, Egypt had existed for two and a half millennia. The pyramids, the symbol of the achievements of that great civilization, had stood already for two thousand years. What Egypt did is without parallel in human history, ancient or modern. In the face of this, Ezekiel had the temerity to declare that Egypt, its cities, its rulers, and its people were vulnerable to the judgment of Judah's God. It was either outrageous delusion or great faith that led the prophet to utter this oracle of judgment against Egypt.

The prophet uses a prophetic commonplace, the day of the LORD (Amos 5:18-20; Isa. 2:12; Jer. 30:7; Zeph. 1:14-18), to assure the exiles that Egypt was about to fall. That fall will be so violent and severe that it will overwhelm Egypt's neighbors, some of whom were Egypt's political, economic, and military allies (Ezek. 30:5). The prophet believed that, just as God's judgment fell upon Israel and Judah, so it was now falling on Egypt and its allies. Here the prophet specifies the instruments that God will use in bringing Egypt to judgment in vv. 10-12. The first of these is Nebuchadnezzar (v. 10). The person who devastated Judah will do the same to Egypt. Even more ruinous would be the disaster that was coming to Egypt when the Nile would "dry up" (v. 12). The Nile, of course, was Egypt's lifeline. Without the Nile, there could be no Egypt.

Finally, the prophet even laid out the path of destruction by listing some of Egypt's cities that would fall. Some of these, such as Memphis, Zoan, and Thebes, were important royal and religious centers. Palaces, temples, monumental buildings, and other architectural marvels made them magnificent cities. Their ruins are impressive even today. Imagine what they looked like when they were in use! The prophet came from a backwater like 6th-cent.

Judah, with an almost insignificant material culture. Still, he did not stand in awe before Egypt, since he foresaw its destruction and fall.

30:20-26 The date given in v. 20 is equivalent to 29 April 587—just three months before the fall of Jerusalem. Even during these final weeks of Nebuchadnezzar's siege, there were people in Judah and in Babylon who still believed that Egypt had the power to lift that siege and save Jerusalem. It is to such people that the prophet directed these words. Although this is the fourth of the oracles directed against Egypt, there is no commission to speak these words to Egypt. This message was for those people who were still seeking human deliverance from what Ezekiel believed to be God's instrument of judgment. To them the prophet avers that no such deliverance will be forthcoming. The prophet makes one last attempt to open the eyes of those who were blind to Jerusalem's fate.

The arm as a metaphor for strength is common enough in the literature of the ancient Near East, including the Bible. Verse 21 implies that God has already taken action against the pharaoh by "breaking his arm." This may be a reference to Hophra's withdrawal from engaging the Babylonians who were besieging Jerusalem. The engagement did lift the siege for a time, but now that the Egyptians left, Jerusalem's fall was a certainty. To those who hope for another intervention from Egypt, God promises to break Pharaoh's other arm (v. 22). What more can the prophet say to dissuade people from relying on Egypt for help? From Ezekiel's perspective, intervention from Egypt is nothing more than a postponement of the inescapable judgment of God. God will break Pharaoh's arms because God wishes to punish Judah. Since Egypt is helping Judah escape divine judgment, it must share Judah's fate: defeat and exile (vv. 25-26).

31:1-18 The fifth oracle against Egypt is a prophecy of judgment in the form of an allegory. The prophet uses the common ancient Near Eastern motif of the tree of life to underscore again the reason for Egypt's downfall. Egypt regarded its greatness as its own achievement. Egypt was a great civilization; there is no denying that. From the prophet's perspective, Egypt's fatal flaw was not its greatness but its error in ignoring God's total sovereignty—even over a great power. When Egypt began to keep Judah from its destiny, it was just a matter of time before God would act. Judah had to experience divine judgment.

Following the introductory verses (31:1-2a), the oracle begins with a poetic description of the great tree that God planted in Eden. There was no tree to rival its beauty and stature (vv. 5, 7). The poem is replete with mythological allusions, but the direct associations with Egypt are nil. There is no implication of any criticism of the great tree that God created. Perhaps these verses are part of a poem that the prophet used to speak about the fall of Egypt. Ezekiel comes to that subject in the prose section of the oracle that follows in vv. 10-18.

Beginning with v. 10, the prophet leaves off his poetic description of the tree and begins to pronounce his words of judgment. The implication of what follows is that Egypt's very greatness is the source of its weakness, just as the tree's height was the source of its pride. The one historical allusion made in this oracle comes in v. 12. There God states that "foreigners, the most terrible of the nations," will deal with the tree they cut down. As high as the tree is, it will never reach to the heavens, and it will always be vulnerable to those who would cut it down. Ezekiel implies that Egypt, despite in greatness, is also vulnerable. Egypt will learn the tragic lesson that kings and nations, no matter how great, will not last forever. Egypt no less than Judah is at risk.

The prophet stretches the metaphor when he has God cast the fallen tree into Sheol. That place is the great leveler. All are equal in Sheol. When it reaches the abode of the dead, Egypt must accept its solidarity with other, less important nations. It too will learn what God's sovereignty means. Egypt has made a serious mistake in thinking that its achievements have secured for it some type of immortality.

The date of this oracle (v. 1) is equivalent to 21 June 587. In just a matter of a few weeks, Jerusalem will fall to the Babylonians. In the allegory of the tree, Ezekiel helps Judah to see its fate from a more universal perspective. Judah is not the only nation that stands under divine judgment. No king and no nation can escape that judgment—not even Egypt.

32:1-16 The messenger formulae in 32:1 and 17 mark this as a unit, and vv. 2 and 16 label this text a lament. As happens often in the book of Ezekiel, this unit is a composite of several different forms. One expects a lament to look backward to compare the former circumstances of the subject of the lament with present difficulties. Except for v. 2b, there is none of that in this unit. Similarly this text, except v. 2, does not follow the poetic meter of a Hebrew lament. The bulk of this text (vv. 3-15) is not a lament but an announcement of judgment.

More crucial for understanding this text is the imagery that Ezekiel used in this sixth oracle against Egypt. Again the prophet reinterprets Babylonian mythology with which the exiles had become familiar. According to the Babylonian creation myth, Marduk, the patron deity of Babylon, defeated the sea monster Tiamat and created the world out of its carcass. Ezekiel demythologizes this ancient story. What the prophet describes is not a battle between two divine beings. Rather, it is Nebuchadnezzar, the king of Babylon, who is acting as God's chosen instrument defeating the Nile dragon, the pharaoh of Egypt (v. 11). The use of this imagery helps to transform these oracles against Egypt from being merely an announcement of punishment to the defeat of evil and chaotic powers. The prophet then is announcing not divine retribution upon Egypt but God's creation of a better world.

The purpose of this "lament" is not to look back at Egypt's lost glory, not to condemn the pride of Pharaoh, not to give vent to the anger of the exiles over the fall of Jerusalem. Instead, the prophet wishes to affirm the power and sovereignty of Judah's God over all the nations of the world. It is a bold assertion, because the prophet makes it shortly after the exiles received the news of the fall of Jerusalem. (The date for this oracle is 3 March 585.) Ezekiel declares that beyond the judgment of Judah and Egypt there is a better world waiting for those who serve God.

32:17-32 The last oracle against Egypt is similar to the taunt against the king of Babylon whose fall was to precede the restoration of Judah (Isa. 14). The text from Ezekiel is not as biting, though it uses the same metaphor: a tour of Sheol where once great powers live among the shadows. This is an appropriate theme for the text that serves as the conclusion to the oracles against Egypt and the whole of Part IV, which contains prophecies against the nations.

The date of the oracle is sometime in 586. (The Hebrew text does not contain the month; the LXX supplies this detail.) The text is not as engrossing as its counterpart from Isaiah because it contains a repetition of stock phrases.

The purpose of the litany of older and now extinct world powers is to affirm that Egypt now joins their number. Like the Mesopotamian powers Assyria and Elam (Ezek. 32:22-25), like Tubal and Meshech from Asia Minor (v. 26), and even like the petty powers Edom and Sidon (vv. 29-30), Egypt's dwelling is now in a remote area of Sheol. There Egypt finds its rightful place.

Though ancient Israel saw Sheol, the abode of the dead, as the fate of all humanity, this text implies there can be distinctions among the dead. The prophet contrasts Egypt and the other once great powers to the "mighty men of old" who died with honor. These "mighty men" are probably the mythological offspring of "the sons of God and the daughters of men" (Gen. 6:1-4). They were not guilty of the crimes that Egypt, Assyria, and the other nations committed. These crimes brought Egypt to its wretched place in the abode of the dead (Ezek. 32:32).

The oracles against the nations end with a vision of once mighty world empires groveling in the dust of Sheol. The prophet acknowledges that God allows the nations to exercise great power for a time. In the end God does judge the powers of evil. The prophet implies that for Egypt God's words of judgment came too late, for there can be no response from Sheol. Once in Sheol, the place of the dead, Egypt can make no efforts to change its fate. The time for such action is past. Words of judgment like these can lead to repentance and new life only for the living. The prophet makes that explicit in Part V, in which he announces God's plans for Judah's future.

PART V
JUDAH'S RESTORATION

Ezekiel 33:1–39:29

The next great section of the book of Ezekiel begins with the parable of the watchman (Ezek. 33:1-20). This fifth part of the prophet's message serves to balance the first three (chs. 1–24), in which the people of Judah display an incredible but ultimately unrealistic confidence in their future. God calls the prophet to speak words of divine judgment to a people who made it almost impossible for themselves to hear this message. Here the circumstances are the reverse. This time the people despair, and with good reason. God calls the prophet to lead the people to faith in their restoration—another impossible task. Overcoming the political obstacles to Judah's restoration was not as difficult as overcoming the obstacle created by the people's own unbelief. Just as Ezekiel had to lead his people to accept God's judgment, so now he must lead them to accept God's salvation.

The place of these chapters in the book of Ezekiel as it now stands is surely the result of an editorial plan. The announcement of Jerusalem's fall in 33:21-22 should follow ch. 24. The oracles against the nations (chs. 25–32) give a hint of what is to follow in chs. 34–39, and 33:1-20 signals a new stage in the prophet's ministry. The proclamation of salvation (chs. 34–39) follows the announcement of judgment (chs. 1–24). Between these two large blocks of material come the oracles against the nations (chs. 25–32) that prepare the dispirited exiles for the unexpected message that follows.

A TRANSITION
TO CONSOLATION
Ezekiel 33:1-33

33:1-20 Chapter 33 serves as the immediate literary transition from all that precedes in the book of Ezekiel to the message of hope that begins with ch. 34. This text also serves to mark off a new stage in the prophet's mission. Ezekiel will now speak of the great miracle of restoration. His words will no longer be harsh and unwelcome; they will be almost gentle and surely consoling.

In 33:1-9 the prophet reuses a metaphor from 3:16-21: the watchman. While the text is ostensibly about the prophet and his mission, its real focus is on the exiles and their reactions to the prophet. The metaphor is clear enough. During the day, some people who lived in a fortified city worked outside the city gates. So that they could go about their work without worry, a guard stood on the city wall scanning the horizon for any sign of an approaching enemy. When the watchman spied hostile forces, he gave a signal to the townspeople in the fields. It was their responsibility to leave their work to return to safety behind the city walls. Both the watchman and the people had clear responsibilities. The watchman was to survey the vista before him and warn of approaching danger. The people were to heed his warnings and react immediately. Verses 7-9 make it clear that Ezekiel is Judah's watchman. He is adamant about fulfilling his responsibilities. Unfortunately, some of those who heard his warnings felt that any response was futile.

Verses 10-20 reflect the objections of the exiles to the implications of the parable. Ezekiel's audience correctly infers that the prophet is broaching the subject of restoration. This is a subject that they will not allow themselves to consider. They believe that their guilt is so great that the revival of their community is just not possible (v. 10). The people also believe that God's ways are "not just" (vv. 17, 20). (Note the NEB translation of vv. 17, 20: "The LORD acts without principle.") In the face of these objections, the prophet avers that God has taken no pleasure in Judah's fall. On the contrary, it is God's will that Judah rise again.

Ezekiel can make this claim because he believed that justice was not the foundation of Judah's relationship with God (v. 20). If it were, Judah's restoration would be impossible. No human being or community could survive divine judgment were its sole criterion justice. The prophet believed that Judah's relationship with God has divine forgiveness as its foundation. Repentance is the sole condition of Judah's restoration (vv. 15-16). Ezekiel believed that God would never refuse forgiveness to those who proved to be genuinely repentant.

Ezekiel makes these assurances to the nation by speaking of the individual's relationship with God. The prophet draws out the implications of individual and corporate responsibility in the metaphor of the watchman. Though the watchman's vocation is that of an individual, his actions affect many people. The categoric and unqualified forgiveness that God offers to the repentant sinner makes it possible for Judah to live again. Ten years in Babylon and the devastating news that Jerusalem has fallen have destroyed the last vestige of confidence that the exiles had about their future. It is precisely at this point that Ezekiel feels free to proclaim God's intention to restore Judah. The only requisite for forgiveness is repentance (vv. 14b-15). If the people of Judah "turn" from their evil, they can expect God's forgiveness and restoration.

Although the prophet uses an old metaphor, he transforms it. The watchman normally kept his eyes open for signs of approaching danger and issued his warning when he believed that trouble was imminent. What Ezekiel, the watchman, saw in the distance was not the approach of another enemy. The prophet saw God coming with forgiveness for all who would accept it through repentance. Judah could look forward to the future with hope if enough people would act on the prophet's word and show the evidence of repentance in their lives. Despite the devastation that Judah experienced, it can have confidence in the future. God's offer of forgiveness is absolutely certain for those who "turn from their sin and do what is lawful and right" (v. 14b). In what appear to be the circumstances of death, the prophet utters an oracle that speaks of life—life that comes through God's response to Judah's repentance.

33:21-22   There are three passages in the book of Ezekiel that speak about the prophet's dumbness: 3:22-27; 24:24-27; and 33:21-33. (For the relationship of these three texts and a reconstruction of events in Ezekiel's life that prompted their composition, see the comment on 3:22-27.) It is likely that at one point in the prophet's ministry he experienced a state of ecstatic dumbness. The most probable occasion for this experience was following his oracles proclaiming the fall of Jerusalem. Once the city had fallen, the prophet was ready to begin a new phase of his ministry. The prophet emerges from his ecstatic dumbness since he has a new message for Judah. The paradox here is that the defeat of Jerusalem enables the prophet to speak about its restoration.

In 24:20-24 God leads the prophet to recognize that the death of his wife was to help him understand the meaning of Jerusalem's fall. Here the prophet learns that indeed the city has fallen. God was "wedded" to Jerusalem by the covenant, and God had to watch as the city "died." When the prophet heard about Jerusalem's destruction he understood why he had to witness the death of his wife. It was to reveal to him that God had "suffered" in and through Israel the penalty for Israel's sin and rebellion. Until that moment Ezekiel had been dumb. He had no "gospel" to proclaim. Now he can speak because he knows of God's love and grace from his own experience. He knows now that rebirth is possible.

The expression "the hand of the LORD" (33:22) appears also in 1:3; 8:1; 37:1; and 40:1. In each case it refers to an extraordinary experience of God. In this passage it denotes a special divine action that enables the prophet to begin speaking again after being silent for some time. Ezekiel has a new message to proclaim: the announcement of Judah's restoration. Until the fall of Jerusalem, he could not offer the exiles any hope for the future. Once the city fell, he could offer the exiles hope—a hope based on God's forgiveness alone. After Judah's final defeat, the exiles could no longer cling to the belief that somehow political alliances, military power, or any human intervention could secure Judah's future. Only God could offer Judah any hope for the future.

There are some problems about the date in 33:21. Solving these problems is not crucial to understanding this text. The most plausible view is that the fugitive from Jerusalem arrived in Babylon about six months after Jerusalem's fall. Since the city fell in July 587/6, the date of the fugitive's arrival is 8 January 586/5.

33:23-29 Verse 24 cites a proverbial saying used to justify the appropriation of the property of the exiles. The mention of Abraham here is unique in the book of Ezekiel. In fact, reference to the promises made to the patriarchs is uncommon in the prophets. Such a reference would lend support to the very idea that most prophets tried to undermine: that God's promises to Israel were unconditional. The prophets stand in the Mosaic tradition whose perspectives Exod. 19:5 expresses clearly: ". . . *if* you will obey my voice and keep my covenant, you shall be my own possession among all peoples. . . ." Prophets like Ezekiel wanted Israel to know that its present circumstances were a direct result of its failure to "obey God's voice."

Those people who remained on the land after the fall of Jerusalem were looking for the kind of security that the prophet denied to the exiles. Ezekiel insists that they cannot insist on their "right" to live on the land. They need to remember that the land is a gift that always remains God's. Israel merely receives the land as an inheritance as long as it remains bound to God through obedience. The prophet accuses the people of idolatry, violation of dietary laws, murder, and adultery (Ezek. 33:25). He asks how people guilty of such offenses can expect to remain untouched by divine judgment. The prophet announces God's judgment, which will take the form of war, disease, and animal attacks (v. 27). Because of the prophet's denunciations the people will recognize divine judgment when it comes to them (v. 29). This judgment did come as a third deportation in 582, which Jeremiah mentions (Jer. 52:30).

By citing the proverb that mentions Abraham and then an-

nouncing the coming judgment upon those who quote that proverb to justify their actions, Ezekiel discredits any claim of those
who survived the fall to Jerusalem to own the land by right. Their
behavior has resulted in the cancellation of those "rights." Their
disobedience shows that they are not interested in responding to
God as Abraham did but in manipulating their religious traditions
to support their land-grabbing. This text paints a graphic picture
of the competition among the survivors of the fall of Judah. It
must have been fierce, inhuman, and violent. How could the
prophet be sympathetic to the claims of the survivors who
"piously" point to the promises made to Abraham as justification
for their actions?

33:30-33   Although an editor joined this oracle to the preceding
one (Ezek. 33:24-29) with a single prophetic word formula in
v. 23, they are two separate units. Whereas the preceding oracle
addressed those who remained in Judah, this one deals with the
exiles. It too unmasks the veneer of religiosity that some people
used to hide their unwillingness to respond to the divine will.
This oracle is unusual. It is a divine proclamation to the prophet
without any commission to say these words to those who were
guilty of the abuse that the oracle describes. It is reminiscent of
Jeremiah's confessions (e.g., Jer. 12:1-6; 15:15-21) in which the
prophet complains to God that people do not respond to his
message. Here it is God who does the complaining. God describes
the attitude of Ezekiel's fellow exiles who love to hear his oracles
but do not act on them.

This oracle assumes that Ezekiel had a very good reputation.
People did come to hear him speak. They enjoyed hearing about
the issues he raised, thinking about the message he conveyed,
discussing the meaning of the oracles he gave. Unfortunately they
were unwilling to act on the prophet's words. When it came to
repentance, the prophet had few converts. Perhaps this was because
some people in exile managed to prosper in their new surroundings. They appreciated the opportunity to hear Ezekiel from an
intellectual and aesthetic point of view. They were not ready to
have his words affect their behavior or alter the position they
achieved in Babylonian society.

God consoles the prophet in what must have been a frustrating circumstance by stating that when Ezekiel's predictions come true people will realize that a true prophet has spoken (Ezek. 33:33). Though Ezekiel knew that the words he spoke came from God, not all his neighbors believed as he did. They did not consider him a prophet but a religious curiosity. His words may have stimulated them, but his oracles did not move many people to change their lives. For too many exiles Ezekiel's prophecies were a form of entertainment (v. 32). The prophet, of course, meant his words to be a call to action. The people were not any more ready to hear the word of the LORD than any Gentile. They were insincere. They considered Ezekiel a fool for believing as he did. They did not put any more stock in the prophet's words than they did in the popular songs of the day.

The stage is ready for the prophet's words of salvation. Chapter 33 serves as a kind of transition from the oracles against the nations (chs. 25–32) to the oracles of salvation for Israel (chs. 34–39). Ezekiel has reasserted his role as Judah's watchman. He has criticized those still in Judah whose feelings of security were ill-founded and those in Babylon who regarded him not as a prophet but as a curiosity. He called people to heed his words. The message was not his but a message that God directed him to convey to the people of Judah in exile *and* those still in the land.

ISRAEL'S SHEPHERDS
AND GOD'S SHEEP
Ezekiel 34:1-31

This chapter has an oracle that condemns Judah's "shepherds" (i.e., its political rulers) and then promises that in the future God will act as Judah's ruler and dispense with human kings who have proven not just ineffective but perverse (vv. 1-16). Attached to this oracle are three other units that have a similar content. The first (vv. 17-22) abandons the shepherd metaphor and speaks of judgment that is coming to the flock itself. The second (vv. 23-24) presents David as the shepherd of God's flock. The final unit (vv. 25-31) abandons the figure of sheep and shepherd (except for v. 31) and speaks of an idyllic future for Israel. As is true with chapters like this one, it is difficult to determine with certainty the words of the prophet and those that are the result of later expansions by the circles that transmitted Ezekiel's words. Since this commentary centers on the final form of the text, determination of the original setting of each unit that makes up this chapter is not crucial. In its present form, this entire unit proposes to address the exiles after the fall of Jerusalem. It attempts to describe the future that God is creating for Judah.

34:1-16 Ezekiel speaks bitterly about Judah's political leaders, whom he condemns as responsible for its fall. In the prophet's eyes they are nothing more than parasites who lived off the people whom they were to protect. To make his point Ezekiel uses an ancient metaphor. The "shepherd" as an image of political rulers goes back to the Sumerian royal tradition (4th millennium B.C.E.). The motif became widespread throughout the ancient Near East. Jeremiah 23:1-6 also uses this image to denounce Judah's political leadership. There is probably no direct literary dependence of the Ezekiel text on the one from Jeremiah. Both prophets made use of the same traditional image in their censure of Judah's failed political system.

Ezekiel asserts that Judah's rulers profited from their positions while doing nothing to exercise the responsibilities of their offices. They did little more than exploit the very people whom they were to protect. The oracle that condemns them (Ezek. 34:2-10) does not serve as a warning for the shepherds. Their discredited rule is over; the likelihood of God restoring it is almost nil. The prophet uses Judah's human shepherds as a foil for the shepherd who will tend the sheep in the future. This shepherd will be none other than the LORD.

The image of God as Israel's shepherd was not the prophet's innovation (cf. Gen. 49:24; Ps. 23). This image still communicates centuries later (see John 10:1-18). In the past God delegated the role of shepherd to the human beings who ruled over Israel and Judah. Since these have proven to be abject failures, this delegation will cease. God will act directly on Judah's behalf to insure its future. What started out as an oracle of judgment ends as an oracle of salvation that speaks directly about Judah's future. The prophet no longer refers to Judah's past and the judgment that it generated. The prophet deals with Judah's future and the salvation that the exiles will experience.

Besides the shepherd motif in this oracle, the prophet also introduces images taken from the Exodus and Settlement traditions in Ezek. 34:13-15. When Ezekiel speaks about Judah's future, he does not use rhetoric that is entirely new. He expresses his good news with images taken from older traditions while affirming that Judah's future will eclipse its past. It could not be otherwise with God as Judah's shepherd.

34:17-22   The subject reverts to judgment, but this time it is not the political leaders whom the prophet addresses but rather the people of Judah themselves. Ezekiel abandons the shepherd metaphor. Instead he uses the image of weak and strong animals in a flock, because the prophet knew that Judah's political leadership was not its only problem. There were great injustices that were the product of Judah's stratified society. The people of means were not content with merely consuming the bulk of the nation's resources. They made it impossible for the poor to profit from the few resources that the rich did not dissipate.

One reason for the failure of Judah's political system was the weakness of its social fabric. The divisions within Judahite society made it impossible for Judah to withstand the political and military pressures that it had to face. From a historical perspective, perhaps it was inevitable that a small national state such as Judah would fall to the expansionist Neo-Babylonian Empire under Nebuchadnezzar. The serious social divisions within Judah made it so much the easier for the Babylonians to complete their destruction of Judah.

God promises to judge between the weak and the strong sheep (vv. 20-22; RSV "fat" and "lean"). The clear implication here is that God will make it possible for the weak to survive by ending the domination of the strong. God always takes the side of the weak against the strong because the strong have been guilty of exploitation. They made it impossible for the weak to enjoy even a small fraction of the "pasture" that should be available for all.

34:23-24 There is an abrupt shift from the promise that God will "judge between sheep and sheep" (v. 22) to the appointment of David to "feed" God's flock (v. 23). Here is a reversion to the theme of 34:2-10, which assumes that God delegates the role of shepherd to human beings. This is at odds with the assertion in 34:11-15 that God will assume the role of shepherd personally. Delegation of this responsibility to human beings will cease. Here Ezekiel envisions a David of the future who will be the shepherd of God's flock.

The prophet asserts that David is the only shepherd for God's flock (v. 23). Apparently Ezekiel believed that the future God had in store for Judah involved reunification with Israel. Though the first David ruled over a united Israel, the unity did not survive long after Solomon's death. Also the prophet may have been aware of the tradition that found expression in 2 Sam. 7, which declares that there was to be no temporal limit to the rule of the Davidic dynasty. Is the text looking forward to the restoration of the Davidic dynasty or the rise of an ideal Davidic figure in the future?

It is difficult to be sure. There are only two other passages in the Hebrew Bible that explicitly refer to a future David: Hos. 3:5 and Jer. 30:9-10. Messianism comes to full expression in Jewish literature produced between the two Testaments.

What is of particular interest here is the title that Ezekiel gives to this future David. In Ezek. 34:24 the prophet does not call him "king" *(melek)* but "prince" *(nasiʾ)*. Most commentators do not find this difference in terminology crucial. Still it may very well give an insight into the prophet's view of the role that the future David will play in the restored Israel. He will not be a typical ancient Near Eastern monarch, but God's "servant" who presides over the kingdom that God rules. This David as God's servant has a certain latitude in the fulfillment of his responsibilities. Still he remains someone who belongs to his master and who is therefore committed to obedience. The prophet's avoidance of the term "king" in speaking about the future David does not necessarily imply a type of demotion of the king. Ezekiel's *nasiʾ* will be exactly what David and the rest of Israel's kings should have remained: God's servants. By insuring Israel's fidelity to Yahweh the *nasiʾ* will fulfill his highest destiny.

34:25-31 The final unit of ch. 34 abandons the metaphors of shepherd and sheep except for v. 31, which ends the entire chapter. The subject of this final unit is Israel's idyllic future. The prophet paints an almost Eden-like picture of that future in which there will be no more wild animals to threaten the people (v. 25). The land's fruitfulness will bring a great bounty so that the people live in peace and prosperity (vv. 26-27). The transition from speaking about the future David to speaking about the land's prosperity and peace may appear to contemporary readers as abrupt, yet ancient Near Eastern and biblical traditions associate the king with cosmic blessing (see Ps. 72).

The polemic against the shepherds with which this chapter began is forgotten. What replaces it is a promise of blessing. Though this promise is similar to that of Lev. 26:4-6, there is probably no direct literary relationship between the two texts. The prophet was familiar with the traditional language of blessing and uses it to help his people grasp his vision of their future. The final verse (Ezek. 34:31) reapplies the metaphor of the sheep that dominates a good portion of this chapter. It also reinterprets the typical covenant formula that Ezekiel uses (see 11:20; 14:11). This verse insures that the prophet's readers will know that his vision was not about the reestablishment of human dominion, but was a revelation of God's determination to be once again the God of Judah and Israel.

JUDGMENT FOR EDOM—
SALVATION FOR ISRAEL
Ezekiel 35:1–36:15

The prophetic word formula in 35:1, repeated in 36:16, suggests that 35:1–36:15 is a unit. A cursory examination of the section's content shows that this is not the case. It is a union of what were two separate units originally. The first foresees disaster for Edom, while the second proclaims salvation for Judah. A closer examination of both subunits reveals that each is a collection of individual prophetic sayings that have come together because of a specific editorial judgment. Though this text's structure is complex, and understanding how its components fit together can be frustrating, its basic meaning is clear. An editor assembled this unit to elucidate one of Ezekiel's fundamental assertions. The prophet proclaimed that the fall of Jerusalem and the exile of its population were not God's final word to Judah.

The purpose of this unit is to highlight Judah's salvation by contrasting it with the judgment that is coming upon Edom. The exiles' years of captivity in Babylon and the fall of Jerusalem undermined the last vestige of their false security. They could now recognize the extent of divine judgment on their infidelity. More than this, Jerusalem's fate prevented some exiles from believing that the future held any possibility for renewing the special relationship that existed between them and their national deity, that is, the covenant made at Sinai. When the prophet began speaking words of restoration, no one heeded him, just as when he spoke words of judgment. The purpose of this unit is to show the reason behind the prophet's announcement of salvation.

The literary relationship between each component of this unit is not easy to explain. Still it is clear why an editor chose to arrange the material we have before us. Ezekiel 36:1-15, the proclamation of salvation to the mountains of Israel, balances the announcement of judgment to those same mountains in 6:1-14. During his proclamation of salvation, Ezekiel contrasts Judah's fate with that of Edom. This led to the editorial judgment to preface 36:1-15 with a collection of prophetic sayings that announce judgment to the mountains of Edom, specifically Mt. Seir (see Num. 24:18, where Seir is a synonym for Edom). This served to set the restoration of the mountains of Israel in a clearer perspective.

35:1-15   Edom has already been the subject of two oracles of judgment (cf. Ezek. 25:12-14). The occasion for these oracles was Edom's complicity in Judah's collapse. This enabled Edom to capture a portion of Judah's territory after the final fall of the Judahite state. The intense rivalry between Judah and Edom probably began when David added Edom to his empire and enslaved its populace (2 Sam. 8:13-14) and continued because of Solomon's commercial exploitation of the region (1 Kgs. 9:26-28). Biblical tradition ascribes this enmity to rivalry between the ancestors of Edom and Judah (Gen. 25:27-34; 27:41-45). The fall of Jerusalem made it possible for Edom to exact its revenge on Judah by appropriating a portion of its territory. This is precisely what Edom did by expanding into the Negeb.

This subunit is a collection of individual oracles, each of which ends with a recognition formula ("you [they] shall know that I am the LORD"; see Ezek. 35:4, 9, 12, 15). Not only is there switching of persons between these oracles, but even within the same oracle there is inconsistency in persons (e.g., v. 8), which modern translations like the RSV smooth out. These oracles list the crimes for which God will judge Edom: hatred, envy, and greed. Edom wanted Judah to collapse so that it could appropriate its land (vv. 10-15). This turns God into Edom's enemy so that its seemingly secure cities will become a wasteland (vv. 1-4). Because Edom was guilty of the slaughter of Judah's citizens, its citizens will experience the same evil (vv. 5-9).

Through these oracles the prophet wanted the exiles to recognize that the expected political consequence of Jerusalem's fall was not the will of God. God did not allow Judah to experience disaster simply to enrich Edom. God's ultimate purpose was Judah's restoration to its special relationship with its God. To make it clear that this purpose will prevail, Ezekiel announces the imminent fall of Edom, the desolation of its cities, and the slaughter of its citizens.

36:1-15 This collection of oracles serves to contrast the immediate past and future of Edom and Judah. Edom has survived the military and political pressure to which Israel succumbed, yet its future is bleak. Judah has experienced a fate that threatened its continued existence yet its future is promising. The collection is the counterpart to 6:1-14, which was an oracle of judgment against the mountains of Judah. These oracles promise that God will restore these mountains to their former beauty and prosperity.

This unit too is a collection of oracles. Usually a prophetic oracle begins with a single introductory formula and closes with a single concluding formula. This unit contains no less than seven introductory formulas (vv. 2, 3, 4, 5, 6, 7, 13) and three concluding formulas (vv. 11, 14, 15). There are three commands to prophesy (vv. 1, 3, 6) and two demands for attention (vv. 1, 4). The work of later traditionalists is clear in this unit. Without getting into a detailed analysis of the contents of this subunit, one probably can point to vv. 2, 5, and 7 as the original nucleus around which the rest of this section grew.

Despite its literary complexity, the basic thrust of 36:1-15 is clear. Verses 1-7 are an oracle of judgment against Edom for appropriating Judah's land. Verses 8-15 comprise an oracle of salvation for Judah. They promise that new life will come to the "mountains of Israel." Farmers will cultivate the land again. People will rebuild their cities. The entire population will flourish again. This is a clear affirmation that beyond Judah's judgment there is hope. This was the message that Ezekiel wanted to convey to the exiles following the fall of Jerusalem. Later traditionalists affirm their concurrence not only by transmitting the prophet's words but by augmenting them to underscore their faith in Ezekiel's vision for Judah's future. The prophet taught his people to believe that God's final purpose for Judah is restoration and salvation. They are to believe that God's purpose will prevail despite any apparent evidence to the contrary.

ISRAEL'S NEW HEART
AND SPIRIT
Ezekiel 36:16-38

Why should God restore the people Israel since God has expelled them from their land for good reason? Ezekiel's proclamation of salvation following upon his insistence on Judah's doom raised this question. This unit attempts to formulate an answer. The prophet's rhetoric is a problem for contemporary readers of the book of Ezekiel. Here the prophet gets carried away with his rhetoric, and this puts aesthetic and theological obstacles in the path of appreciating his message. Here the prophet's two principal metaphors cause some difficulties. First, he explains the Exile as the result of ritual impurity. This image is foreign to many of his readers, and his illustration in Ezek. 36:17 is particularly offensive to women. Second, the prophet insists that in the future Israel will be incapable of disobedience. This appears to transform people into moral automatons so that real freedom is no longer a possibility. The prophet's choice of illustrations in v. 17 is unfortunate. His insistence that God will program Israel into obedience in v. 27 is too strong. The prophet used exaggeration for effect. His words in v. 17 are offset by 18:31. The prophet was not making moral judgments about women or human potential for good. Ezekiel was trying to convince the exiles that his message of restoration was worth listening to. Apparently his fellow exiles needed convincing.

36:16-21 After the initial messenger formula, God surveys Israel's history for the prophet. Israel was unfaithful. The prophet compares the effects of this infidelity to those of ritual impurity that rendered a person unfit for public worship (36:17). The nation has rendered itself ritually impure and therefore could not

162

remain in God's presence. God's only alternative was to have the people led into exile. This course of action had its own problems, since the nations viewed Israel's exile not as a means to preserve God's holiness but as a failure of Israel's national deity. Instead of protecting God's honor and majesty, the exile of Israel and Judah called them into question. God could not allow these circumstances to go on.

36:22-23 The tradition about the wilderness wanderings preserves the memory of similar circumstances. God had determined to destroy the people who had escaped from Egypt because of their disobedience. Moses convinced God to spare them for the sake of God's own honor (Num. 14:11-23). Here God discloses that the Exile will end—not because of Israel's merit, but to preserve God's reputation among the nations. Restoration will take place for God's sake and not Israel's. When the nations see Israel's return to its land, they will draw only one conclusion: Israel's national deity has acted to save the people. By restoring Israel to its land, God could uphold God's own dignity before the rest of the world.

36:24-32 Though the prophet asserts that the restoration will take place to vindicate God's honor, it will nonetheless affect the people and land of Israel. Picking up on the metaphor of ritual uncleanness, Ezek. 36:25 speaks about a sprinkling that will rid Israel of its impurity (see Num. 19:9-22). Ezekiel then moves to metaphors that he has used earlier: a new heart and spirit (see Ezek. 11:19). Israel's restoration will mean an inward renewal for the people. In the ancient world the heart was the center for volition and the intellectual catalyst for feeling and action. A "heart of stone" implied inflexibility and willfulness, while a "heart of flesh" meant submission and compliance. The "new spirit" suggests that God will empower Israel for obedience. This "new spirit" is the spirit of God, who is the source of all life. The gift of God's spirit became a common way to speak about God's movement in Israel's life (see 39:29; Joel 2:28-29; Acts 2:4-21, 33; 10:44-47; 15:8; 19:2-7).

Ezekiel believes that forgiveness which cancels guilt is not

163

enough to reestablish Israel's relationship with God. Forgiveness is necessary, to be sure, but Israel needs something else to insure that it will not founder again. Earlier, the prophet had all but said that Judah was incapable of obedience (Ezek. 2:3-4), just as Jeremiah implied (Jer. 13:23). Accordingly, the people must be remade so that disobedience becomes an impossibility for them. Jeremiah makes the same affirmation (Jer. 31:31-34). Here both prophets become carried away by their rhetoric. What Ezekiel wanted to affirm was that without God's initiative a genuine conversion on Israel's part is impossible. He wants to declare how difficult it is to overcome the bondage of past evil. He does not wish to turn Israel into a nation of moral robots whom God has programmed to obey. If disobedience is impossible, so is obedience.

The restoration of Israel to its land will have some external effects. Ezekiel promises that the land will enjoy unparalleled fertility so that Israel will never again experience famine. Famine was always a danger to the region in antiquity. The land did not have any great river system to provide irrigation as did Egypt and Mesopotamia. Israelite farmers had to depend entirely upon adequate rainfall to support their crops. Any year the rain did not come in sufficient quantity, the people suffered from famine. The people of the ancient Near East knew this to be a characteristic of Palestine (Ezek. 36:30). Ezekiel asserts that once the restoration takes place, famine will be a phenomenon of the past.

36:33-38 The final external effect of the restoration will be the repopulation of the land and the rebuilding of its cities. The restoration will be so dramatic that people cannot help noticing the Eden-like quality of the land. War and exile have depleted the population of the land. Restoration will make a marked increase in the number of people who will find their support in a land that had been desolate because of Israel's disobedience. Not only will God transform the nation from within, but a newly fertile, famine-free land will support a great population.

THE DRY BONES WILL LIVE
Ezekiel 37:1-14

Ezekiel's vision of dry bones taking flesh and coming back to life at the command of God is the most familiar passage of this entire book. This vision has stimulated not only the speculations of theologians but also the imagination of artists and composers. It has inspired diverse cultural expressions from an American black spiritual to a political cartoon strip in a modern Israeli newspaper.

This text describes one of the prophet's ecstatic visions, but its imagery is not as bizarre as are others in the book nor is its meaning difficult to determine. It has attracted the interest of several patristic commentators, most of whom found here biblical warrant for the Christian belief in the resurrection of the dead. (A notable exception was Jerome.) Early rabbinic commentators, too, found the Jewish belief in the resurrection supported by this text. Part of the synagogue wall at Dura Europos depicts Ezekiel's vision of the dry bones, but clearly the winged creatures in the mural represent the individual souls of the dead—a notion far from the idea behind this passage. Whatever this text came to mean for later believing communities, it is clear from the book of Ezekiel that the prophet disclosed his vision of the dry bones as part of his attempt to convince his fellow exiles that God's power was about to restore Judah to its land, the source of its life.

The notion of death that lies behind this vision of dry bones bleaching in the sun diverges somewhat from the pre-apocalyptic idea. An important component of the earlier Israelite view of death centered on Sheol, a place of shadowy half-existence where the dead dwell. This passage imagines a type of disintegration of the dead as in Eccl. 12:7. The assumption of the prophet as the vision begins is that this disintegration is irreversible.

165

Unlike the other visions in this book, the present text provides no date to suggest the temporal setting of this passage (cf. Ezek. 1:1; 8:1). God quotes the exiles' assessment of their status in 37:11b. This text reflects a moment after all the illusions about Judah's future ended and before significant hope for restoration was stirring among the exiles. The prophet then reveals the contents of his vision at a very low moment in the lives of the exiles.

From a structural point of view, this text is among the simplest in the entire book. There are two subunits here: vv. 1-10, which make up the vision proper, and vv. 11-14, which provide an interpretation. The oracle in vv. 11b-14 makes perfect sense apart from the report of the prophet's vision. This does not mean that the vision report is a secondary addition serving to introduce the oracle. There is no compelling reason to deny the vision report to the prophet. Indeed, the vision makes the oracle in vv. 11b-14 all the more dramatic.

37:1-10   The expression "the hand of the LORD was upon me" (v. 1) is a formulaic expression in Ezekiel. It marks a moment when the prophet experienced an extraordinary divine influence in his life (see also 1:3). What we have here is a report of another ecstatic episode in the prophet's life. During this episode the prophet sees a plain with human bones strewn all about. These are bleaching in the sun. In the midst of this overwhelming encounter with the power of death, God commands Ezekiel to speak to the bones and prophesy their regeneration (37:4). Once the prophet speaks the words commanded by God, the bones rejoin and bodies form around them. God commands the prophet to prophesy again, but this time to the four winds (v. 9) to breathe upon the bodies. They obey, and the newly reformed bodies come to life.

In this report of Ezekiel's ecstatic vision, the same Hebrew word *(ruah)* appears in three different senses. Different English words are necessary to render each of these senses. In v. 1 *ruah* is the "Spirit" of the LORD that conveys the prophet into his ecstatic state. In v. 5 *ruah* is breath—the animating principle of human life. In v. 9 *ruah* refers to the "winds" that bring the breath of life to the bodies awaiting their vivification. This is reminiscent of the *ruah* (the wind/breath/Spirit) that hovered over the chaotic waters and infused order and life into inert matter (Gen. 1:2).

In contrast to the account of the creation of Adam in Genesis, here the "four winds" bring the breath of life. In Genesis God does this directly. The use of the same Hebrew word with its wide semantic field provides a thread that weaves together this passage in Hebrew. This is not possible in translation when different English words attempt to convey the precise connotation for each particular use of *ruah*. While this may be helpful to some extent, it means the loss of the rich allusive power of the Hebrew term.

An important line of continuity between the prophet's vision and the account of creation in Gen. 2 is the two-stage regeneration of the dried bones. Ezekiel 37:4-8 records the formation of bodies around the bones, followed by the animation of those bodies in vv. 9-10. In Gen. 2:7 God first forms Adam from the ground and then breathes into his nostrils the breath of life. Ezekiel wants to prove to his fellow exiles that it is the LORD who is about to bring Judah back to life. Here the LORD follows the same pattern as in the creation of Adam.

Significant features of the bones that the prophet saw in his vision were their numbers and aridity (Ezek. 37:2). The people from whom these bones came were dead for a long time. There could be no reasonable hope that the bones could be part of a living body again. At least there was no way that the prophet could see any possibility of that happening. To the exiles Judah's future looked as bleak. The nation, its institutions, its political power were dead. There was nothing to suggest that circumstances would change.

37:11-14 This is precisely the point of the exiles' despairing remark in v. 11b. The prophet learns that they are wrong as God affirms that what Ezekiel saw in his ecstasy was the regeneration, the reanimation, the resurrection of "the whole house of Israel" (v. 11a). The interpretation of the vision takes the form of a disputation with the exiles' resigned evaluation of their plight. For the exiles, the nation is a graveyard full of very dry bones. Life has long since gone out of the bodies that these bones supported. God can cause these bones to rise, receive new flesh, and live.

Unlike in Ezek. 36:16-38, the prophet here offers no explanation for what God is going to do for Israel. There is no apparent motivation; it is a completely gratuitous act on God's part. Restoration when it comes will be the result of a free decision of God. Israel (the dry bones) can only be passive recipients of God's power and benevolence.

In 37:12b-13 the imagery changes somewhat from the valley of dry bones to "graves." These verses may be the work of a later traditionalist adding his reflections to the words of the prophet. These words, more than anything else in this text, have led people to find here not simply an oracle that promises restoration to the exiles but also an even greater miracle—the resurrection of the dead. The image that the prophet saw in his vision was not something about Judah alone. It speaks to a universal human experience. The metaphor of the dry bones arising to life communicated to the people who first heard it, but it was also open to later reinterpretation very easily. Verses 12b-13 represent a first stage in that reinterpretation.

Beginning with ch. 33 we have noticed a dramatic transformation in the prophet. He is no longer simply the proclaimer of human failure and inadequacy. He has become the evangelist of God's power to forgive and restore. The first part of his ministry makes its clear that he is not one to see Judah's future as its own creation. Ezekiel was certain that it was impossible for the people of Israel to make any significant change in their political and religious status. The only way matters could change was for God to act. Moreover, the prophet did not see the prospect of divine action as just a vague possibility. He was certain that God's movement for Israel's benefit was imminent. Once the restoration will take place, Israel and the nations will know that Israel's God is LORD (37:14).

THE TWO STICKS
Ezekiel 37:15-28

After the prophet's ecstatic vision in the previous unit, the prophetic action and its interpretation given here seem prosaic. The point that Ezekiel is trying to make here is obvious. In his vision of restoration, the political separation of what were once the two Israelite kingdoms will be no more. Ezekiel's vision of a "reunited" Israel rests on a theological rather than historical view of the unity of the Israelite people.

The book of Joshua presents Israel's entrance into Canaan as a military conquest accomplished by the militia of a united Israel. Nonetheless, it is unlikely that the acquisition of the land was as simple as that. Various Israelite groups settled in regions of Canaan. Gradually and independently of one another, they became dominant in their respective regions. The book of Judges makes it clear that the tribes engaged in concerted action when under pressure from a common threat. Even so, it was difficult to get more than the tribes immediately affected into action (see Judg. 4–5). It was not until the Philistines posed such a great danger to all the Israelite tribes that they agreed to unite under Saul. David was able to parlay his military success against the Philistines and others into political unity among the tribes and the establishment of a national state. This unity was fragile and did not outlive Solomon his successor.

Ezekiel stands in the tradition that believed that political unity among the tribes under the leadership of a Davidic monarch was the divine will. The traditionalists from the Deuteronomic school were other strong proponents of this notion that there was one God, one people, and one king. This perspective came to dominate the biblical tradition.

169

The structure of this unit is obvious. It is also clear that there was some development from the prophet's original words to the final form of this passage. Following an introductory formula (Ezek. 37:15), there is a description of a symbolic action that the prophet is to do at God's direction (vv. 16-17). This action should elicit questions about its meaning (v. 18). This gives Ezekiel the opportunity to affirm that the unity of Israel is God's will. The prophet believed that when restoration came, God wished *all* the people to participate in it (v. 19).

The theme of the original action and its interpretation was the unity of God's people. This oracle acted as a kind of magnet. It attracted expressions of what later traditionalists saw as components of the prophet's vision for Israel's future: return to the land (v. 21), restoration of the Davidic dynasty (vv. 22, 24), reform of Israel's worship (v. 23), and reestablishment of the everlasting covenant between God and Israel symbolized by the permanence of the temple (vv. 26-28). Beginning with v. 24 there is a subtle but clear shift from the theme of unity to that of *permanence*. The prophet does not look for a "new" covenant as Jeremiah did (Jer. 31:31). Rather, he believes that the covenant between God and Israel is "everlasting" (Ezek. 37:26). The temple was the sign of God's eternal presence in Israel's midst.

Ezekiel's primary concern here was to affirm that the unity of all God's people is a central piece in his vision of Israel's restoration. The prophet's vision went unfulfilled because of the centrifugal forces among the various groups that made up the Israelite people. These were always stronger than the forces that tried to encourage unity. Between the Settlement and the rise of David the tribes developed in two clusters. One was in the north, with Ephraim and Manasseh (the two Joseph tribes) dominant in this region. Another cluster was in the south, with Judah as the dominant force. It was David's political skill, military achievements, and charismatic personality that achieved a type of unity that was but a temporary measure at best. There were always those who saw the divine will in David's rise to power. They believed that the northern tribes' attempt to reassert their independence was rebellion not simply against the Davidic dynasty but against divine rule as well. Despite the prophet's words and various attempts, the

170

divisions between north and south remained. In the NT period, these divisions were clear enough in the animosity between Jew and Samaritan.

In vv. 22 and 24 the prophet uses the term *melek*, "king," to refer to the future ruler of the restored Israel. The term he usually uses for this person is *nasi'*, "prince." See the comments on 46:1-18 for a discussion of these two terms.

THE GOG AND
MAGOG ORACLES
Ezekiel 38:1–39:29

Until now the prophet expressed his vision of Israel's restoration in conventional language. The prophet now moves into the type of idiosyncratic imagery with which he has become identified. These two chapters help to give a distinctive turn to the prophet's words about the place of the Davidic dynasty in his vision of Israel's future. The way Ezekiel spoke about the dynasty and Israel's restoration in previous oracles implies that he believed in restoration as the result of a new Davidic king in Jerusalem who would obey Yahweh—unlike most of the earlier kings (34:23-24; 37:24-25). In these oracles it becomes clear that Ezekiel did not believe that the restoration could occur as the result of what an ordinary king could do. The restoration would have to be the direct work of Yahweh. It will come after Yahweh defeats Gog, the mysterious enemy of Israel, with fire and brimstone from the sky. After this great victory Yahweh will restore Israel to its land and will pour the Spirit upon the people.

In developing these thoughts, the prophet had at his disposal an ancient tradition that envisioned an assault upon Jerusalem by the kings of the nations. According to this tradition such an assault will be futile, since as the home of Yahweh Jerusalem is inviolable (e.g., see Ps. 48). The invasion of Gog will fail, since it attacks the city where Yahweh dwells. Jerusalem fell to the Babylonians precisely because Yahweh left the temple (Ezek. 8–11). The prophet derived this view from the mythic traditions of Canaan that saw the dwelling place of the gods as impregnable. At the basis of the Israelite form of this tradition is the belief that Yahweh founded Zion. The very architecture of Jerusalem reveals the nature of Yahweh. The testimony to

172

Yahweh's presence, then, is not merely belief or theological recital. It is visible and tangible.

Without this mythic background, these two chapters are among the most difficult to appreciate. They have become prey for Christian fundamentalist commentators who have interpreted them as dealing with an invasion of the modern state of Israel by Russia. The basis for this improbable interpretation is the LXX's misreading of the Hebrew word *ro'sh* in 38:2 as a proper name, "Ros." Popularized by the Scofield Reference Bible, fundamentalist belief holds that the prophet was speaking about the modern state of Russia. Besides the geography (Russia is north of Israel), this interpretation has nothing to commend it.

One cause of difficulty in understanding these chapters is that apparently the prophet in part moves beyond the historical circumstances of his day. He uses eschatological language and imagery to speak about the final victory of Yahweh over the forces of evil represented by Gog. This is precisely the way the book of Revelation understands these two chapters (see Rev. 20:8). Because these chapters appear to be an allegory of the last days, dispensationalists who believe that they are living in "the last days" have felt free to "decode" Ezekiel's words. Their interpretations are as bizarre as some of the prophet's imagery. In this scheme, Ezek. 38–39 contain prophecy that is yet unfulfilled. Supposedly they provide a literal description of some future battle involving the modern state of Israel and the Soviet Union.

In reality, this unit is a testimony to Ezekiel's faith in the final victory of Yahweh over the forces of evil. The prophet believed that restoration was coming for Judah, but he also knew that Judah would still be in precarious economic and political circumstances. It would still have to contend with nations as powerful and aggressive as Babylon. To encourage those who were part of the restored Judah, Ezekiel assures them that the eternal conflict between good and evil will end one day. At a time that Yahweh foresees, the powers of evil will make a final and futile effort to subject the good. This gives Yahweh the opportunity to seal the fate of these evil powers definitively. Though the restoration that the prophet foresaw was a monumental achievement of Yahweh's mercy and power, there is still one more such intervention that is yet to come.

The other chapters of Part V deal with the near future, while chs. 38–39 fix their attention on the distant future. Excising these chapters from their present position in the book would make the transition between Parts V and VI smoother than it is, since chs. 40–48 describe a vision of a restored Jerusalem and its cult—a vision that also deals with the immediate future. From the perspective of chronology it appears as if chs. 38–39 are out of place. One interpreter has suggested that this unit may have once served as the conclusion to the book of Ezekiel. The final redactors kept chs. 38–39 in their present position because they are similar to the preceding chapters in form. The concern of these two chapters with the distant future has led some to see chs. 38–39 as another example of proto-apocalyptic in the book of Ezekiel.

In terms of its approach to reality, one may define apocalyptic as "a Judeo-Christian world-view which located the believer in a minority community and gave his life meaning by relating it to the end, soon to come, which would reverse his present status" (William A. Beardslee, "New Testament Apocalyptic in Recent Interpretation," *Interpretation* 25 [1971]: 424). In terms of its literary form, one may define apocalyptic as a revelation given by God through a mediator to a seer about future events (cf. Paul D. Hanson, "Apocalypse, Genre," *Interpreter's Dictionary of the Bible,* Supplement, ed. Keith Crim [Nashville: Abingdon, 1976], 27).

Chapters 38–39 do bear a somewhat superficial likeness to apocalyptic. This results from the presence of some motifs that are usually found in apocalyptic texts. What these chapters describe is a great battle between the forces of good and evil. The move against God's elect will take place at an undefined time in the future (38:8). God will defeat the forces of evil and deliver the elect after cataclysmic occurrences in nature (vv. 19-22). Both Ezekiel and genuine apocalyptic writers emphasize divine sovereignty in fulfilling the God's plan.

What chs. 38–39 lack is the eschatological thrust of apocalyptic. The war against Gog may be a decisive battle and one that Yahweh will fight for Israel. Still, it is not the eschatological conflict that later apocalyptic texts describe. Portions of these chapters refer to

Yahweh's final victory over evil powers in the future, but their position in the book of Ezekiel mutes their effect. In their present context, chs. 38–39 do not lead the reader to imagine the final victory of Yahweh over the forces of evil. They move into a reflection on the restoration of Israel that will take place in the near future. Followed as they are by chs. 40–48, these chapters do not move the reader to envision the end of history, but Israel's new life in the land. While there are strong similarities between this text and later apocalyptic literature, the literary context of chs. 38–39 keep the readers' attention focused on this present world and Israel's immediate future.

This unit begins with an undated messenger formula in 38:1. Within it are four commissions to speak that set off four subunits: 38:2-13; 38:14-23; 39:1-16; and 39:17-29. These neat divisions are the result of the work of redactors. The text is much more complex than it appears at first glance. Without going into a detailed discussion of all the problems here, it is possible to assert that redactors commented on and reworked an original oracle of Ezekiel on Gog. The original oracle comprised most of 38:1-9; 39:1-5 and 17-20.

Here Ezekiel blends two traditions. One is the motif of "the foe from the north," which surfaces several times in Jeremiah (Jer. 1:13-15; 4:6, 15-16; 5:15; 6:22) and Zephaniah (1:14-18). There is, of course, a basis in Israel's experience for this motif since any nation invading the region, except Egypt, would come from the north. A second motif is the Holy War tradition. This motif goes back to the very origins of ancient Israel when it experienced Yahweh as totally sovereign in war. Here Yahweh incites Gog to wage war (Ezek. 38:4) and then utterly defeats him (vv. 19-23). The spoils of victory belong to Yahweh (39:9-10).

38:1-13 After the messenger formula in 38:1, the text begins with Yahweh's commissioning of the prophet to prophesy against a certain "Gog, of the land of Magog" (v. 2). In other oracles, the prophet addresses people well known to everyone (e.g., Egypt's pharaoh), but it is likely that Ezekiel's readers had no more clue to the identity of Gog than we do today. Though there have been many attempts to identify Gog, none is completely convincing. Some interpreters, noticing the absence of any oracle against Babylon and its rulers in the book, suggest that oracles against Gog from Magog fulfill that role. More likely, Gog was a legendary ruler who headed a coalition of threatening powers. These powers came from the edge of the then-known world.

Ezekiel uses the figure of Gog as a vehicle to proclaim his faith in Yahweh, who controls the destiny of all nations and who will one day defeat every evil power. The location of Magog is unknown. It is as legendary as its supposed ruler, though Gen. 10:2 lists it in the Table of Nations. The prophet has already identified Meshech and Tubal (Ezek. 27:13; 32:26) as trading partners of Tyre with a reputation of ferocity. (Identifying Meshech as Moscow and Tubal as Tobolsk is dependent on the LXX's misreading of *nesi' ro'sh* [38:2] as "prince of Ros" and the later identification of "Ros" with Russia. The RSV is correct when it renders this phrase as "chief prince.")

These mysterious names contribute to the sense of anxiety that Ezekiel is trying to arouse in those who hear or read this oracle. Verse 5, which lists others in the coalition, is probably a later addition. The inclusion of Persia dates this addition to a time after Ezekiel. Cush and Put are to the southwest of Israel and would hardly join a coalition from the north. Apparently v. 5 came from someone who did not know geography very well. The coalition members named in v. 6 are more probably partners in a group of invaders from the north. Beth-togarmah was a trading partner of Tyre, according to 27:14. This is the first time the prophet mentions Gomer. It is probable that he refers to the Cimmerian nation that settled in what is now Armenia after defeating the kingdom of Urartu in the 8th cent. B.C.E.

Clearly the prophet does not regard Gog as Yahweh's instrument in punishing Israel; therefore, it is unlikely that Magog is Babylon. Furthermore, in the other oracles against the nations Yahweh punishes individual countries because of crimes committed in the past. Here Yahweh is inciting Gog so that Yahweh could move against Gog and his allies to defeat them completely sometime in the future. The approach to Magog and Gog is unlike that taken with the other nations and rulers who come in for condemnation by the prophet. It appears as if Yahweh wants Gog to attack "the mountains of Israel" (38:8). This attack would provide the opportunity to defeat Gog and the vast army he assembled. The vague expressions "after many days" and "in the latter years" make it clear that Ezekiel is not speaking of something that awaits Israel in the immediate future. The editorial decision to place chs. 38 and 39 in their present context does leave the reader with a different impression.

Beginning with 38:10 there is a clear shift in emphasis. Here Gog is responsible for devising the "evil scheme" to invade Israel. Since the newly-restored Israel will be without significant military power, it is a tempting prize for acquisitive nations like Magog. The effect of vv. 10-13 is to show that Gog's moves against Israel took place because of Gog's inordinate desire for the spoils of war waged against a defenseless opponent. The text transforms Yahweh's judgment against Gog into an act of justice. This stands in tension with vv. 1-9, which have Yahweh inciting Gog to gather his coalition and move against Israel.

Verses 10-13 are the result of a later expansion of the original prophetic text. They soften the image of Yahweh's moving Gog to invade Israel in order to have a pretext to defeat Gog. These verses speak of divine retribution for Gog's cupidity and violence. The place that Gog invades is no longer "the mountains of Israel" (v. 8) but "the center of the earth" (v. 12). (For a discussion of this expression, see the comment on 5:4b-17.) Here this expression is less an ethnocentric assertion and more an attempt to underscore the significance of Gog's invasion of Israel. It is not just another oppression of the weak perpetrated by the strong. It provokes a decisive and world-changing reaction from Yahweh, who springs to Israel's defense by utterly destroying the power of evil to afflict Yahweh's elect.

"The center of the earth" is Jerusalem, which this text conceives as being more than a political capital or religious center. It is the very basis of the world's historical order. Ezekiel 38:10-13 may not be the work of the prophet. These verses are probably from later traditionalists who expanded the words of the prophet for their theological ends. This expansion transforms Yahweh's defeat of Gog into a victory of divine justice whose consequences will be felt not just in Israel but throughout the world.

38:14-23   The second commissioning formula introduces the next subunit, which contains further additions to Ezekiel's original prophecy about Gog. This text combines the two different explanations for Gog's invasion of Israel. According to vv. 14-15 Gog takes the initiative in moving against Israel; according to v. 16b it is Yahweh who "brings" Gog against Israel. The assumption behind the latter assertion is that the conquest of evil is part of Yahweh's plan. Yahweh then takes the initiative to cause the final and decisive battle. This battle will end with Yahweh's complete victory over the powers of evil. The restoration of Israel is no longer part of the vision here. The emphasis is on the cosmic battle between good and evil that the battle between Yahweh and Gog personifies. The cosmic dimensions of the battle are clear from nature's witnessing of Gog's defeat. Another familiar motif here is the earthquake that is the harbinger of Yahweh's victory (v. 19). Palestine is in a geologically unstable area. In antiquity people believed that the power and devastation caused by a severe quake could be nothing but a manifestation of the divine. The final goal of Yahweh's battle against Gog is to insure that all nations will recognize Yahweh's holiness (v. 23).

39:1-5   This is the second strophe of Ezekiel's original oracle against Gog. After the prophet announces the invasion of Israel by Gog in 38:1-9, he receives a second commission from Yahweh (39:1). This time the prophet is to announce Gog's utter defeat. This subunit announces the total destruction of the forces of evil because of divine intervention. Verse 2 recapitulates 38:1-9 briefly: Gog comes from "the uttermost parts of the north" against "the mountains of Israel" under compulsion from Yahweh. Portraying Gog as an archer, Ezekiel asserts that Yahweh will render him ineffective (vv. 3-4a). The usual way of holding a bow was with the left hand, the right being free to take arrows from the quiver. Yahweh will strike both bow and arrow from Gog's hands. The oracle ends with the definitive formula: "for I have spoken, says the Lord GOD" (v. 5). Because the battle takes place on the "mountains of Israel," Yahweh's defeat of Gog underscores the fidelity of Yahweh despite the nation's infidelity. Yahweh's victory will show to all who witness it that God is faithful.

178

39:6-16   This subunit is an expansion of the prophet's original word of doom that announced Gog's defeat. What we have here is a series of expansions of Ezekiel's oracle. Verses 6-8 provide an interpretive framework within which to understand the divine purpose for the defeat of Gog. God has moved definitively against the power of evil so that all peoples will recognize that Yahweh alone is God. The oppression of Israel that is the result of Gog's invasion brings dishonor to Yahweh's name, but Gog's crushing defeat brings about universal recognition of Yahweh's holiness. Verse 8 declares that the "day" of Gog's defeat is the day of judgment that the prophets have announced (38:17).

Beginning with v. 9 there are attempts to provide readers with graphic representations of the consequences of Gog's defeat for the people of Israel. Usually weapons left by a defeated enemy would be added to the victor's cache of arms. After all, there would be other battles to fight. The war against Gog was to be no ordinary war. It will be the final battle, whose conclusion will make armaments obsolete. What the Israelites are to do with the refuse of the battlefield is use it for fuel. That the supply of combustible weapons (spears, shields, javelins) will feed Israel's fires for seven years shows the magnitude and finality of the battle against Gog. One practical effect of Yahweh's victory over Gog is that the Israelites will not have to harvest their forests to provide firewood for a very long time.

Another token of the significance of Yahweh's victory over Gog is found in vv. 11-16, which describe the burial of the fallen soldiers from Gog's coalition. The location of the burial site is not clear. "The sea" of v. 11 could be either the Mediterranean Sea, the Dead Sea, or the Sea of Galilee. In any case, the burial site is unclean and therefore blocks the way of those who would travel through it. This probably explains the name of the valley, the "valley of the Travelers."

The burial is necessary to purify the land that is covered with the corpses of Gog's army destroyed by Yahweh's power. The burial will take place in two stages. First, the whole of Israel must take part in the burial of Gog's army. Their work will take seven months, so immense were Gog's forces and so complete was God's victory. The Israelites contribute nothing to this victory; they merely clean up the battlefield. After this first stage of activity, a group specially appointed for the task goes through the area again and marks where any bones remain. Burial details will follow them to inter the remains. This section concludes with an explanation of the origins of a city-name for a site located near the burial place. The place of burial was *ge hāmon gog*, that is, "the valley of Gog's army." The significance of the wordplay with the name Hamonah is not clear.

39:17-20 Since the previous subunit describes the burial of Gog's annihilated army, the invitation to birds and animals to scavenge among the corpses is out of place. This grisly scene formed the original conclusion to Ezekiel's oracle against Gog. After destroying the invading army of Gog, Yahweh adds a horrid indignity to the fate of the fallen warriors. Their corpses will be a sacrificial meal that birds and animals will consume. It is a stunning reversal. Instead of human beings consuming the animals of sacrifice, it is the animals who consume the human beings sacrificed for Yahweh's honor. Such an ending to the oracle against Gog befits the sometimes bizarre imagery that the prophet uses so effectively.

39:21-29 These last verses of ch. 39 are less a conclusion to the Gog prophecy than a conclusion to the entire section dealing with Judah's restoration that begins in ch. 33. They make no clear allusion to Gog but speak in a general way about Yahweh's mastery of human events—a mastery that God exercises in righteousness. The result of God's righteous deeds is the universal recognition of Yahweh's sovereignty (39:21). It follows then that Israel too will finally recognize Yahweh as its God (v. 22). Verses 23-24 recapitulate what chs. 1–23 have stated about God's motive for the judgment that Israel came to experience in its exile. This judgment exercised before the entire world gives evidence of God's righteousness. The Exile was God's judgment on Israel's infidelity.

The prophet uses the expression "I hid my face" in vv. 23, 24, and 29 and nowhere else in the book. The imagery envisioned here is that Israel will prosper only when God's face is toward Israel. When God is absent from Israel disaster results. No doubt

Ezekiel borrows this imagery from the blessing of Aaron in Num. 6:25-26. It is also common in the Psalms (e.g., Ps. 13:1; 22:24). The final five verses (Ezek. 39:25-29) review the promises of salvation that the prophet announced beginning with ch. 33.

The Hebrew of 39:26 may be translated "they will take upon themselves their shame. . . ." The RSV emends the text to read "they shall forget their shame. . . ." Although this emendation requires no change in the consonantal text of the Hebrew, but only in the Masoretic pointing of a single letter, ancient versions such as the LXX support the Hebrew text as it stands. If one accepts this reading, the theological implication is that restoration does not mean that Israel will ignore the pattern of behavior that led to its downfall. Israel's pardon and new life in the land is not a charter of forgetfulness but a call to rejoice in the power of God's mercy and forgiveness. Israel's exile and its restoration will be a sign to the nations of Yahweh's divine sovereignty. God secures Israel's future by the gift of the divine Spirit (v. 29).

The Gog prophecy is the way that the prophet chose to speak concretely about the salvation that he was proclaiming to Israel on God's behalf. Ezekiel presents it in the form of a final act of the drama that began with Israel's election, reached its critical point in Israel's exile, and now finds its denouement in God's restoration of Israel to its land. This prophecy forms a fitting conclusion to the oracles of salvation that begin in ch. 33. These final verses of ch. 39 serve to conclude not only the Gog prophecy but Ezekiel's entire message of salvation and restoration.

PART VI
THE KINGDOM OF GOD

Ezekiel 40:1–48:35

This concluding section of the book of Ezekiel restates the message of Part V in a new key. Chapters 40–48 replace the conventional prophecies of chs. 33–37 with imagery that is primarily mythic. The prophet chooses to speak about Jerusalem's future by recasting imagery deriving from the ancient Near Eastern mythic motif of the "cosmic mountain." To do so Ezekiel's rhetoric fuses three Israelite versions of that motif: the Eden, Sinai, and Zion traditions (cf. Jon D. Levenson, *Sinai and Zion* [Minneapolis: Winston, 1985]). To appreciate the prophet's rhetoric it is important to remember that his vision does not limit itself to historical possibilities. That is precisely why he uses mythic language.

These chapters also contain some legislation. This made the book of Ezekiel somewhat of a problem for the early rabbis. Ezekiel 40–48 contain the only body of laws that the OT does not place on the lips of Moses. This was one problem. A greater problem was that some laws in these chapters contradict those of the Torah. In effect, Ezekiel becomes "the prophet like Moses" (cf. Deut. 18:15) through whom God reveals the divine will for the restored Judah and Jerusalem. Rabbinic tradition preserves the memory of a Hananiah ben Hezekiah. He kept the book of Ezekiel from being suppressed by studying the apparent contradictions between it and the Torah and explaining them all away. The tradition implies that this was no easy task. Hananiah used three hundred barrels of oil illuminating the room where he studied these texts to clear up the contradictions.

The legislation found in Ezek. 40–48 distinguishes Ezekiel from the other prophets who spoke of Judah's restoration—especially Second Isaiah. Ezekiel provides specific direction to Judah on what must happen to transform his vision into reality. What the prophet describes is the kingdom of God. It is to replace the historical reality that was Israel. The principal focus of the vision is the relationship between God and Israel and the service that Israel owes to its God. This final vision understands that service to be liturgical. The prophet describes what comprises acceptable worship and what Israel's life is to be like as it concentrates *totally* on the liturgical service of its God. Ezekiel wishes the new Israel to replace the historical entity that existed before the Exile and was unable to render proper service to God. That is why the Israel of this prophetic vision bears little resemblance to the Israel of history.

It is difficult to speak of these final chapters of the book of Ezekiel as forming a literary unity. Whatever unity they appear to have is purely artificial. Combining visions and legislation cannot be smooth. The tone and purpose of these two literary forms are very different. The restored community apparently did not regard what has the form of legislation in Ezek. 40–48 as legally binding. The book survived because people saw this legislation as part of the prophet's vision for the future despite how strange this may appear to the contemporary reader.

The visionary passages (e.g., 40:3-37; 40:47–41:4) were the original core of these chapters. Examples of later materials are the liturgical ordinances in 44:3–46:24. Because chs. 40–48 differ so markedly from the rest of the book of Ezekiel, there has been an inclination to ascribe them to someone other than Ezekiel. That conclusion is unnecessary. As occurs with the rest of the book, these final chapters are the result of literary additions to what was an original core of material that came from the prophet himself. What makes the decisions regarding the origin and date of individual passages difficult is that copyists have not been as careful as they could have been in preserving that material in Ezek. 40–48.

These chapters function to bring the book to its conclusion: the restoration of Israel in its land. As such they form a counterpart of chs. 8–11. In Ezek. 8–11 the prophet had a vision of the people's cultic sins and the consequent departure of God from the sanctuary. In Ezek. 40–48 the prophet foresees the return of God's glory to the temple and receives the new cultic regulations. Observance of these not only makes up for past offenses but insures God's continued presence in the sanctuary. From this sanctuary flow waters of blessing and fertility (47:1-12). These blessings come to the new Israel living within its land with the temple at the very center of that land (47:13–48:35).

The contents of these final chapters are a mixture of prophetic vision of the future with some suggestion of how Israel can arrive at that future. There is a blend of idealism and realism here. After all, the prophet could not conceive of Israel's restoration apart from a return to Jerusalem and a restoration of Yahweh's cultus there. The final chapters of the book are the result of years of reflecting on Israel's past, its present circumstances, and its prospects for the future. These reflections lead to an extraordinary vision of the temple. During this vision, the prophet's hopes for the future take concrete shape.

Since Ezekiel was a priest, it is not surprising that this vision centered on the temple. At times readers today may become exasperated with the attention that the prophet gives to matters that they may consider to be of little importance. In spite of this difficulty, it is easy to understand and appreciate the fundamental thrust of these final chapters. They assert that God will dwell in the midst of Israel again and Israel will find its fulfillment in the service of this God. These final chapters of the book represent the crowning achievement of the prophet. Here he directs his fellow exiles' attention toward what lay ahead for those whom the LORD will bring back to Zion. These visions had no effect on the actual rebuilding of the temple and the reordering of the liturgical life of Judah after the return from exile. Nonetheless, they show how deeply the prophet felt about his responsibility to his people at a desperate moment in their life (Moshe Greenberg, "The Design and Themes of Ezekiel's Program of Restoration," *Interpretation* 38 [1984]: 208).

THE TEMPLE VISION
Ezekiel 40:1–42:20

The closest biblical parallel to this vision is that of Moses, to whom God revealed "the pattern of the tabernacle . . . on the mountain" (Exod. 25:9, 40). What happened to Moses on Sinai now happens to Ezekiel on "a very high mountain" (i.e., Zion; 40:2). There is another Mosaic parallel here: Ezekiel can see the land that is the focus of his preaching, but only in a vision. He does not settle there himself. The prophet is to tell the exiles of his vision and give them the laws that God revealed to him while on the mountain. Similarly, Moses did not enter the land to which he was leading the Israelites. He received a glimpse of it just before his death as he gazed on it from Mt. Abarim/Nebo (cf. Num. 27:12-13; Deut. 32:48-52; 34:4).

There are some similarities between the temple of Solomon and the one that the prophet sees in his vision. Still, there are enough differences to lead the reader to conclude that the temple that Ezekiel envisions is different from the one that the Babylonians destroyed. The minute details that Ezekiel gives regarding the new temple may appear to be uninteresting and even irrelevant. It is nonetheless important to remember that these materials became a stimulus for later Jewish mystical speculation. Meditation on these seemingly esoteric details led Jewish mystics to an experience of the divine.

40:1-4 The date of the vision as given in Ezek. 40:1 is 28 April 573. God grants the prophet a type of "parole" from the Exile. Ezekiel receives a vision in which he sees the restoration of the temple and the land. This vision is a foretaste of the final redemption of Jerusalem that still is to come. What the prophet sees, of course, is the divinely established security of Jerusalem, though he does not mention the name of the city. He also saw and told of the fall of the historical Jerusalem in chs. 8–11. What he sees in this vision is the supra-historical Zion that can never fall because it is the dwelling place of Yahweh. The imagery that the prophet uses here has a very long pedigree. "The very high mountain" of 40:2 is reminiscent of ancient Canaanite mythology of the cosmic mountain (cf. Richard J. Clifford, *The Cosmic Mountain in Canaan and the Old Testament.* Harvard Semitic Monographs 4 [Cambridge, Mass.: Harvard University Press, 1972]). As occurs with Ps. 48:1-2, this imagery does not concur with the geography of Jerusalem. Nevertheless, it serves to affirm that Zion is the abode of God.

"The very high mountain" to which the LORD takes Ezekiel is Zion, to be sure. It is also the garden of Eden that the prophet characterizes as "the holy mountain of God" (Ezek. 28:14). Like Zion, Eden is a place where God is immediately accessible. In chs. 28 and 31 Ezekiel describes Eden as a place of great beauty, with astonishing mineral wealth, and with a miraculous river because God's presence blesses Eden. This imagery recurs in chs. 40–48 as the prophet describes the Zion of the future. In the prophet's mythic consciousness Zion and Eden merge. It is perfectly natural then that Ezekiel describes the restored Jerusalem with metaphors whose origin is in the Eden tradition.

As happened in chs. 8–11 (see 8:2), a "guide" accompanies the prophet (40:3). His appearance and his speech make it clear that this guide is not a human being, but a messenger from heaven. God brought Ezekiel to the city so he might see what his guide would show him. He is to relate in turn the content of this vision to Israel. This pattern, a vision interpreted by a heavenly guide for a seer, became a commonplace in the apocalyptic tradition.

40:5-46 The prophet assumes that his readers are familiar with how a temple complex looked. While his original readers may have had the experience that makes this text understandable, this is not so for readers today. Surrounding the temple building itself was an inner courtyard whose boundary was a wall. Surrounding that wall was an outer courtyard also enclosed with a wall. This complex of structures had an east-west orientation. There were gates in the eastern, northern, and southern sides of the outer and inner walls. There were no gates in the western wall, since the temple itself abutted it. The impression with which Ezekiel wants to leave his readers is that the utmost care went into the building of the temple that he saw in his vision. Its exact symmetrical proportions testified to that. Appreciating the prophet's excitement about what he saw is difficult for modern readers, who see the temple as nothing more than a building. For Ezekiel and his readers, the temple was *the* mode of God's presence in the world. The problem in appreciating the prophet's vision, of course, is with us. It made a great impression on those to whom the prophet directed his words.

The basic linear measure used throughout is the cubit. Apparently the cubit used in Palestine, as determined by archaeological research, was the royal cubit of Egypt. It was 52.5 cm. (20.67 in.) in length. The RSV refers to it as "the long cubit." The measurements made by the guide reveal the architectural beauty of the new temple. For Ezekiel this was proof of the building's extraordinary character. It was fit to house the divine presence.

Directional orientation in this vision is no small matter. It is significant that the entrance into the temple is from the east, since it was toward the east that God left the temple according to 11:23. The prophet then faces west and cannot face the east, since there are no western gates. The building described in 41:12 takes up the area to the west of the temple. Ezekiel does not name the function of this building. Walther Zimmerli remarks that its only purpose was to prevent an access to the area behind the temple (*Ezekiel 2*, 378-79). This would eliminate a repetition of the outrage that Ezekiel described in 8:16-18. According to that text a group of elders with their backs to the temple faced the east as they worshipped the sun.

The detail given in the prophet's description of the gates makes it obvious that these were more than entranceways. In antiquity, gates to cities or to important buildings were elaborate structures in their own right. They had small rooms that opened on the passageway. Some had a vestibule on the outside that provided a transition space between the outside world and the structure that one was entering. Ezekiel states that the vestibule of the northern gate was where the slaughter of the animals destined for sacrifice took place (40:40-43). This prescription was important from Ezekiel's perspective, since laymen could not go beyond the outer court to the inner court where the actual sacrifice took place. Similarly they could not slaughter animals destined for sacrifice. The prophet has all this taken care of by Levites, who formed a class between the laity and priests.

The prophet mentions priests for the first time in vv. 45-46. Ezekiel implies that there are two categories of priests. One group deals with the maintenance and security of the temple. The other manages the more important sacrificial worship. Still, both categories of temple personnel are priests. Other texts in the book of Ezekiel do make a clear distinction among the personnel of the temple: 43:19; 44:6-16; 45:4-5; 46:19-21, 24; 48:11.

The possibility of offering God true worship in Solomon's temple no longer existed, for it was in ruins. Ezekiel has a vision of a new temple. He describes how they who enter it gradually arrive at the place of God's holiness as they pass through the gates in the outer and inner walls (see 40:6-16). This gradual introduction to the presence of God impressed the prophet's readers with the sacredness of the temple. They realized the privilege it was for them to stand in its precincts. It was a building whose very dimensions God has determined. This vision reflects the premium that antiquity placed on sacred space and its use.

40:47–41:4　　This section describes the dimensions of the inner court and temple building itself. It had a single entrance and incorporated three rooms arranged in a series that went from the entrance at the eastern end to the innermost room at the western end. The first room is the vestibule (40:48-49). One entered this room by ascending ten steps from the western end of the inner court. The temple then stood on a platform that elevated it above the floor of the inner court. Alongside the entrance of the vestibule were two pillars. The function of these pillars is not clear. Solomon's temple had such pillars (1 Kgs. 7:15-22). The next room is the nave (Ezek. 41:1-2). In Solomon's temple this room housed the altar of incense, the table for the bread of the presence, and ten gold lampstands (1 Kgs. 6:20-22). Here the text does not describe the contents of the room but only its dimensions. Then the guide proceeded to measure the innermost room. Apparently Ezekiel did not enter this room. Perhaps the prophet wished to show his reverence for the most sacred place in the temple. In Solomon's temple this room contained the ark of the covenant. The ark probably was destroyed when the Babylonians razed the old temple. Again, this text does not mention the contents of this "most holy place." Ezekiel provides only its dimensions. The very architecture of the building spoke of its special character. Its holiness would derive not from the accoutrements of liturgical service but from the very presence of God within the new temple.

41:5-15a   This section describes some auxiliary buildings, platforms, and open spaces associated with the temple building as envisioned by Ezekiel. Since the text does not describe a structure that ever existed, those who handed on this text did not always know what precisely the prophet had in mind and so they made "corrections" in the text they received. The result is that this text is very difficult to unravel. A straightforward reading of the text makes little sense, and some changes are necessary. Despite these difficulties, the prophet apparently wanted his readers to be aware of a series of rooms that ran alongside the northern, southern, and western sides of the temple building itself (Ezek. 41:5-9). He did not say what the function of these rooms was, though storage seems a real possibility. There are doors in the northern and southern chambers that open out to the platform on which the temple building stood. Apparently there was also a wall on the northern and southern ends of the platform. These walls served to separate the holy space from the outer courtyards beyond them. To the west of the temple building was another structure (vv. 12-13, 15) that the prophet calls simply "the building." An open space ("the yard" of vv. 14-15) separated it from the western wall of the temple building. The prophet does not specify the function of "the building."

41:15b-26   This passage contains a description of the interior decoration of the temple building. The doors that provided access to the vestibule, nave, and innermost room were double doors that met in the middle. Hinges held each side of the door to the entranceway so that the doors could be folded back against the wall. The walls of the first two rooms had paneling, and designs of palm trees and cherubim adorned them. Ezekiel did not describe the decorations of the innermost room, since he had not entered it. The prophet wishes to impress his readers with the care given to the decoration of the rooms that made up the temple building.

42:1-20   This is the final portion of Ezekiel's tour of the temple complex. Verses 1-14 describe sets of rooms for priests that were on either side of "the building" that was just to the west of the temple building itself. These rooms had several functions. First, they were probably storage areas. Second, they housed the kitchens that prepared the food that came to the priests as part of their dues for service in the temple. Finally, they contained wardrobes for the priestly vestments. After completing their service in the temple, the priests would enter these rooms from the inner court. They were to remove their sacred vestments and change into their secular clothes before leaving the temple area by way of the outer court. This elaborate procedure was necessary to avoid profaning the temple or endangering the area outside the temple with the sacred vestments. In the final part of the vision (vv. 15-20), Ezekiel's guide takes his last measurement. The entire temple complex is five hundred cubits square. The symmetry is perfect. The entire complex is set off by a wall that serves to separate the sacred from the profane.

This painfully detailed description of the ideal temple, a vision of which God granted the prophet, underscores the importance of the new temple. It was of course the means by which God's presence in the world becomes tangible. For Ezekiel God's presence in the temple was not a casual affair; it was something serious. The proper response of someone in the presence of God is awe. The elaborate and beautiful architecture of the temple is to inspire that awe in Israel. Yet throughout this description of the prophet's vision there has been no reference to the actual presence of God in the temple. The buildings, despite their beauty, symmetry, and splendor, remain nothing more than buildings. In the next section Ezekiel will describe the return of God to the sanctuary.

THE RETURN
OF GOD'S GLORY
Ezekiel 43:1-12

The vision of the temple and its dimensions have prepared the reader for the reentry of God's glory, which had departed the temple in an act of judgment on Israel's sins (chs. 10–11). The return of God's glory will be the ultimate sign of Israel's restoration. The guide brings Ezekiel to the eastern gate. The experience is overwhelming (43:3). What is most significant is that the prophet hears the voice of God assuring him that the glory of God will remain "in the midst of the people of Israel for ever" (v. 7). The first seven verses of this chapter are the core of chs. 40–48: the coming of the invisible God to the new temple marks the end of the Exile and the beginning of a new relationship between Yahweh and Israel.

These verses announce the arrival of the divine presence of God at the new temple. They mark the climactic moment in the prophet's vision of Jerusalem's restoration: "the glory of the LORD" has entered the temple (43:4). It is important to recognize that the significance of the temple lies not in its use as a place of worship. The temple is the place where the presence of God abides. Once Yahweh returns to the temple the restoration is complete. These words are the most significant that the prophet has uttered, for they give ultimate meaning to his entire life and ministry. Verses 1-5 function as God's rededication of the temple. Thus this unit is the complement to chs. 8–11, which announced Yahweh's abandonment of the old, defiled sanctuary before its destruction by the Babylonians. According to 11:22-23, the abominations practiced as part of the old temple's ritual led to the departure of God's glory out of the eastern gate. Now in 43:2-4 that same glory returns from the same direction by which it left (40:6).

Ezekiel 43:9 alludes to the cultic sins that made the departure of God's glory necessary.

Verses 6-9 issue a warning against desecrating the place of God's presence by "idolatry" or by ignoring the sacredness of the site. In particular they warn against placing the burial place of the kings too near the temple and thus defiling it. People in ancient Israel believed that the dead were a source of ritual impurity (Num. 5:2-4; 19:11-13). All contact with the dead was to be avoided. While priests could bury members of their immediate families, the high priest was forbidden to bury his parents in order to insure his ritual purity (Lev. 21:11-12). Israel now had to be careful to avoid the type of behavior that scorned the holiness that belonged to the temple because of God's presence there.

The prophet's vision of God's glory returning to the temple is a summons to commitment and loyalty (Ezek. 43:10-12). Ezekiel assures Israel that fidelity to God is not in vain, since his words speak of a new relationship between God and Israel. The prophet foresees a new order in which Israel's obedience will not be a matter of supreme human effort; it will be a natural response. The sentiments expressed in vv. 10-12 serve to build a bridge between the visions of chs. 40–48 and the cultic legislation found there. Ezekiel implies that Israel's future is dependent upon the fulfillment of the cultic laws in the temple which reflect the divine plan that he had seen and which he is sharing with his readers. The cultic ordinances that follow in the next section propose to prevent Israel from repeating the sins that led to God's departure from the old temple.

TEMPLE LEGISLATION
Ezekiel 43:13–46:24

In chs. 40–42 the prophet described a spectacular building that was not in use. It could not fulfill its purpose without the presence of God filling the rooms designed to house God's glory. Now that God has returned to the temple (43:1-12), it is necessary for the prophet to provide ordinances that will regulate the temple's use. The center of the temple complex is the altar, so the prophet begins with it. The legislation that follows sets forth what Israel must do to begin the immediate use of the altar.

43:13-17 Although this text deals with the altar of burnt offerings, as does the following section (43:18-27), its impersonal form makes it unlike what follows. Its purpose is hard to determine. The altar's stepped arrangement runs contrary to Exod. 20:25-26. The place where the sacrifice was to be offered was large but not very accessible, so the legislation is not very practical. The requirement that the steps of the altar face east (Ezek. 43:17) probably intends to avoid the misdirected worship of 8:16. The altar itself incorporated three large blocks: the two lower stones formed the pedestal, and the third was the surface for offering the sacrifice. Each block was smaller than the one beneath it. This made for the stepped appearance. There were four "horns" protruding from the top stone. Though the text does not mention it, the altar would have been sunk into a trench. This would allow the blood of victims to flow into the trench without staining the surface of the platform. The structure was 3.6 m. (12 ft.) high, and the priests reached it by way of stairs on its eastern side. While servicing the altar, then, the priests would be facing toward the west—in the direction of the temple building. The altar symbolized not only the distance that existed between God and human beings but also the means to overcome that distance.

43:18-27 Ezekiel gives these liturgical instructions the form of a prophecy with the messenger formula of v. 18: "Son of man, thus says the Lord GOD. . . ." Apart from the framework that gives this section the appearance of an oracle, what remains is legislation for a ritual for consecrating the altar of burnt offerings. The body of the oracle describes the steps in the process of consecration as in Exod. 29:36-37; 40:9-11; and Lev. 16:18-19. The person addressed by the oracle is, of course, Ezekiel. This is comparable to the way Moses functions in the legislation in the Pentateuch: the prophet is to carry out the consecration. Here again this passage appears to portray Ezekiel as the new Moses (cf. Deut. 18:15). The prophet also speaks of a new exodus, a new covenant, a new allocation of the land. Further, like Moses, he sees the new promised land from a distance. At the very least, what this text presents is a prophet who opens the way for a renewed worship by a new people of God. Israel's restoration then receives prophetic warrant. It is according to the word of God. The departures from pentateuchal legislation, though embarrassing to the early rabbis, should not be the focus of the reader's attention. What is important is that Israel again could offer proper worship because the LORD will say then "I will accept you" (Ezek. 43:27).

A ritual of consecration is necessary to transfer the altar from the realm of the profane into that of the sacred. Once the transfer has taken place, the altar is fit for divine service so that similar rituals can take place that transfer persons from the sphere of the sinful to that of the holy. Once this happens it is possible for the people to share the peace offering with God. God receives the prescribed portion of the offering from the altar; the people receive theirs in the outer court. The ritual of consecration was so elaborate because of the unique function of the altar. At the altar the restoration and maintenance of the people's relationship with God took place. Moreover, the people of antiquity did not have as casual an approach to the divine as Westerners do today. It was no small matter to approach God at the altar to seek forgiveness.

197

44:1-3   The term "sanctuary" here and in most of what follows in the book of Ezekiel refers to the temple complex and not the temple building alone. Because God's presence in the temple is permanent, the gate by which the divine glory reentered the temple never needs to be open again. The gate here is a structure containing several rooms, one of which the prince may use while eating ritual meals (44:3). That the prince can use rooms within the gate is not an exception to the prescription that the gate be sealed, since the gate no longer functions as a means to enter the temple area. This sealing of the gate is another way Ezekiel asserts that the coming restoration of Jerusalem is the final and complete one. The closure of the gate then is not a menacing symbol but an encouraging one. Behind this symbol is the idea that there should be royal doors reserved exclusively for the passage of the great king. Since Yahweh entered the temple through this gate, it is unseemly that others should use it. Since God will never leave the temple again, the gate will remain closed.

44:4-5   An earlier text (43:11) mentions the entrances and exits to the temple. These verses mention the entrances to introduce the requirements for admission in the following section and in 46:1-10. Ezekiel does not ignore the need to specify such requirements. The prophet firmly believes in the restoration that God will cause. Still, he cannot ignore the folly that led to the destruction of the temple and the departure of the divine presence. The need for holiness in those who will participate in the temple's rituals derives from these painful memories.

44:6-16   This text makes a clear distinction between those of the temple personnel who are concerned with sacrifice and those who are not. The former are priests; the latter are Levites. According to this passage, the existence of this two-tier clergy is one consequence of the infidelity of the Levites, the group that makes up the lower clergy. In this text there is a difference between the higher and lower caste of those who serve in the temple. Ezekiel 40:45-46a makes no such distinction. It is probable that 44:6-16 represents a development in the thought of those who treasured and transmitted the words of Ezekiel. His focus on the prerogatives of the Zadokite priests contained the seeds of this more radical distinction between these priests and the Levites.

This text explains that the Levites' subservient status results from an act of infidelity in which the descendants of Zadok took no part. The Chronicler preserves a genealogy of Zadok that makes him a descendant of Aaron's son Eleazar (1 Chr. 6:3-8). It was Eleazar's son Phineas to whom God promised "the covenant of a perpetual priesthood" because of the fidelity he showed in a time of rebellion (Num. 25:6-13). Some scholars consider this genealogy to be little more than an attempt to legitimate the priesthood of the Jerusalem temple. According to their reconstruction of the history of ancient Israel's priesthood, Zadok became a priest of Yahweh once David incorporated Jerusalem into his Israelite kingdom. Previously Zadok was priest-king or at least high priest of the Jebusite Jerusalem. It is improbable that those who are responsible for Ezek. 44:6-16 believed that the priests of their day were descendants of one who was not an Israelite.

The tradition of a rebellion of the non-Zadokite Levites stands in sharp contrast to the tradition preserved in Exod. 32:25-29. This text is the Zadokite theology of Ezek. 44 in reverse! In Exod. 32 it is the Levites who are loyal and steadfast while Aaron fashions the golden calf. Here the ancestor of the Jerusalem priests is guilty of introducing idolatry. It was the Levites who purged Israel of the idolaters. Clearly there was some conflict over control of the Jerusalem temple. The Deuteronomist does not favor either side to the exclusion of the other. Deuteronomy asserts the equivalence of Levite and priest (Deut. 18:6-8). Though Ezek. 40:45-46a seemed to share that perspective, 44:6-16 favors the claims of the Zadokites. This is the only OT text in which Zadok appears as the ancestor of legitimate priests of the Jerusalem temple.

Reconstructing the history of ancient Israel's priesthood is a task beyond the scope of this commentary. It is enough to say that the shape of this history is not entirely clear. What is obvious here is that this text assumes that the temple will be served by two groups. The Zadokites will serve the altar. In addition, there will be a lower class of liturgical personnel, the Levites, who serve as helpers to the priests. The lower status of the Levites is a consequence of their failure to remain loyal to Yahweh. What we see here is probably the final stages of a conflict between the priests of the Jerusalem temple and the priests of the "high places," the local shrines that were no longer legitimate places for worship (cf. Paul D. Hanson, *The People Called: The Growth of Community in the Bible* [San Francisco: Harper & Row, 1986], 253-268).

This text uses the language of an old pentateuchal ruling (Num. 18:1-7, 22-23) to reach a very different conclusion. There are several links between these two texts. Both establish a priestly and levitical hierarchy to insure that only proper groups enter the temple and perform the rituals. In both texts a crisis precedes the establishment of the hierarchy. Numbers 18 is the result of the rebellion of Korah and the fear of the Israelites to approach the tabernacle. Ezekiel 44 is the result of Israel's idolatry (vv. 9-12). There are important differences between the two texts. According to Num. 18 the priests are responsible for the profanation of the shrine (Num. 18:1). The Levites are to serve the priests, take charge of the shrine, and insure that no unauthorized persons enter the shrine. Ezekiel 44 blames the laity for allowing foreigners into the temple (vv. 6-7) and for appointing some of them to serve in the temple (v. 8). The prophet condemns certain Levites who abetted those responsible for these abuses. Ezekiel then prohibits any layperson from offering sacrifice. The priesthood is not open to the Levites. Only "the sons of Zadok" may be priests.

One way to explain this intention of this passage is to see it as the outcome of conflict between priests and Levites. Supposedly Ezekiel takes the side of the priests. What is probably at stake here is not the resolution of a political conflict between these two groups. The main concern is the prophet's vision of a liturgy whose holiness far surpasses that of the present. Ezekiel's strict perspective on ritual holiness did not find acceptance in postexilic Judaism, which adopted the less strict rules found in the Pentateuch.

What seems a too scrupulous concern for the ritual purity of the ministers of worship in the temple had as its goal the inculcation of a scrupulous concern by the worshipping community for ethical purity as prerequisite for worship. Israel's past failures were moral ones. By making the service of God in the temple a sacred and momentous act, the prophet was trying to instill an attitude of reverence and awe to impress those who would worship an all-holy God with the need to live a holy life.

44:17-31   This section is a pastiche of materials taken from the laws in Leviticus that stipulate the requirements of the holiness appropriate to priests: Ezek. 44:17-19 = Lev. 6:10-11; Ezek. 44:20 = Lev. 21:5; Ezek. 44:21 = Lev. 10:9; Ezek. 44:22 = 21:7; Ezek. 44:23-24 = Lev. 10:10-11; and Ezek. 44:25-27 = Lev. 21:1-3. The case is different for Ezek. 44:28, which explains that God is the inheritance of the Levites and therefore there is no inheritance of land for them. Here the prophet repeats an old theological justification for a social practice whose origins are not certain. The prophet repeats the traditional explanation for the landless condition of the Levites: the Levites have God as their inheritance (Num. 18:20; Deut. 10:9; 18:2; Josh. 13:33). In making provisions for the priests who are without any agricultural holdings (Ezek. 44:29-31), Ezekiel makes use of the priestly tradition again: Lev. 2:3, 10; 6:23, 26, 29; 7:6, 31-35; Num. 18:13, 18-20. The prophet emphasizes continuity between the old order and the new vision that God had granted him. The underlying assumption is that this time the priests will carry out the divine will.

45:1-9   The division of the land among the various tribes is the subject of Ezek. 47–48. Here the text deals with only one part of the land: the location of the temple and the holy city. This land belongs directly to the LORD, while the rest of the land is the inheritance of the tribes. The land belonging to God directly is approximately 166 square kilometers (64 sq. mi.). Three parts comprise this area. The northernmost portion comprising some 65 square kilometers (25 sq. mi.) belonged to the Levites. Next came a strip of the same size that was available to the priests. It also was the site of the sanctuary. The last strip, which was about 34 square kilometers (13 sq. mi.), was for the city itself. The land to the east and west of this sacral land was for the prince. The rest of the land of Israel belonged to the tribes.

This section deals more specifically with the question of land occupied by priests and Levites. According to 45:4, the land that priests have is not "an inheritance" like that of the other tribes.

It is simply a place to build their homes and to keep their livestock. The situation with the Levites is different. They own land. Their holdings are expansive enough to build cities (v. 5). The Levites have this land because in the new order it is only the priests who will offer sacrifice and have God as their "inheritance." The future that the prophet envisions is, in part, continuous with past practices, but it also involves a new pattern. This break with the past is necessary because of the more stringent requirements of holiness that come with the restored temple and its ministers.

While on the subject of land, Ezekiel asserts that the holiness of the restored Israel will not permit the type of land-grabbing through which the powerful were able to dispossess the powerless (vv. 8b-9). The prophet will reassert this in 46:18. The new order that the prophet foresees for his people has no room for the abuse of power like that described in 1 Kgs. 21. That text shows how royal and judicial power conspired to divest Naboth, who was unwilling to give up his family inheritance to King Ahab. The royal house has a role in the prophet's vision of the restored Israel, but it will be a royal house committed to justice.

Anyone familiar with the topography of the region recognizes that Ezekiel's plan for the division of the land is unrealistic. The prophet shows more concern for symmetry than he does for the realities of geography. The prophet's idealism has an important pedagogical function. Israel got into difficulties precisely because it ignored God. Here the prophet insists that God be at the "center" of things. The holiness that God requires of Israel makes it essential that Israel never forget God. The location of the sanctuary in the land that Israel again will come to possess is a living symbol of the central role that Yahweh is to have in Israel's life.

45:10-17 The emphasis on justice at the end of the previous section leads to an insistence on just weights and measures. Unfortunately, it offers no practical suggestions about how to achieve this goal. It was the responsibility of the "prince" to establish and maintain just standards. The failure of the monarchy to do this before the fall of Jerusalem was the principal deficiency of the earlier system. It is impossible for a society to flourish when injustice thrives. This leads the prophet into a discussion of a tax that will provide for regular sacrifices. The prince is responsible for insuring that funds collected are at the disposal of those who are responsible for offering the sacrifice. Ezekiel does not specify how the prince is to collect the tax. The origin of this text is the prophet's idealism and not lived experience. It is vague on practical specifics, yet the assumption behind these prescriptions is as old as Israel. The capacity to offer a gift to God is a consequence of God's prior gifts. The prophet calls Israel to return just a portion of what God has already given it. This is an act of recognition by which Israel admits that what it has comes from God. The offerings that Israel made for the temple were to be its way of acknowledging that it acquired nothing by its own initiative and strength.

When the restoration took place there was no prince to fulfill this responsibility. The temple had no endowed lands or estates to underwrite the expenses of prescribed sacrifices. One approach taken by the Jewish community during Nehemiah's day was a voluntary tax earmarked for the temple sacrifices (Neh. 10:32-33). During the Greek period, the Seleucid rulers of Judah bore the expense of supporting the temple sacrifices as the ruler's privilege (cf. 2 Macc. 3:1-13).

45:18-25 This unit deals with two subjects: an annual ritual for the purification of the sanctuary (Ezek. 45:18-20) and the rituals connected with the major festivals (vv. 21-25). The prophet's treatment of the major festivals is fragmentary. He does not even mention Pentecost (the Feast of Weeks or Shabu'ot). Verse 25 deals with the Feast of Booths without mentioning it by name. Only the Feast of Passover/Unleavened Bread receives any extensive treatment. There are considerable differences between Ezekiel's ordinances and the pentateuchal laws (Num. 28–29). The pentateuchal version eventually prevailed in early Judaism. A most notable difference between the two calendars is the Day of Atonement that Lev. 16 describes. The observance of this day takes place on the tenth day of the seventh month. The prophet does provide for the expiatory rites connected with Leviticus' Day of Atonement by the rites of the first and seventh days of the first month (Ezek. 45:18-20). Despite the differences between the two calendars, they share a common assumption. The people have a responsibility for con-

203

tributing to the maintenance of the public worship of God. Ezekiel also assumes that one of the prince's duties is to administer the contributions made by the people.

46:1-18 Throughout his discussion of the minor festivals (46:1-15) the prophet refers to "the prince," and in vv. 16-18 he deals with the prince's rights regarding the land. Ezekiel's vision of a new Zion includes a human ruler. The prophet has already spoken of an inner transformation of human nature that will exchange people's "heart of stone" for a "heart of flesh." He nonetheless sees a role for an external structure: the monarchy.

The term that Ezekiel uses for the human ruler in his visionary Zion is *nasi'*, which the RSV translates as "prince." The prophet has used this word several times when speaking of the Davidic head of state: 7:27; 12:10, 12; 19:1; 21:30; 34:24. In 7:27 he uses it in parallel with *melek,* the word for "king." Ezekiel's preference of *nasi'* is deliberate. It probably reflects the prophet's hesitancy to endorse the kind of monarchy that produced the abuses that marred the Davidic dynasty. Most of the times *nasi'* appears outside the book of Ezekiel it surfaces in the Pentateuch. Perhaps by using this term to designate the human ruler of the community Ezekiel wished to place the monarchy under the aegis of the covenant of Sinai. Ezekiel does not discard the Judahite monarchy; he refashions it. The prophet had a place for a monarch but not for the monarchy, that is, the social, political, and economic system associated with the king. Ezekiel states that the prince's chief function is to be the patron of the liturgy. The *nasi'* is to devote himself entirely to the liturgy, just as Deuteronomy's king is to devote himself entirely to the study of the Law (Deut. 17:18-20). In effect, the *nasi'* acts as a high priest, an official that does not appear in the book of Ezekiel.

In other prophetic traditions the royal figure plays a more central role as the agent of God's deliverance of Israel (cf. Isa. 9:2-7; 11:1-9). Messianism, the belief in the future coming of an ideal royal figure, developed in Judaism when it became clear that the Persians would not allow the restoration of Judah's native monarchy. The restoration of the monarchy became part of early Judaism's vision of the future. As it developed, messianism became a more complex set of beliefs.

While the Davidic figure remained prominent, the people of Qumran looked for a priestly messiah as well. The Samaritans hoped for a Moses-like "restorer." The NT affirms that Jesus was the fulfillment of the messianic expectations that revolved around both David (Matt. 16:13-19; 21:1-11; Rom. 1:3-4) and the priestly figure (Heb. 1:1-5; 2:14-18; 4:14-16; 6:19–7:3; Rom. 8:31-34). In his presentation of Jesus' Sermon on the Mount, Matthew (Matt. 5–7) consciously portrays Jesus as a second Moses.

Ezekiel 46:6 and 7 form one of the texts that made it difficult for the rabbis to accept the book of Ezekiel as inspired. This text contradicts the laws of the Pentateuch. Here the offering specified for the new moon is different from that specified by Num. 28:11. Ezekiel does not offer any explanation for the differences between his legislation and that of the Pentateuch. There was probably no polemical interest behind these differences. What the prophet wanted to emphasize is the role of the prince in these matters. "When they go in, the prince shall go in with them" (Ezek. 46:10) underscores the role of the prince in the restored community. He is *with* the people as they worship God. His role in the community is not so much political as it is liturgical. His prominent role in worship derives not from any priestly status but from his position as representative of the people. Israel's kings probably had more freedom in the worship of the Jerusalem temple than Ezekiel allows his *nasi'*. David not only brought the ark to Jerusalem, he danced before it (2 Sam. 6:14). His sons were priests (2 Sam. 8:18b). Solomon officiated at the dedication of the temple (1 Kgs. 8).

The gates of the temple are another subject in this unit. The eastern gate has a special status, since it is the one which God used upon reentering the sanctuary. Since the outer eastern gate is not open and there is no western gate, this section describes how the people are to use the northern and southern gates to enter and leave the temple.

In Ezek. 46:16-18 there is a shift from the liturgical role of the prince to his property rights. Though such a shift is abrupt, the prophet includes this topic to forestall what had been a serious problem in the preexilic period. Ezekiel does not want a repetition in the restored community of the circumstances that led to the breakdown of Israelite society earlier. The prophet did not want royal property to grow at the expense of ordinary citizens. Ezekiel specifically forbids the prince from giving the property of citizens to his family and friends. If the prince wishes to make a gift of land to anyone, that land must come from his own holdings.

Ancient Israel's economic, political, and social system had as its foundation the ownership of land. The land provided people with economic support and the means to contribute to the proper worship of God. While the prince too would have his land, Ezekiel knew that Israel had to be warned about royal prerogatives in this regard. He wanted to help Israel avoid falling into the pattern of royal greed that was endemic before the fall of Jerusalem. This greed contributed to the breakdown of Israel's social structure. Though the prophet's vision of Israel's future is often idealistic, here he is realistic. He recognized the potential for corruption that came with the monarchic system.

This collection of liturgical regulations deals with two moments in Israel's worship: its daily worship and the festal worship. There were to be special times of worship accenting God's redemptive acts on Israel's behalf. There was also to be worship in the temple each day. Maintaining a rhythm between these two moments was essential to the prophet's vision of the restored temple.

46:19-24 Each of the two subunits (vv. 19-20 and 21-24) that make up this section describe similar installations in the temple which the priests use to process the food that the Israelites offer as sacrifices. The purpose of this legislation is to protect the holiness of the temple by isolating certain activity that must go on in its confines. The people need to be kept away from such activity. The holiness of God in the temple is so concentrated that any unauthorized contact with it can lead to death.

It is important to remember that much of what the people were to offer in sacrifice was later eaten by priests and people. This feature of Israelite worship shows how concretely the people expressed their belief that God has made provision for the most basic of bodily needs: the need for food. It also symbolizes the union between God and Israel. The worship that went on in the temple was not confined to word and gesture. It included the eating and the experience of fellowship that comes from sharing a meal.

206

LAND OUTSIDE THE TEMPLE
Ezekiel 47:1–48:35

47:1-12 After dealing since 44:4 in legislation for the restored temple, Ezekiel resumes recounting the vision he had of the temple and its environs. Here he speaks of a river that flows from the temple. Ezekiel shifts his emphasis from the life-threatening holiness of God in the temple to the life-enhancing holiness of God that flows from the temple. The river that flows from the temple will make the salt-saturated Dead Sea into a fresh water lake full of fish. God's power changes a place of death into a place of life.

The prophet uses what was, even for him, ancient Canaanite imagery: the motif of the sacred stream. Canaanite epics spoke of the god El's dwelling at the source of two rivers. Isaiah makes use of that same imagery in speaking of a fabulous stream that gushes forth at Zion (Isa. 8:6-7; 33:20-24). When Ezekiel speaks of the restored Zion he includes the tradition that speaks of the miraculous stream of Zion. What Isaiah mentions without much elaboration, Ezekiel develops in great detail. The return of God to the temple is what brings healing to the land. From the door of the temple flow streams that provide sustenance for the fish and plants that derive their life from them. Ezekiel uses this imagery to affirm that the new temple, like the old, will be a font of blessing for Israel. This Edenic symbolism shows the depth of yearning for complete restoration that gripped the prophet. It also shows how powerful were these images of the past for Ezekiel as he described his vision of Israel's future.

The prophet's vision of a restored Israel, with God at the center of the land and its people, led him to speak of Israel's future with surprising enthusiasm. He maintained that the transformation that would take place in Israel's life would be akin to the transformation

207

of the briny waters of the Dead Sea into the sweet water that would support life in it and around it. The prophet believed that, with God at the center of Israel's life, this transformation was sure to happen. To insure this, Ezekiel here focuses his attention on the temple and its worship. He does not hesitate to concern himself with the smallest detail of that worship. He is certain that a people dedicated to serving God in the temple would place God at the center of its life. With God at the center of Israel's life, a transformation that is miraculous beyond telling will take place.

47:13-20 Very little of the legislation of Ezek. 40–48 had a discernible influence on the practical decisions that had to be made by the community during the Restoration. What we have in these chapters is not a body of functional legislation. It is an eschatological vision: the shape of the prophet's hope for an Israel restored not to its former glory but to a firm and lasting relationship to God. In what follows in the rest of the book, Ezekiel provides Israel with his vision of a new allotment of the land. He begins with a description of the borders of Israel. Ezekiel 47:15-20 delineate the borders of Canaan. Numbers 34:1-12 gives a similar description of these borders. A strong admonition to rid the region of corrupting Canaanite practices precedes that description (Num. 33:50-56). The prophet gives no such admonition because from his perspective the Canaanites were not the problem. Similarly, Ezekiel makes no allusion to the monarchy in setting up these borders and in making the tribal allotments that follow in Ezek. 48:1-29. The principal role for the prince in Ezekiel is cultic rather than political.

47:21-23 The Pentateuch prescribes humane treatment for the aliens living in Israel (cf. Exod. 22:21; 23:9; Lev. 19:10, 33-34; 23:22; Deut. 14:29; 24:14-15, 17-22). Such treatment is a moral obligation that derives from Israel's experience as aliens in Egypt. Ezekiel goes far beyond the Torah's legislation. The prophet insists on the integration of aliens into Israelite society by allowing them to own land. Earlier legislation treated aliens as objects of charity who could be nothing else since they could not own land in what was an agricultural economy. Ezekiel's vision fully integrates the alien into the Israelite economic system. According to Deuteronomy, the holiness of Israel distinguishes it from all other peoples. Apparently, Ezekiel sees that holiness derives from the land. All those who live on the land—whether Israelite or not— are holy and are to enjoy the protection afforded by the covenant.

48:1-29 By Ezekiel's time several old Israelite tribes no longer existed as definable entities. Nonetheless, when the prophet speaks of reallocating the land the pattern he follows is similar to that in Josh. 13–21. Just as there will be a new exodus (Ezek. 20:32- 38) and a new covenant (34:23-30; 37:21-28), there will be a new allotment of the land tribe-by-tribe. There are some important differences in Ezekiel's scheme.

First, the three Transjordanian tribes (Reuben, Gad, and half of Manasseh) no longer occupy land east of the Jordan. Earlier traditions recognize occupation east of the Jordan as an anomaly (Num. 32; Josh. 22). Ezekiel corrects this by granting these tribes territory west of the Jordan that, historically, had never been theirs. Second, the order of the allotments is also not according to any historical precedent. It is the product of genuine idealism. The Levites are no longer scattered in cities throughout the land (Josh. 21), but live in the region immediately surrounding the temple (Ezek. 48:13-14). Immediately surrounding the Levites are Judah to the north and Benjamin to the south. This is a reversal of the historical situation. Perhaps this is Ezekiel's way of saying that the traditional animosity between the northern tribes and the house of David will not be a part of the future he is describing. The tribe of Benjamin gave Israel Saul, and Judah gave Israel David. The location of these tribes next to Levi shows the importance of the "prince" in the worship of Yahweh.

There is more north-south balance to the tribes. Two of the tribes who had been in the north, Zebulun and Issachar, will come south to join Benjamin, Simeon, and Gad. This attempt at getting geographical balance in the allotments serves to place the temple at the center of the land as befits the "center of the earth" (38:12). A central feature of the prophet's vision was its intention to isolate the temple. Only the Zadokite priests occupy the territory immediately surrounding the temple (see 44:6-31). The holiness of the central region may be the reason behind the more central location given to the tribes descended from Jacob's wives, Leah and Rachel.

The tribes whose matriarchs were the servant girls, Bilhah and Zilpah, are on the fringes of Israelite territory.

There is no evidence that there was any attempt to realign any tribal territories during the actual restoration. What we have here is a product of Ezekiel's idealism. It does have some precedent in the tradition that described the arrangement of the camp in the wilderness (Num. 2; 3:21-29). The tent of meeting was in the middle of the camp. Immediately surrounding it was the encampment of levitical clans. The other tribes camped on the perimeter of the camp—three tribes on each of the four sides of the camp.

Ezekiel makes certain that the royal enclave and the territory of Judah are separate from the area of the temple. Solomon's temple was a royal chapel attached to the area of the palace. The prophet considered it unseemly that the kings shared a common wall with the temple (Ezek. 43:8). Between Judah and the temple are the Levites and the Zadokite priests. Perhaps this is the prophet's way of insisting that Yahweh's rule replaces that of the Davidic dynasty.

48:30-35 This final section of the book of Ezekiel stands in tension with what immediately precedes it. In 48:10 the temple was in the priestly territory and the "city" belonged to a separate strip of land (vv. 15-19). Here apparently the text assumes that the temple is both separate from and a part of the city. Each side of the city has three gates named in honor of the ancestors of the tribes. The tribes descended from Leah, the first of Jacob's two wives, have the gates on the north and south named after them. The two sons of Rachel are honored by having the eastern gates named after them. (The temple was to face the east [43:1-5; 44:1-3; 46:1-3], and the "glory" of God entered the temple by the eastern gate [43:2].)

The one remaining eastern gate is named after Dan. The gates on the west side of the city honor the tribes descended from the other sons born to Jacob's two servant girls. The name of the temple city (formerly Jerusalem) is *Yahweh shammah* ("the LORD is there"). Perhaps this new name for Jerusalem is necessary because the prophet once stated that the city's name was "polluted" (22:5). Ezekiel mentions no other city as he describes the restored land of Israel. Jerusalem played too central a role in the prophet's vision of the future to be ignored.

210

EPILOGUE

We conclude our study of the book of Ezekiel with no illusions.
We have not solved every problem connected with its interpretation; we have not even raised every problem. What we have tried
to do is to come to some appreciation of the work of a man who
so believed in the future of his people that he could not see the
Exile as the final chapter in the life of Israel. Ezekiel was also a
man who keenly felt God's absence despite the visions and other
experiences with which this book abounds. The book this man
composed is a monument to his faith in a future in which God
would be at the very center of Israel's life. This would insure
Israel's future.

The book of Ezekiel is a book of extremes. The prophet is
harsh and pitiless when speaking of God's judgment on a sinful
Israel; he is kind and sympathetic when he speaks of Israel's
restoration. His oracles of judgment are total darkness and his
oracles of salvation total light. He can hurt without any remorse
and heal with great compassion. He speaks most effectively about
the shame of Israel's sin and most eloquently about the grandeur
of its salvation. He describes almost dispassionately the departure
of God's glory from the temple. He rejoices in his vision of the
return of that glory to a new temple that will arise in the midst
of a new people.

The book of Ezekiel is a testament of the imagination of a
prophet without equal. No one who reads the book can come
away without an experience of judgment and redemption. The
prophet's imagination conjured up visions of a chariot of fire and
a field strewn with dry bones. These images and others seize the
reader. Ezekiel will not allow his readers to have a pleasant expe-

rience with his book. His words, his metaphors, his images catapult the reader into years of agony and exile that the prophet and his compatriots experienced in Babylon. We too experience the frailty of Israel's relationship with God, the breakdown of its society, and the nightmare of its punishment. But the prophet's rhetoric also entices us with the irresistible power of his dreams. That is why the Synagogue could not put this book aside despite the theological problems it raised for the generation that made the Pentateuch the supreme and normative revelation.

Another problem the early rabbis had with this book was that reading it could lead some people to inquire about the divine vehicle in Ezek. 1 and 10. Such inquiries were popular among Jews who did not accept rabbinic authority. It is no wonder than that many early rabbis were not enthusiastic about the book. An anonymous opinion in the Mishnah holds that ch. 1 should not be read in the synagogue service (*Megillah* iv.10). Other authorities objected to Ezek. 16 because of its insult to Jerusalem. These opinions are not normative. The synagogue reads ch. 1 on the first day of the Shabu'ot (the Feast of Weeks or Pentecost).

What made the book of Ezekiel so irresistible to the rabbis despite its difficulties was its belief that redemption, when it would finally come, was to be the product of God's mercy and not Israel's repentance. The prophet came to realize that if Israel's future were dependent upon its potential for repentance and faith, there could be no future. Israel's future would be the product of God's mercy and not Israel's potential. Such a perspective will not allow any people to believe that they are beyond hope for redemption. Even if their sin makes them unworthy of God's grace, God will give that grace nonetheless. This vision of God's grace is something that every generation needs to experience. Elie Wiesel points out that Ezekiel's visions took place in some specific time frame—all except one: the vision of the dry bones. The promise that is inherent in that particular vision cannot be linked to a specific time or place.

Ezekiel believed that Israel's relationship with God is ultimately dependent upon what God wills and not what Israel does. Despite its gross infidelity, Israel's future is one *with* God rather than *without* God. For the prophet, God is sovereign but bound to

Israel by an inexplicable love. Israel's life with God is a product of this love rather than of its own fidelity or even repentance. This is a stunning assertion coming from someone living in exile. It is a testament to faith. The writers of the NT, particularly Paul, will ask for that same faith from those who believed in Christ.

The prophet went beyond his assertion that Israel again would experience God touching its life. He declared that there would never again be a rupture in Israel's relationship with God. Regarding Israel, he envisioned "a new heart and a new spirit" that would make disobedience an impossibility. Regarding God, the prophet saw the eastern gate of the temple remaining permanently sealed after God's glory returned to the temple. Ezekiel did not intend the first of these images to mean that Israel would become a moral robot incapable of evil. That would suggest that Israel would also be incapable of good. Similarly, the prophet did not intend the second image to become another unconditional promise of divine favor. That could easily degenerate into a guarantee that did not require a moral response from Israel. Too much had happened to Israel for his words to be misunderstood. If the Exile taught Israel anything, it was that there are no guarantees. The Exile brought Israel face to face with the power of its infidelity. What Ezekiel saw was a future in which Israel and God would become so close that infidelity on Israel's part would be unthinkable. A cynic would say that the prophet was hoping against hope.

When Ezekiel was putting his visions into words that people could understand, the Athenians were building the Acropolis and the Mayans were building their temples. Aesop was spinning his fables and Lao-tse was sharing his wisdom. The 6th cent. before Christ was an age of burgeoning culture throughout the world. Ezekiel's achievement was that he could see beyond the torment of his existence to a time in the future when people could *experience* God's presence in a most tangible way. This was an amazing contribution from a man who felt so keenly God's absence. His faith overcame the lessons of his experience, and this faith enabled his generation and others as well to experience God's presence touching their lives.

BIBLIOGRAPHY

Books

Boadt, Lawrence. *Ezekiel's Oracles against Egypt: A Literary and Philological Study of Ezekiel 29–32.* Biblica et orientalia 37 (Rome: Biblical Institute Press, 1980).

Brownlee, William H. *Ezekiel 1–39.* Word Biblical Commentary 28 (Waco: Word, 1986).

Carley, Keith W. *Ezekiel among the Prophets: A Study of Ezekiel's Place in Prophetic Tradition.* Studies in Biblical Theology, 2nd ser. 31 (Naperville: Allenson and London: SCM, 1975).

Cody, Aelred. *Ezekiel.* Old Testament Message 11 (Wilmington: Michael Glazier, 1984).

Craigie, Peter C. *Ezekiel.* Daily Study Bible (Philadelphia: Westminster and London: SCM, 1983).

Craven, Toni. *Ezekiel, Daniel.* Collegeville Bible Commentary (Collegeville, Minn.: Liturgical Press, 1986).

van Dijk, H. J. *Ezekiel's Prophecy on Tyre: A New Approach.* Biblica et orientalia 20 (Rome: Pontifical Biblical Institute, 1967).

Graffy, Adrian. *A Prophet Confronts His People: The Disputation Speech in the Prophets.* Analecta biblica 104 (Rome: Pontifical Biblical Institute, 1984).

Greenberg, Moshe. *Ezekiel, 1–20.* Anchor Bible 22 (Garden City: Doubleday, 1983).

Howie, Carl Gordon. *Ezekiel, Daniel.* Layman's Bible Commentary (London: SCM and Richmond: John Knox, 1962).

Jacobson, Howard. *The Exagoge of Ezekiel* (Cambridge and New York: Cambridge University Press, 1983).

Joyce, Paul. *Divine Initiative and Human Response in Ezekiel.* JSOT Supplement 51 (Sheffield: JSOT Press, 1988).

Klein, Ralph W. *Ezekiel: The Man and His Message* (Columbia, S.C.: University of South Carolina Press, 1988).

Kutsch, Ernst. *Die chronologischen Daten des Ezechielbuches.* Orbis biblicus et orientalis 62 (Fribourg: Universitätsverlag and Göttingen: Vandenhoeck & Ruprecht, 1985).

Levenson, Jon D. *Theology of the Program of Restoration of Ezekiel 40–48.* Harvard Semitic Monographs 10 (Missoula: Scholars Press, 1976).

Lust, Johan, ed. *Ezekiel and His Book: Textual and Literary Criticism and Their Interrelation.* Bibliotheca ephemeridum theologicarum lovaniensium 74 (Louvain: Peeters and Leuven University Press, 1986).

Mays, James Luther. *Ezekiel, Second Isaiah.* Proclamation Commentary (Philadelphia: Fortress, 1978).

Stalker, David Muir Gibson. *Ezekiel: Introduction and Commentary.* Torch Bible Commentary (London: SCM and Naperville: Allenson, 1968).

Steinmann, Jean. *Le Prophète Ézéchiel et les débuts de l'exil.* Lectio divina 13 (Paris: Éditions du Cerf, 1953).

Taylor, John Bernard. *Ezekiel: An Introduction and Commentary.* Tyndale Old Testament Commentaries 20 (London and Downers Grove: Inter-Varsity, 1969).

Wevers, John W. *Ezekiel.* New Century Bible Commentary (Grand Rapids: Eerdmans and London: Marshall, Morgan & Scott, 1982).

Widengren, Geo. *The King and the Tree of Life in Ancient Near Eastern Religion: King and Saviour IV.* Uppsala universitetsårsskrift, 1951/4 (Uppsala: Lundqvists, 1951).

Zimmerli, Walther. *Ezekiel 1.* Hermeneia (Philadelphia: Fortress and London: SCM, 1979).

———. *Ezekiel 2.* Hermeneia (Philadelphia: Fortress and London: SCM, 1983).

BIBLIOGRAPHY

Articles

Abba, Raymond. "Priests and Levites in Ezekiel," *Vetus Testamentum* 28 (1978): 1-9.

Ahroni, Reuben. "The Gog Prophecy and the Book of Ezekiel," *Hebrew Annual Review* 1 (1977): 1-27.

Alexander, Ralph H. "A Fresh Look at Ezekiel 38 and 39," *Journal of the Evangelical Theological Society* 17 (1974): 157-169.

Allan, Nigel. "The Jerusalem Priesthood during the Exile," *Heythrop Journal* 23 (1982): 259-269.

Astour, Michael C. "Ezekiel's Prophecy of Gog and the Cuthean Legend of Naram-sin," *Journal of Biblical Literature* 95 (1976): 567-579.

Biggs, Charles R. "The role of *nasi* in the programme for restoration in Ezekiel 40–48," *Colloquium* 16 (1983): 46-57.

Brownlee, William H. "The Aftermath of the Fall of Judah according to Ezekiel," *Journal of Biblical Literature* 89 (1970): 393-404.

————. "Ezekiel's Parable of the Watchman and the Editing of Ezekiel," *Vetus Testamentum* 28 (1978): 392-408.

Bullock, C. Hassell. "Ezekiel, Bridge between the Testaments," *Journal of the Evangelical Theological Society* 25 (1982): 23-31.

Cassuto, Umberto. "The Arrangement of the Book of Ezekiel," in *Biblical and Oriental Studies* (Jerusalem: Hebrew University and Magnes, 1973), 1:227-240.

Childs, Brevard S. "The Enemy from the North and the Chaos Tradition," *Journal of Biblical Literature* 78 (1959): 187-198.

Darr, Katheryn Pfisterer. "The Wall around Paradise: Ezekielian Ideas about the Future," *Vetus Testamentum* 37 (1987): 271-79.

Day, John. "The Daniel of Ugarit and Ezekiel and the Hero of the Book of Daniel," *Vetus Testamentum* 30 (1980): 174-184.

DeVries, Simon J. "Remembrance in Ezekiel: A Study of an Old Testament Theme," *Interpretation* 16 (1962): 58-64.

Dressler, Harold H. P. "The Identification of the Ugaritic Dnil with the Daniel of Ezekiel," *Vetus Testamentum* 29 (1979): 152-161. [Reply by Baruch Margalit, "Interpreting the Story of Aqht," *Vetus Testamentum* 30 (1980): 361-65.]

Fox, Michael V. "The Rhetoric of Ezekiel's Vision of the Valley of the Bones," *Hebrew Union College Annual* 51 (1980): 1-15.

Freedy, K. S. and Redford, D. B. "The Dates in Ezekiel in Relation to Biblical, Babylonian and Egyptian Sources," *Journal of the American Oriental Society* 90 (1970): 462-485.

Geyer, John B. "Mythology and Culture in the Oracles against the Nations," *Vetus Testamentum* 36 (1986): 129-145.

Good, Edwin M. "Ezekiel's Ship: Some Extended Metaphors in the Old Testament," *Semitics* 1 (1970): 79-103.

Grassi, Joseph A. "Ezekiel XXXVII.1-14 and the New Testament," *New Testament Studies* 11 (1965): 162-64.

————. "The Transforming Power of Biblical Heart Imagery," *Review for Religious* 43 (1984): 714-723.

Greenberg, Moshe. "The Design and Themes of Ezekiel's Program of Restoration," *Interpretation* 38 (1984): 181-208.

Habel, Norman C. "Ezekiel 28 and the Fall of the First Man," *Concordia Theological Monthly* 38 (1967): 516-524.

Haran, Menahem. "The Law-Code of Ezekiel XL–XLVIII and its Relation to the Priestly School," *Hebrew Union College Annual* 50 (1979): 45-71.

Hsieh Show-Shong. "Ezekiel Chapter 33–48: A Study of Hope," *South East Asia Journal of Theology* 14/2 (1973): 115-16.

Klein, Ralph W. "Yahweh Faithful and Free—A Study in Ezekiel," *Concordia Theological Monthly* 42 (1971): 493-501.

Lemke, Werner E. "Life in the Present and Hope for the Future," *Interpretation* 38 (1984): 165-180.

Lindars, Barnabas. "Ezekiel and Individual Responsibility," *Vetus Testamentum* 15 (1965): 452-467.

Luc, Alex. "A Theology of Ezekiel: God's Name and Israel's History," *Journal of the Evangelical Theological Society* 26 (1983): 137-143.

McConville, J. Gordon. "Priests and Levites in Ezekiel: A Crux in the Interpretation of Israel's History," *Tyndale Bulletin* 34 (1983): 3-31.

McKenzie, John L. "Mythological Allusions in Ezek 28:12-18," *Journal of Biblical Literature* 75 (1956): 322-27.

Michael, J. Hugh. "Gog and Magog in the 20th Century," *Expository Times* 61 (1949): 71-73.

Newsom, Carol A., "A Maker of Metaphors—Ezekiel's Oracles Against Tyre," *Interpretation* 38 (1984): 151-164.

217

BIBLIOGRAPHY

————. "Merkabah Exegesis in the Qumran Sabbath Shirot," *Journal of Jewish Studies* 38 (1987): 11-37.

Niditch, Susan. "Ezekiel 40-48 in a Visionary Context," *Catholic Biblical Quarterly* 48 (1986): 208-224.

Smith, Morton. "The Veracity of Ezekiel, the Sins of Manasseh, and Jer. 44:18," *Zeitschrift für die alttestamentliche Wissenschaft* 87 (1975): 11-16.

Tuell, Steven. "The Temple Vision of Ezekiel 40-48: A Program for Restoration?" *Proceedings of the Eastern Great Lakes Biblical Society* 2 (1982): 96-103.

Van Seters, John. "Confessional Reformulation in the Exilic Period," *Vetus Testamentum* 22 (1972): 448-459.

Vawter, Bruce. "Ezekiel and John," *Catholic Biblical Quarterly* 26 (1964): 450-58.

Weinfeld, Moshe. "Jeremiah and the Spiritual Metamorphosis of Israel," *Zeitschrift für die alttestamentliche Wissenschaft* 88 (1976): 17-56.

Williams, Anthony J. "The Mythological Background of Ezekiel 28:12-19?" *Biblical Theology Bulletin* 6 (1976): 49-61.

Wilson, Robert R. "An Interpretation of Ezekiel's Dumbness," *Vetus Testamentum* 22 (1972): 91-104.

Woudstra, Marten H. "Edom and Israel in Ezekiel," *Calvin Theological Journal* 3 (1968): 21-35.

Zimmerli, Walther. "The Message of the Prophet Ezekiel," *Interpretation* 23 (1969): 131-157.

————. "Plans for Rebuilding After the Catastrophe of 587," in *I Am Yahweh* (Atlanta: Knox, 1982), 111-133.

————. "The Word of God in the Book of Ezekiel," *Journal for Theology and the Church* 4 (1967): 1-13.